GOVERNING URBAN INDIA
Policy and Practice

About the Author

Dr. A. Ravindra, an officer of the Indian Administrative Service (IAS), served in various capacities in government and retired as Chief Secretary to the Government of Karnataka. He holds a PhD in Urban Studies. He has been a Secretary to the Government of Karnataka in the Housing and Urban Development Department, Administrator and Commissioner of the Bangalore City Municipal Corporation, Chairman of the Bangalore Development Authority (BDA), and has been in a leadership role in several other state and city level public institutions responsible for urban infrastructure, finance and planning.

Dr. Ravindra was instrumental in reforming the property tax system in Bangalore, and in a first for an Indian city, mobilizing development funds through municipal bonds. He was also central to initiating the Bangalore Metro Rail project and setting up *Swabhimana*, a platform for improving urban governance with people's participation. After retiring from the IAS, Dr. Ravindra served as an Advisor (Urban Affairs) to the Chief Minister of Karnataka.

Dr. Ravindra heads the Center for Sustainable Development (CSD), a non-profit social enterprise focusing on urban sustainability, and has also served as the Chairman of the Institute for Social and Economic Change (ISEC), as well as the Public Affairs Center (PAC). Dr. Ravindra has published extensively on issues of public policy, urban governance and of general interest. His previous books include *Urban Land Policy, Metropolitan Bangalore: A Management Perspective; Governing an Indian State: Karnataka in Focus* and; *Bangalore Multiplicity*, a coffee table book on Bengaluru.

GOVERNING URBAN INDIA
Policy and Practice

A. Ravindra

CONCEPT PUBLISHING COMPANY PVT. LTD.
NEW DELHI - 110059

ISBN: 978-93-5594-790-1

First Published 2024

Published and Printed by

Concept
Since 1974

Concept Publishing Company Pvt. Ltd.
A/15-16, Commercial Block, Mohan Garden
New Delhi-110059 (India)
T: +91-11-41101460
E: publishing@conceptpub.com, *W*: www.conceptpub.com

Cataloging in Publication--Courtesy: D.K. Agencies (P) Ltd. <docinfo@dkagencies.com>

Ravindra, A., 1942- **author.**
Governing urban India : policy and practice / A. Ravindra.
pages cm
Includes bibliographical references and index.
ISBN 9789355947901

1. Urbanization--India--History. 2. Urban policy--India--History. 3. City planning--India--History. 4. Municipal services--India. 5. Municipal government--India. I. Title.

LCC HT384.I4R38 2024 | DDC 307.760954 23

Foreword

In recent years, there is increasing recognition in Indian policy circles of the paramount role cities and urban regions play in furthering national development goals, including increase in economic growth and per capital income, reduction of poverty and inequality as well as fostering democratic values of citizenship. Historically, cities are economic engines, employment generators and hubs of innovation, apart from being cultures of plurality. While urban policy has received some importance, especially since the 1980s, recent years have seen a shift in acknowledgement of the strategic role of the city, within larger national development goals. However, we still have a long way to go in terms of genuine devolution in urban governance, even after thirty years of the 74th Amendment. This is an imperative which will crucially determine our key responses to national challenges and will become a force multiplier in our efforts towards developing India especially in the next 25 years.

It is in this context that Dr. A Ravindra's book **Governing Urban India: Policy and Practice** is of great importance. The author has been a distinguished public servant, having served as a member of the Indian Administrative Service (IAS) in the top echelons of the Government of Karnataka, including holding leadership positions in almost every important urban body in Karnataka. He therefore has a ring side view of some of the most important decisions taken (or not taken) in urban affairs in Karnataka, especially in Bengaluru. This rich insight borne from experience is informed by a rigorous analytical mind who is deeply interested in the subject as an academic area of study in itself. This combination of erudition and practical orientation makes this book a ready reference to urban policy and governance in India. This overview is comprehensive in its sweep, referring to history and policy as the narrative moves. Dr. Ravindra is diligent in quoting Megasthenes (who in his Indica, interestingly mentions municipal boards in Mauryan Pataliputra) as well as Jane Jacobs ('without cities, we would all be poor'). He looks back at urban formations in India from ancient, medieval and modern times; and traces the roots of our current crises in governance to the British colonial administration. In doing so, he does not miss the (failed) efforts of Lord Ripon who wanted to decentralise urban administration or the salutary efforts of individuals such as Otto Konigsberger and Patrick Geddes in humanising town planning in practice. The author delves into various aspects urban planning in detail without losing perspective on what ails governance at the systemic level. He rightly points to strategic neglect of the city in the early years of India, manifested in disjointed and fragmentary five year plans. He quotes Angus Maddison the British economist on how India's share in the world economy declined from 24.4% in 1700 to 4.2% in 1950, a number that accompanied the decline in the position of urban areas as well. The policy aspects of city governance and the failure to implement the 74th Amendment in entirety are addressed in great detail.

I found three aspects of the author's approach of great value. First, he has an integrative approach, which looks at cities and urban regions as a multi/inter disciplinary area of study and practice, which cannot be tackled by land-use plans alone. This connection between spatial and economic plans is of special interest to me. Second, he has a genuine sensibility towards fostering citizen-centric participatory approaches, and he mentions initiatives that he had undertaken as a city administrator. I found some of his vignettes from his work particularly interesting, including honest analysis of how some efforts did not see the desired results, in spite of best intentions. Third, the author has a forward looking mindset which is focused on finding systemic structural solutions. This has particular pragmatic value without losing sight of the big picture.

I am convinced that our manner of responding to cooperative federalism and urban governance will determine the future of this country. Democratic decentralisation by roping in the third tier is critical to solving the complexity of India's challenges. Such decentralisation, read with the subsidiarity principle, will truly allow a multi-level play of enormous significance. Decentralisation comprises delegation, decongestion and devolution. The first two are akin to agency transfers and mainly dictated by considerations of pragmatism and efficient management but the third aspect namely, that of devolution is rather more substantial. It is the very soul of the tenet of decentralisation and completes the characterisation of decentralisation. Unfortunately, the expectations of the 74th Amendment have been belied, with most states unable to devolve to the urban local bodies as per the subsidiarity principle. The urban local bodies are still considered as the creatures of the states as they once were, prior to the 74th Constitution Amendment. Their validity as the legitimate, third tier of the government, is still not a reality and indeed is not recognised as such. Bringing in the third tier of government within the fold of the overall architecture of fiscal federalism may actually help secure a more solid relation between the three levels of government and allow for the prospect of cooperation between all three, with all of them willing to accommodate each other. This will allow a multi-level perspective for thinking productively about India's federal structure.

At the structural level, we need a successor to the 74th Amendment which is able to usher in genuine devolution in our urban areas and addresses the limitations of the 74th Amendment. For one, we need to put in place a way by which we are able to share the GST with the third tier. As we know, the urban local bodies are weak and disempowered and so unable to fulfil the mandates. We will require a Constitutional Amendment firstly to create a consolidated fund at the local bodies level and secondly in the makeup of GST which could be shared between the centre, state and the third tier involved. This is only fair since the GST is a consumption tax and the taxpayer must see direct benefits accruing for their payment. This will also boost the supply of governance and make available higher quality of local public goods and amenities. The other important facet of decentralisation is the 3Fs namely, functions, functionaries and finance, which must be clearly assigned to the local bodies so as to provide for funded mandates.

It is important for the centre and the states to share an equal percentage of the GST, i.e. CGST and SGST with the third tier. This will provide a buoyant fiscal base to the third tier and more importantly align interests of the elected officials with their citizens as GST is essentially a consumption-based tax. Towards this, I would propose the following rates: A single GST rate of 12% with CGST and SGST of 6% each and both centre and state would share at least 1/6th of this with the third tier. This would enable providing a fiscal base of not less than 1% of GDP to the third tier in a predictable manner. Given growing urbanisation and the increasing role of the cities in maintaining the country's growth momentum, an adequate fiscal base for the cities can alone ensure the supply of required public goods such as urban mobility, solid waste management, public health, etc. Such a measure will also generate a considerable amount of fiscal resources with high buoyancy. For instance, this year alone it can generate more than Rupees Two Lakh Crores and grow by more than 10% every year. These large resources would be additional to the resources from the property taxes that will continue to be levied by the local bodies. There is, of course, need to reform the property tax system as well. Such strengthening of the fiscal base can give a major boost for greatly improving the urban infrastructure and strengthen our cities as a powerful engine of growth. With a predictable fiscal base, the well-run local governments can also raise additional resources via issuance of long-term bonds.

While the future of India is decidedly urban, unfortunately, the 74th Constitutional Amendment was almost an afterthought (after the 73rd Constitutional Amendment) and did not go far enough. Urban was perhaps seen in policy circles as a necessary evil that need not be cultivated. The capacity building required specifically for urban governance, planning and delivery were neglected. There were no specific HR policies to hire bureaucrats with specialised calibre. We need new world class interdisciplinary institutions such as the Indian Institute for Human Settlements (IIHS) that can create new knowledge at the urban scale across the country. The devolution via the State Finance Commissions (SFCs) has been negligible, hence the urban local bodies are not empowered. This has resulted in poor delivery and chaotic management of our cities. As a consequence, our cities have become grossly suboptimal in terms of provision of local public goods to the detriment of cities and indeed to the detriment of India's long term economic prospects. It is in that context that we need a new Constitutional Amendment that empowers cities and urban regions, and creates new avenues for cooperative federalism with the centre and the states.

Dr. Ravindra's book is a step in this direction and details the various forms of structural possibilities to deal with the challenges and opportunities presented by India's growing urbanisation. Since urbanisation is now finally and belatedly regarded as essential to the country's future, it is time now for a rigorous relook at the governing structures in our cities and both imagine and put in place new governance arrangements for our cities to deal with the increasing challenges of poverty, infrastructure, inequality and services. A more empowered city in terms of fiscal resources and functional autonomy is key to fulfilling the promise of our cities being indispensable to our national development story. It is with this hope that I commend this book to the attention of our citizens, policy scholars and policy makers.

Vijay Kelkar
Indian Institute for Human Settlements,
Bengaluru
Chairman 13th Finance Commission
and
Former Secy,
Government of India

Preface

I live in the city of Bangalore or Bengaluru as it is now called and have been a witness to its growth and the myriad changes it has gone through over the years, since mid-twienth century, for good and bad. What was once known as a garden city with salubrious climate, clean with beautiful tree-lined streets and slow-paced, has now transformed into a megacity with a population of over 13 million. It is now famously called the Silicon Valley and IT capital of India, with a prospering middle class, glitzy malls and luxury apartments, but also facing problems of poor infrastructure, severe traffic congestion (recently tagged as the most congested city in the world), deteriorating environment and unsatisfactory public services. People are raising questions about what has gone wrong with a city that was so good and beautiful.

There are similar stories about many other cities in India and we often hear the term 'urban crisis' being used. Even as I am penning this Preface, I see a news flash—'Air Emergency in Delhi'—the Air Quality Index (AQI) having crossed the danger score of 400 and at times 500 and a thick haze enveloping the national capital. Schools have been closed, movement of heavy vehicles prohibited and other restrictions imposed to control air pollution. Mumbai has also reported heavy air pollution and people choking for breath. A week back, a leopard entered Bengaluru city causing a big scare, an indicator of intensifying human-animal conflict.

As an IAS officer, I had the opportunity of working in the urban sector in different capacities both at the policy-making and field levels that provided rich experience in different facets of urban policy, planning and practice. I also became a passionate student of the 'Urban' discipline and tried to understand how cities function across countries, developed and developing. While cities in the former stood on a separate footing, those in the latter shared several common features—increasing urban population, efforts to improve economic growth and infrastructure, poverty and inequality, and local governments struggling for adequate financial resources. My own reflections and interactions with various stakeholders have led me to believe that the most critical issue in urban India is what I might call the 'Conundrum' of Urban Governance, and this is what I have primarily tried to address in this book.

There will, of course, be different perceptions and opinions about how to find solutions to the urban challenges we face, and it is not an easy task. As Saskia Sassen put it, "Cities are complex systems. But they are incomplete systems. In this incompleteness lies the possibility of making—making the urban, the political, the civic as a sort of new frontier zone for the circulation of development processes and for the making of new types of economies…" (Sassen, *Cities: New Frontier Zones in Development Processes,* 2012). Our efforts should be oriented towards not adopting some western models, but in the first place make Indian cities functional with basic amenities and effective services, and design new development processes integrating the urban and the rural and at the same time make the major cities globally competitive in terms of economy, infrastructure, technology and human resources.

The purpose of this book will be served if it can spark debates and conversations on cities, especially on governance issues and the possible solutions, which may vary from state to state and city to city.

A. Ravindra

Acknowledgements

Words cannot adequately describe my sense of gratitude to Dr. Vijay Kelkar for having readily agreed to write a foreword for the book. The foreword reflects his deep understanding of urban issues and the importance of urbanisation to India's future growth. As a renowned economist, his suggestion on sharing a part of the Goods and Services Tax (GST) collections with local governments needs serious consideration by the Central and State governments. My immense thanks to Dr. Kelkar.

This book could not have been published without the assistance of several persons. First, I wish to place on record the unstinted support of Mr. Gurucharan, Director, School of Social Sciences, MSR University, and former Director of Public Affairs Centre (PAC), Bengaluru. His cooperation extended from providing the services of the staff of the Centre and engaging researchers, to his personally going through my manuscript and offering his valuable comments. My profound thanks to Mr. Gurucharan and the staff of PAC.

Mr. Swastik Harish, a specialist in Urban Development and Housing, stood beside me like a pillar, meticulously going through the manuscript, offering comments and suggestions on every chapter and compiling Tables and Illustrations. He has also shown enormous patience in incorporating the several revised versions of the manuscript. Without his help, I could not have completed the book by this time. Let me convey my deep appreciation and gratitude to Mr. Swastik for all that he has done.

I now come to those who provided research assistance. Dr. K.C. Smitha, Assistant Professor, Centre for Political Institutions, Governance and Development Science, Institute for Social and Economic Change (ISEC) was of great help in migration study, data analysis and providing the required information on matters that I asked for, particularly on Five Year Plans. Mr. Rahul, Research Officer at PAC, could produce whatever I demanded in quick time and was very helpful during my visit to some cities in other states. Ms Amrutha, Research Assiastant, ever eager to assist, could provide information on different cities. Ms. Juhi Jotwani and Ms. Chavali Phanisri Soumya did a very good job in editing and referencing. My sincere thanks to all of them.

A major source of assistance came to me from Mr. Aromar Revi, Director, Indian Institute for Human Settlements who provided me an opportunity for interaction with the Institute's faculty and research staff, Ms. Pooja Sagar in particular, which proved very useful in giving shape to the book. My special thanks to Mr. Revi and his staff.

I would particularly like to thank Dr. Narendar Pani, reputed economist, National Institute of Advanced Studies (NIAS) and Dr. K. Kumar, Professor of Entrepreneurship, IIM, Bangalore, for sharing their ideas and providing valuable insights.

I must make special mention of Concept Publishing Company Pvt. Ltd. who agreed to take up publication of the book. They had earlier published my book on Urban Land Policy more than two decades back. I would particularly like to express my gratitude to Mr. Ashok Mittal, Managing Director and Mr. Nitin Mittal, CEO, for their cooperation.

It is possible that I have missed out some others. Suffice to say, the assistance I received from so many was invaluable and also showed their personal regard for me. My sincere thanks to all of them.

A. Ravindra

Contents

List of Figures, Tables and Boxes

FIGURES

TABLES

BOXES

Introduction

Who Governs Our Cities and How?

An Invisible Virus Stops City Life

January 23, 2020, is the day when activities in Wuhan, the capital city of Hubei province in central China came to an abrupt stop. The bustling metropolis with eleven million people was locked down. Transport to and from the city was banned, schools and colleges were closed indefinitely, all shops were shut, except those selling food and medicine. Movement of all private vehicles and most of public transport was stopped. People were asked to stay indoors; and only one family member could go out every two days to buy essentials.

That was the beginning of COVID-19, the devastating pandemic that caused unprecedented damage to human health, physical and mental, across the world. Essentially an urban phenomenon, the deadly virus dealt a severe blow to city residents. It did not damage the physical form but rather disrupted city life: the economic, social and cultural activities, the movement of people and vehicles, and the health and livelihoods of millions of human beings across the globe. In India, the first phase that started some time in February 2020 witnessed a national lockdown for a period of two months (March 25 to May 31, 2020), confining people to their homes for an agonisingly long period, a concept quite alien to city dwellers. Overnight, the pandemic rendered lakhs of people jobless, particularly the poor and the migrant workers, driving them back to their villages. The urban middle class and the elite had to adjust to a new way of life, a 'new normal' as it has been called—working from home, unable to go out for work or shopping or recreation or any outdoor activities, forced to get food parcels delivered at residence, and the entire family staying together at home 24 hours a day, with all its blessings and constraints. The more difficult part was dealing with the pandemic itself, unprecedented since the Spanish Flu of 1918 over a century ago. It posed enormous challenges to the government and all sections of people, and most importantly, to those infected with the disease itself, and their families.

As the first phase subsided around September 2020 and people resumed their normal activities, a new set of problems awaited them. They were mandated by the government to follow certain instructions—wearing a mask when they went out, social distancing or maintaining a distance of six feet between two individuals while in a crowd, and frequently sanitising or washing one's hands. Unused and unwilling to facing such restrictions, most urbanites flouted them with impunity. As attention turned to reviving economic activity and it was presumed that the pandemic had vanished, the virus came back. The second phase that started during March 2021 proved more disastrous than the first. The rapidly rising number of people getting infected and rushing to hospitals left the government and hospital authorities in a quandary. Shortage of beds, intensive care facilities, oxygen cylinders and drugs posed serious problems. Even elite hospitals in large metropolitan cities, boasting the best of medical facilities and doctors, were unable to cope with the situation. Administering vaccines was considered the only viable option to control the deadly virus. Manufactured only in a few countries including India with the utmost speed possible, the supply of vaccines proved inadequate to meet the needs of the large population. It seemed to be a race between vaccination and the virus. In spite of best efforts, COVID-19 took a toll of over six million lives worldwide and over 5,00,000 in India, leaving millions of others in post-pandemic distress.

The hardships of the people continued in some form or the other. According to a study by the International Institute of Population Studies (IIPS), India in October 2021, life expectancy reduced by nearly two years. A study on the effect of the crisis on self-employed, casual and regular wage workers across 12 states in India between mid-April and mid-May 2020, carried out by the Centre for Sustainable

Employment of Azim Premji University reported a 64 per cent drop in earnings. The fourth round of the Delhi-NCR Corona virus telephone survey conducted between December 2020 and January, 2021revealed that 80 per cent of the respondents suffered economic hardships including salary cuts, job losses, difficulty in finding work, business closures or decline in business incomes, with salaried workers and small business owners bearing the brunt. With COVID-19 entering the third year, the overall impact has been devastating. As per an estimate by the US-based Pew Research Centre, India's middle class shrank by 32 million or a third in 2020 and the number of poor (those with an earning of $2/Rs. 150 or less per day) more than doubled, an increase of 75 million. The Centre for Monitoring Indian Economy (CMIE) reported 53 million people remaining unemployed as of December 2021.

While the pandemic has caused enormous suffering to the people and severe damage to the economy, it did create some positive impacts. It provided an impetus to the quick adoption of modern digital technology for activities like work-from-home, education, conduct of meetings and conferences. The extensive use of whatsapp for online delivery of services and the manifold rise in digital transactions have revolutionised social life in cities. More than 40 million people shifted from feature phones to smart phones in 2021, signalling a major shift to online consumption and interaction. A significant decrease in air pollution was noticed in large cities during the lockdown period on account of the highly restricted use of motor vehicles.

The global crisis caused by the COVID-19 pandemic has stoked a debate about a new urban crisis spread across economic, social and environmental sectors—loss of economic growth, the migrant problem triggered by the long lockdown periods, loss of jobs, seriously affecting the livelihoods of the poor and vulnerable sections of society, the adverse impact on education of children and the youth consequent on the indefinite closure of schools and colleges, and on the physical and mental health of a large number of people. Despite the setbacks, the crisis can be used as an opportunity to revisit the policies we have pursued to promote economic development, and the urban lifestyles that have been responsible for some of the problems we are facing and what can be done to reclaim our cities and recreate them as more resilient, healthy, inclusive urban habitats.

India@75: The 'Urban' Significance

In a coincidence, the current pandemic is leading us to the 75th year of India as an independent nation. During this period, the development scenario of the country presents a mixed picture of impressive economic gains, coupled with underachievement in certain sectors that have placed us at a lower level compared to many other developing countries. Broadly, two distinct approaches to development can be discerned in the post-independence period: first, during the 45 years from 1947-1991, what may be called the 'planning era'; and second, the three decades since 1991, generally described as the post-economic liberalisation era. The first phase was marked by stagnant economic growth and slow or steady progress in the social sector areas like education and health. In the second phase following economic reforms, India's growth accelerated and it has now emerged as the fifth largest economy in the world with a Gross Domestic Product (GDP) close to $3 trillion.

Three forces that have shaped the course of events in the modern world in a very substantial way are: **Urbanisation, Globalisation and the Tecnological Revolution**. They have together impacted the national and global economies, political developments, social change and movement of people across countries. In the beginning of the 20th century, just about 16 per cent of the world's population lived in towns and cities; today, over half the world's population (4 billion) lives in urban areas and 70-75 per cent of world's GDP is generated in cities, where most of the world's wealth is concentrated. While the more developed countries in what is termed the 'global north' have achieved a high degree of urbanisation (70-90%), those in the less developed regions of the 'global south' are urbanising in varying degrees.

For India, the significance of urbanisation is three-fold: first, the demographic shift from rural to urban; second, the increasing contribution of the urban economy to the country's GDP, and third, the social transformation on a scale never witnessed before. Although oft-quoted, the context demands recalling what Mahatma Gandhi had famously said: "India lives in her villages". That was in 1925 and was literally true as nearly 90 per cent of the country's population was living in rural areas. By 1947, soon after independence, this figure had declined to 83 per cent and 75 years down the line, in 2022, the rural population has further reduced to about 65 per cent. In other words, India has become more urbanised and the country has changed in significant ways.

India's pace of urbanisation till 2001 must be considered slow, with only 31.2 per cent living in urban areas in 2011. But the signs of an increased pace of urban growth were evident when for the first time, the Census recorded a faster rate of growth of urban population compared to the rural during the decade 2001-11. According to UN estimates, by 2030, this figure will edge up to 37 per cent and by the 100th year of India's independence in 2047, over half the country's population will turn urban. India's current urban population of 430 million, more than the total population of the United States of America and the United Kingdom combined is expected to reach 590 million and by 2050, it will surpass 800 million and account for nearly 20 per cent of world's urban population. Thus, in sheer numbers, urban India presents enormous opportunities in terms of human capital and social capital.

In the economic sphere, cities act as centres of industrial production, trade and commerce with multiple avenues for employment, accounting for 55 per cent of India's GDP and 85 per cent of its tax revenue. By 2030, their share of GDP is projected to rise to 70 per cent and they will account for 70 per cent of the net new employment. The same year, 91 million urban households would turn middle class, over four times the number of 22 million in 2010. Thus, the role of cities in generating resources for India's development is of crucial importance.

In the social and human development sector, cities provide the foundational requirements of education and health facilities, and create the ethos for a muti-cultural society. They function as centres of higher education and sophisticated health care. The large metropolises in particular attract the best talent in practically all fields of human activity—in science, technology, social sciences, art and culture. They provide the space for vibrant social interaction, intellectual debate and discourse, and an environment for cultural efflorescence.

Yet, the challenges that urban India faces are truly daunting. In the first place, it calls for huge investments to meet the ever growing infrastructure requirements of our cities: 1.2 trillion dollars according to some estimates and Rs. 39.2 lakh crores or $822 billion over a 20-year period as per the Government of India. Secondly, urban planning in India, spatial as well as developmental, has been shoddy, with the result our cities, by and large, present a picture of chaos and neglect: poor state of roads, traffic congestion, pollution and inadequate civic services. Third, the stark contrasts and inequalities in urban society, the co-existence of poverty and prosperity in close proximity, posh luxury housing juxtaposed with squalid slums, fast moving modern motor vehicles zooming past the pedestrains looking for safe walking space and long waiting commuters at bus stops, the poor street vendors trudging along the glitzy malls and glass-cased show rooms, labouring to eke out their livelihoods, are disturbing sights to anyone with even the least social conscience. While the deteriorating urban environment is a matter of serious concern, the problems posed by climate change pose a grave threat to sustainable urban development. Finally and crucially, the broken city governance system, unable to respond adequately and at times minimally to the basic needs of the citizens, has puzzled the ordinary people as much as the urban experts, while those responsible for managing the cities offer their own 'systemic' explanations.

Some basic questions arise:

- In spite of the rapid strides in science and technology and emerging as the fifth largest economy in the world, why are our cities in such a chaotic state?
- Why is India home to 11 out of the 20 most polluted cities in the world?
- Why do most Indian cities rank at the bottom of the UN Livability Index?
- Why do minimum decent housing and basic amenities elude 20 per cent of the urban population, with slums still dotting the urban habitat?

- Why, in spite of the high quality of managerial talent that can efficiently manage huge companies and banks, we are unable to effectively manage our towns and cities?

The central issue we need to reflect upon is our *governance system,* even as India grows in numbers, and with what may appear to be intractable political, economic, social and environmental problems. This boils down to two critical questions:

- Who governs our cities?
- How are cities governed?

As cities hold the key for the economic future of the country, India @75 is an opportune time to review the urbanisation process the country has traversed till now and take stock of how we have planned and designed our cities in the last few decades.We need to think afresh about the policies and strategies required to build a more resilient and inclusive India encompassing not only the 'urban' but also the 'rural'.

Absence of an Epistemology of Urban Development

The 'city' represents many things: the urban form expressed through its buildings, streets and open spaces; the economy that generates employment, trade and commerce; the geography that provides space for people to live and for production of goods and services; the society that enables interaction amongst citizens; the centre for education and health and; the ethos that promotes art, literature and culture. Hence, the urban perspective varies depending on the lens through which one visualises it. The geographer views it through the lens of migration, people moving from rural to urban or small towns to big towns and the settlement patterns that emerge; the architect looks at the urban form, the buildings and the built environment; the urban planner is concerned with demographic growth, the spatial character, land uses and regulations; the economist looks at the opportunities for investments and the potential to generate wealth; the ecologist is concerned about how the environment is impacted by all these activities. The city is all of these and much more.

To understand a city in its entirety and the way it is transforming itself from time to time, for better or worse, we need a conceptual framework. It is not merely what is happening in a city and its surroundings that is important but the 'how' and the 'why' of it. Unfortunately, the epistemology of urban development has been sorely lacking in India. This has been a great handicap in understanding the urban processes: the spatial and population growth trends, the forces that operate in propelling a city's economic growth and social change, the politics and governance and all that contributes to its chaos or beauty. This has been my experience as an urban policy-maker and practitioner.

As far back as the fifth century BC, the great Greek historian Herodotus, taking note of the rise and fall of great places observed: "For most of those which were great once are small today, and those that used to be small were great in my own time. Knowing, therefore, that human prosperity never abides long in the same place, I shall pay attention to both alike" (Herodotus, *The Histories,* trans. Aubrey de Selincourt, 1954). During the time of Herodotus, great cities of the past like Ur and Nineveh had declined and cities like Baylon, Athens and Syracuse had grown to glory which again declined after some time, making way for other great cities like Alexandria and Rome. Alexandria in Egypt has been described as the first great cosmopolis, thanks to the urban legacy of Alexander, Emperor of Macedonia, who in his ambition to conquer new territories, exported Hellenic urban and commercial culture beyond its previous sphere of influence, even into India itself. Later, Rome grew into a massive sprawling megacity with a population of over a million. No historian or writer has left behind any record of the rise and fall of cities of ancient or medieval India. It is remarkable though, that prominent ancient cities such as Pataliputra and Kashi while declining in glory, have survived and are getting revived in the 21st century in their modern form as Patna and Benares (Varanasi). So have Kancheepuram and Madurai in the south under the same names. Medieval cities like Delhi and Lucknow continued to grow under Muslim patronage and taking on new forms under British rule. Celebrated cities like Vijayanagar in the south suffered due to the ravages of war but have revived (modern Hampi-Hospet) in the 21st century.

Dealing with the important question of what makes cities great and what leads to their gradual decline, Joel Kotkin in his book, *The*

City: A Global History which provides a historical insight into the growth and decline of cities, has argued that three critical factors have determined the overall health of cities: first, the creation of sacred space, second, the provision of basic security, and lastly, the host for a commercial market (Kotkin, 2005). By and large, this argument holds good for Indian cities. In particular, the first factor of sacred space has been a key feature of Indian towns and cities throughout its history across ancient, medieval and modern times. The temple, the mosque and the church have become part of Indian tradition and urban fabric providing a continuity to its religious and social life, although in recent times they have been coated with a communal colour. Security and commercial activity have always remained relevant for the growth of any city and their importance has only increased with the growth of urban civilisation.

From a global perspective, cities and urban agglomerations represent centres of economic growth. As such, empowering cities and urban communities is seen as an important political dimension of urbanisation in India. This entails revisiting the structure of city governments, the authority vested in them, the sustainability of their finances and the powers and functions devolved on them. The 74th constitutional amendment of 1993 envisaged empowering urban local bodies through decentralisation of powers but the translation of that mandate into reality has been constrained by the complexities of inter-governmental relationships. This is manifesting itself in the unplanned and often ad hoc patterns of urbanisation, especially in the over 60 metropolitan cites including the mega urban agglomerations. In turn, this has seriously compromised delivery of essential services, notably urban waste management, water supply and sanitation. This has also constrained infrastructure growth including affordable housing, public transport and health care services, seriously impacting migrant and informal sector workers.

One interesting feature of a modern city is that it breaks down cultural sterotypes and narrow denominational categories that tend to act as barriers to culture, economy and society. In what is expected to be the 'Asian Century', this is happening at the intersection of three grand processes—globalisation, migration and urbanisation—shaping the economic and political future of the Global South. Its defining feature is the rapid pace at which the social and cultural forces drive and are driven by the migration of knowledge. This raises important questions: how do individual or group identities in urban settings shape the migration of knowledge, and how they themselves are shaped by the migration of knowledge that accompanies them? In what ways is this influencing the quality of urban governance and managerial efficiency? How can we democratise urban governance and professionalise the management of our cities? These are the major questions the book will traverse.

Indian cities defy the logic underlining the discourse of a hierarchy of cities that play a command-control role in the process of globalisation. Nor are they at the commanded and controlled end of such global circuits. Indeed, it is difficult to apply conventional urbanisation theory to the path of urbanisation that is unfolding in India. The major cities do not fit into the conventional but varied narratives of 'the most important cities of capitalist accumulation' (Friedman, 1986, 2002: 154); cities that are large but do not necessarily dominate the process of globalisation' (Castells, 1996); as part of the global economy predominantly comprising 'those components of industries which are operating across borders' (Sassen, 2001: 347).

It is, therefore, important to understand what defines the 'Indian City'. Surely, it is unlike any western city or the developed cities of Asia. A former Prime Minister of India wanted to transform Mumbai into a Shanghai and a former Chief Minister of Karnataka dreamt of making Bangalore a Singapore. Such ideas are not only unrealistic, they are likely to distort the image of what can be a good Indian city. Visualising the future without understanding the past and without a clear perspective of the present can have the effect of vitiating the very process of urban policy making and planning. Urban epistemology is interdisciplinary with urban economics, politics, sociology, science, and social science in dynamic interaction. New forms of urbanisation unfolding around the world that challenge inherited conceptions of the urban as a fixed, bounded and universally generalised settlement type have given rise to debates about the future course of urban development (Brenner & Schmidt, 2015). In more recent times, inequality, migration, zoonotic pandemics and the disruption they bring in their wake, combined with the emergence of million plus cities and megacities growing out of the rural hinterland or devouring the rural, as it were, compels us to rethink urbanisation.

The crucial and widely discussed issue of local autonomy needs to be addressed more objectively. In an increasingly globalising economy, can cities decide their own future? Will devolution of power to the city government propel economic development and ensure good governance? How has urban local democracy worked in India? It may even be contended that there is hardly any democracy at the city level compared to rural India where panchayats enjoy greater autonomy. The concept of local autonomy may vary from place to place, depending on the level of development and local capacity. Arguments for both state control and city control are valid and are in conflict with each other (Frug, 2014). Can we consider *a new form/model of urban local government* that suits the Indian ethos and the local conditions?

The focus of the book will be more on the processes of urban governance: the 'Urban Practice', which can provide better insights into how a city functions and how a city government works, and who makes them work? While the process of urbanisation and its impact has been dealt with elaborately in urban literature, the process of urban governance has not, unfortunately received the attention it deserves. In this book, I have tried to adopt a holistic approach with city-centric illustrations to identify and discuss the issues pertaining to the growth and development of Indian cities and to explore the ways and means of reclaiming them from the ad hoc, compartmentalised approach that has characterised their growth till now.

While each city is unique with its own special features, certain characteristics appear common across the urban centres. First, they exhibit dual features: the old and the new, one representing the traditional ways of life and styles of architecture, with narrow and congested streets, and the other, planned and developed according to British styles. Secondly, several cities and towns in India have an administrative base, serving as the headquarters of a district, taluk and a further sub-divisional level of what is termed as hobli. Third, there are the post-independent newly built cities like Chandigarh and Lutyen's Delhi and industrial townships like Bhilai and Rourkela, and now the newly conceived smart cities, each typology contributing to the ideas of development in new and older cities. Fourthly, in every state, there are rapidly growing metros with their changing landscapes. Finally, the political economy acts as the overriding driver for the spatial and temporal patterns. While it is not the case that these characteristics manifest uniformly across all cities, they do provide a starting point to develop a framework for a new urban historiography. Urban policy and city planning need to respond to the unevenly developing urban geographies and the diverse conflicts and competing demands the cities engender.

Future Challenges

Niti Ayog in its document 'Strategy for New India @75' has attempted to define "clear objectives for 2022-23 in a diverse range of 41 areas that recognise the progress already made, and challenges that remain, identify binding constraints in specific sectors, and suggest a way forward to achieving the stated objectives", and included two areas pertaining to urban development: 'Smart Cities for Urban Transformation' and 'Modernising City Governance for Urban Transformation'. This is a welcome recognition by the government of the importance of cities and in evolving a strategy to make them 'smart' and 'well governed'. Smart cities are aimed at "driving job creation and economic growth, significantly improve efficiencies in serviced delivery and leverage technology for inclusive, sustainable and participatory development by 2022-23". The objective of modernising city governance is "to transform our cities into economically vibrant and environmentally sustainable habitats that provide equitable access to basic infrastructure, public services and opportunities to all citizens and platforms for democratic participation".

The COVID-19 pandemic has thrown up new challenges as well as opportunities. The recovery agenda will have to address the following three critical issues:

1. carrying the huge health care burden arising from the density of the urban population and migration, and strengthening public health and related infrastructure,
2. boosting employment opportunities for the youth, the informal sector workers, migrant population and other deprived sections, and

3. making cities 'livable' for all citizens: ease of living that includes transparent and simplified government processes by which citizens can access infrastructure and public services.

The key challenge, from a policy and planning perspective, is to *rethink the development paradigm* and consider an *integrated urban-rural development model*, a model that positions a urban-rural command area as a growth centre, and adopt a strategy of focusing on productivity-inclusiveness-employment-generation, entrepreneurship, environmental sustainability, and a set of essential services and infrastructure that erases the distinction between the rural and the urban, between the village and the city.

From a global perspective, some critical issues arise, pertaining to the future of cities in the context of global pandemics and the recent Russia-Ukraine and Issad-Palestine wars. The former has forced us to revisit our assumptions about human health and medical progress while the latter has demonstrated as it were that cities painstakingly built over years can be reduced to a rubble in no time. Both pose a threat to the survival of mankind.

Secondly, international migration has emerged as an important dynamic in determining the economic future of cities and nations. With declining populations in developed countries and rising populations in several developing countries, movement from the latter to the former is bound to increase, especially of the youth seeking new avenues of education and employment and new lifestyles. Forced migration on account of international political conflicts is a hard reality as evident from the mass exodus from some of the Arab countries to Europe and across some countries in Asia and Africa. Climate change giving rise to intense heat conditions and other natural disasters will induce movement to safer places.

As interconnectedness between cities across the world, increasingly facilitated by modern technology gets closer, while nationalist tendencies get stronger, we may speculate *if cities will become more important than nation states?* Can cities while owing allegiance to their national sovereign state authorities, develop a non-national identity? Will city leaders, keener than national leaders about local public order, local development and the welfare of their citizens, be able to exhibit greater responsibility in avoiding conflicts and promoting peace, and a safer living environment? What will be the role of citizens, and what will be their power in these evolving circumstances, *vis-a-vis* the government.

Finally, and perhaps most importantly, what kind of policy interventions and governance framework are needed to translate the desired goals into reality? This book will explore a new historiography of urban India and seek to develop a framework to better understand the challenges of urban development praxis for the future.

Part I
The Urban Legacy

Chapter
1

Pre-Colonial India

> The city, as one finds it in history, is the point of maximum concentration for the power and culture of a community. It is the place where the diffused rays of the many separate beams of life fall into focus. The city is the form and symbol of an integrated social relationship: it is the seat of the temple, the market, the hall of justice, the academy of learning. Here in the city the goods of civilisation are multiplied, and manifolded; here is where the human experience is transformed into viable signs, symbols, patterns of conduct, systems of order. Here is where the issues of civilisation are focused: here, too, ritual passes on occasion into the active drama of a fully differentiated and self-conscious society.
>
> (Lewis Mumford, 1938)

Rise and Fall of Ancient Indian Cities

At the midpoint of the twentieth century, in 1950, a little over two years after achieving political independence, India became a sovereign democratic republic with its own constitution. We emerged as a modern nation with an ancient civilisational past and a proud urban legacy. At the dawn of Independence, the country was mostly rural, with 80 per cent of its people living in villages. This, however, ought not to create an impression that, in the past, India was all non-urban. As a country with over 2,500 years of recorded history, a look back to the beginnings of urbanisation in India would serve as a useful link to the present.

India's urban heritage can be traced back to the Bronze Age (3300-1800 BCE), when the Indus Valley civilisation flourished between 2600 and 1600 BCE, along with other great civilisations of antiquity such as the Egyptian and the Mesopotamian. Cities were an important feature of this civilisation, prominent among them being Harappa, Mohenjodaro, and Ganeriwala, now located in Pakistan, and Dholavira, Kalibangan, Lothal, and Rakhigarhi in present-day India. These cities reveal remarkable features of town planning. Streets were broad and laid out according to a plan, with a roadside drainage system and underground drainage for sewage disposal. The street design, with a grid pattern, seems strikingly modern. The people displayed a high sense of cleanliness, as evidenced by the existence of public and private baths. Dholavira, considered one of the best preserved urban settlements, and now a UNESCO World Heritage site, shows evidence of good town planning, with well-designed streets, houses, drainage, cemetery, stadium, ceremonial ground, and a series of reservoirs (Chandra, 2021; Harish, 2009).

The 'second urbanisation' in India occurred during the Iron Age (sixth to third century BCE) when new urban settlements emerged along the Ganges and Indus rivers. The use of iron weapons facilitated the formation of large territorial states. In addition to kingdoms, evidence shows that several republics that flourished during this period. Pataliputra emerged as the capital of the powerful Mauryan Empire, along with cities such as Kausambi, Kashi, Champa, Ujjain, Vaishali, and Takshashila. Major seaports of the time included Bharukachcha (Broach in Gujarat), Suparaka (Sopara, north of Bombay), and Tamralipti (Tamluk in West Bengal), and references to sea voyages and trading journeys to the coasts of Burma, Malaya (Suvarnabhumi), and Ceylon. Kashi and Shravasti served as centres of inland routes. Traded articles included silk, ivory, gold, embroidery, and jewellery. The demand for such goods fostered arts and crafts, leading to the emergence of social groups comprising artisans and merchants. For the first time, the use of coins made of metals, including copper and silver, came into circulation in cities, with copper (*karshapana*) being the standard unit of value. Coins were also considered evidence of

The expected regional planning of the Harappan Civilization

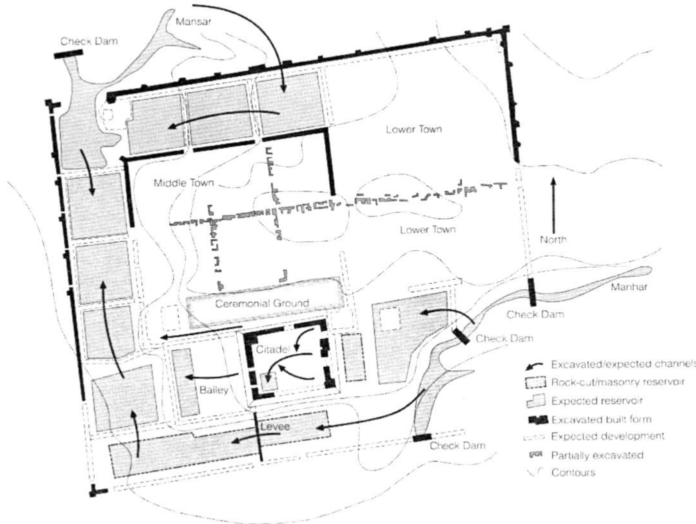

Excavation plan of Dholavira, showing the main features of the city plan

Fig. 1.1: The regional plan of the Indus Valley Civilisation and the city plan of Dholavira. The city of Dholavira is one of the ancient world's finest examples of a planned city, with provisions for infrastructure such as water tanks and drainage systems, and public spaces such as a *maidan* and markets.

Source: Swastik Harish, based on various excavations and historical reports.

commodity production and trading. There are references to the existence of crafts and occupations during this time and an estimated 100 occupations in Rajagriha and Kapilavastu. Excavations have unearthed various types of pottery, dyes, textiles, glass, ivory and iron workers (Sharma, 1991).

Trade has flourished in India since ancient times. Referring to India's tradition of trading, Sir William Hunter, a Scottish historian and a member of the Indian Civil Service (ICS), wrote: "From the earliest days, India has been a trading country. The industrial genius of its inhabitants, even more than her natural wealth and her extreme sea-board, distinguished her from other Asiatic lands. In contrast with the Arabian peninsula on the west, with the Malaya peninsula on the east ..., India has always maintained an active intercourse with Europe" (Hunter, 1898).

Recent archaeological excavations have revealed another ancient civilisation where vibrant urban life flourished at least 2,600 years ago (c580 BCE) at Keezhadi, a village 12 km south-east of Madurai city in Tamil Nadu. Brick structures, gold ornaments, iron implements, terracotta toys, figurines, beads of glass, black and redware have been unearthed. The discovery of ancient ring wells indicates that the inhabitants used groundwater. With the discovery of new artefacts during 2018-20, two more villages—Agaram, a habitation site and Konthagal, a burial site—have been added to the Keezhadi cluster (Sivapriyam, 2021).

The period of Gautama Buddha was characterised by the growth of towns and the development of town life, closely associated with the growth of industry and commerce. The Buddhist scripture, *Mahaparinibbana Sutta* refers to great cities (*mahanagara*) like Champa, Rajagriha, Sravasthi, Saketa and Kusinagara. While some towns were built as fortress towns, commercial towns developed as a result of flourishing trade.

According to Sharma (1991), early historic urbanism reached its peak in India between 200 BC and 300 AD. "Rajagriha, Vaishali, Banaras, Shravasti, Kaushambi and Athrajinkera are some of these towns. Not far from Dharwad is Vadgaon-Madhavpur, a Satavahana site excavated by Karnatak University, Kaveripattinam in Tamil Nadu. These sites, prosperous in terms of coins, structures, semi-precious stones, ivory, glass articles" (*ibid.*). 50,000 Satavahana coins can be seen in the State Museum of Hyderabad.

Governance in Ancient India

Although ancient India was marked by the existence of towns and cities, there are no reliable records about an urban governance system, as separate from overall governance. According to Z. Khan, public administration in ancient and medieval India consisted of structures, procedures and behaviours which ruling dynasties and emperors employed for running their governments. It is speculated that during the Indus Valley period, there might have existed something like a municipal government which made arrangements for looking after the needs of the people. Later, with the rise of powerful kingdoms, a monarchical system of government began to take shape and the King came to be recognised as supreme head of the government. In exercising administrative functions, the king was assisted by ministers and councillors.

During the Buddhist period, empires faded away and republican states (*Mahajanapadas*) had emerged, such as Avanti, Gandhara, Kashi and Kosala. Power was vested in the *Sabhas* (Councils) comprising the common people and the elite. The head of the *Sabha* was elected for a fixed period and was accountable to the *Sabha*.

The Mauryan empire (321-185 BCE), the first large empire in ancient India, exhibited features of a well established administrative system. With a centralised form of government, the system of administration was monarchical and hierarchical. The king was the head of the administration and was assisted by a council of ministers known as *Mantri Parishad* and secretaries. Administrative power was distributed among various administrative units or departments and each department was headed by an *Adhyaksha* or superintendent assisted by clerks, accountants and other officials, including spies. Two important officials were the *Samharta* or collector-general of revenue and *Samhidata* who was in charge of the treasury.

To enable provincial administration, the empire was divided into two parts: one under the direct rule of the king and the second that consisted of vassal states. The former, under the control of the king was divided into a hierarchical structure of provinces, districts and tehsils. The vassal states is said to have enjoyed a great deal of autonomy.

The governance system of the Mauryas attached great importance to the treasury (finance) and collected revenue through taxes and rents. All land was considered as belonging to the king and those cultivating land were to give one-sixth of their produce to the king. Interestingly, taxes included water tax as in modern times (water charges), apart from forest tax and excise duty. On its part, the government undertook welfare measures, material well-being of the people being of primary concern, especially during the reign of emperor Asoka. Justice was dispensed according to the principles of *Dharma*. While the king was the head of the judiciary, there were subordinate judges and the king served as the highest court of appeal.

While there is no evidence of a separate urban governance system, during this period, Megasthenes, the Greek historian who described India in his book *Indica*, refers to the administration of Pataliputra, the capital of the Mauryan empire. According to him, there was a Municipal Board to govern the city; the Board consisted of thirty members and there were six committees, each committee comprising five members and entrusted with specific functions such as trade and commerce, supervision of manufacturing, collection of excise and customs duties and registration of births and deaths.

During the rule of the Guptas (3rd-6th century CE) considered a golden age in Indian history, monarchy continued, with the king assuming titles like *Rajadhiraja* and *Maharajadhiraja*. There was a Ministerial Council called *Mantri Parishad* to assist the king in his functions. The empire was divided into provinces headed by a governor (akin to a modern District Magistrate), which were subdivided into *bhuktis* administered by *Uparikas* appointed by the king. The bureaucracy comprised officials carrying high sounding names such as *Rajapurusha*, *Rajanayaka* and *Rajaputra*. The judicial officer was named *Mahadandanayaka*. As under the Mauryas, all land belonged to the king and revenue was collected through taxes. The Gupta system of administration is said to have influenced the subsequent rulers like Kalachuris, Chalukyas and Rashtrakutas.

Ancient Cities of South India

After the collapse of the Mauryan empire, the northern part of India faced several invasions, causing political instability, except for a brief period of Gupta rule (mid-late third century to sixth century CE). This led to a slowdown in urbanisation, except for the growth of some fortress towns along travel routes and rivers. However, south India demonstrated greater continuity in urbanism, mainly because of the absence of foreign invasions. Tamil classical literature of the Sangam period provides evidence of an independent urban civilisation in the south, with mentions of cities like Madurai, Kancheepuram, Puhar, and Urayur.

Megasthenes, an ancient Greek historian and Indian ethnographer, referred to the first two of these cities in his travel accounts, and Kautilya's *Arthashastra* notes trade relations between these cities and the Mauryas. The southern cities had also established trade contacts with the Arabs, Greeks, and Romans around 1000 BCE. Incidentally, the original manuscript of *Arthashastra* was discovered in the Oriental Library in Mysore city in the twentieth century.

It is worth noting that India, along with China, was one of the largest economies in the world much before the British arrived. Angus Maddison, a British economist, estimated in his remarkable research on global economy that incomes in western Europe in the year 1,000 were lower than in India and China (Maddison, 2001). According to Maddison (2001), India's share of the world economy declined from 24.4 per cent in 1700 to 4.2 per cent in 1950. As described in the earlier section, several Indian cities were prominent centres of trade and commerce, whose glory was also captured by foreign travellers visiting India. Although India was a major centre of urban civilisation during the Mauryan Empire between the fourth and second centuries BC, "India would ultimately fall into a decline with its urban centres largely atrophied, warring competitive states wreaked havoc on one another, and long distance trade suffered as a result" (Blake, 1991).

Why did towns decline after 300 AD? According to Satish Chandra Misra, historian and a former Chairman, University Grants Commission (UGC) (*ibid.*), three factors contributed to the decline: (1) Indo-Roman trade stopped from third century AD onwards, (2)

Fig. 1.2: Excavations at Keezhadi, speculated to be an ancient Sangam-era city, near present-day Madurai, Tamil Nadu.
Source: Government of Tamil Nadu, Department of Archaeology.

the Satavahana empire which brought a lot of gold from outside ended, and (3) Central Asian trade tapered off. These led to a social crisis reflected in social progress being accompanied by social inequality, a phenomenon we are witnessing today—economic growth and social transformation of cities resulting in greater socio-economic inequalities.

Revival of Urban Life during Muslim Rule

In the medieval era, during Muslim rule in India between the thirteenth and seventeeth centuries, there was some revival or urban life. Business activities were observed in towns such as Lahore, Multan, Kashi, Mathura and Ujjain. Medieval towns were spread across fertile lands, taking advantage of land and water routes for cultivation of a variety of local products. Some were well populated; Agra had a population of 6,60,000 in the 1630s and Patna had 2,00,000. The Mughal rule, from Babar to Aurangazeb for about two centuries (sixteenth and seventeenth) provided some stability to the administration and it was during this period that new towns like Agra and Fatehpur Sikri were built. *Pax Mughalica* is credited with having accelerated the growth of urbanisation in the medieval period, and the flow of surplus revenue having contributed to such growth. Abul Fazl, author of *Akbarnama*, wrote that Akbar's empire was divided into 105 *sirkars*, each having a number of towns. Arguably, urbanisation in Mughal India overshadowed the growth of towns in western Europe (Abu'l-Fazl, 1902).

The Deccan region witnessed the emergence of new urban centres such as Bidar, Bijapur, and Golconda. Southern cities such as Tanjore, Tirunelveli, Calicut and Rajahmundry became prosperous business centres on account of their trade connections with other countries. Foreign travellers like Ibn Batuta, Domingo Paes, and Marco Polo described cities like Vijayanagar, the capital of the famous Vijayanagar Empire, in glorious detail. Barbosa, the Portuguese traveller visited Vijayanagara in the early sixteenth century during the reign of Krishnadevaraya, regarded as the kingdom's greatest emperor. The praise bestowed by Barbosa on the empire makes a specific reference to its cities, "the empire is very rich, and well supplied with provisions, and is very full of cities and large townships" (Kamath, 2001).

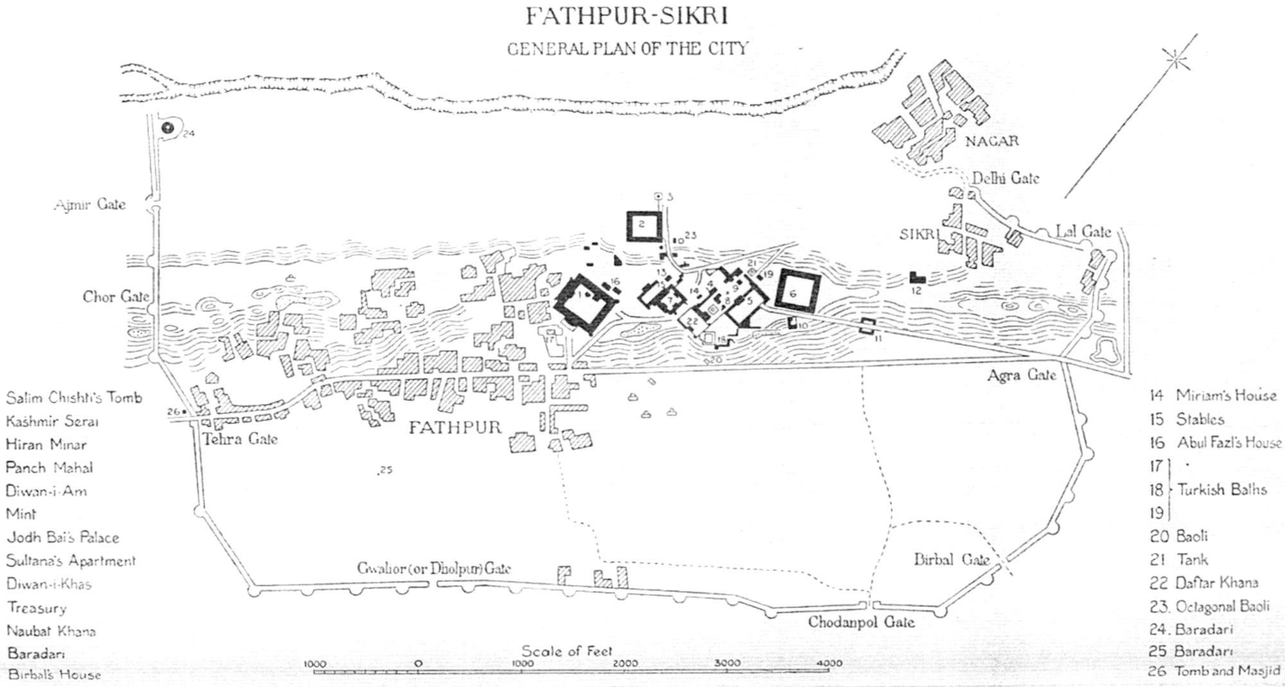

Fig. 1.3: General plan of the city of Fatehpur Sikri, near Agra, Uttar Pradesh.
Source: Vincent Arthur from *Flickr Commons*.

Madurai, Thanjavur, and Kancheepuram were also well developed cultural centres.

Urban Governance in Medieval India

In medieval India, covering a long period (6th-16th century CE), we witness a greater degree of urbanisation with the emergence of a number of secondary towns which may be classified into three categories: administrative towns, temple towns and centres of commercial activities. The administrative towns generally happened to be the capital of the kingdom from where the king carried on the administration with his retinue of officials. In temple towns, many activities centred around the temple, and in commercial towns, manufacturing and trade were the major activities. Some of them however combined two or more activities. Thanjavur, for instance, was the capital of the Cholas surrounded by temples while Surat developed as a centre of textile industry. Hampi was the capital of Vijayanagar empire and renowned for its architecture and sculpture. Somnath in the west and Kancheepuram, Madurai and Tirupati in the south were prominent temple towns. Masulipatam on the east coast, originally built by the Dutch and had the sole distributorship for textiles and spices.

A number of towns and cities were developed during the course of the Mughal rule spanning over two centuries. Agra, Delhi, Fatehpur Sikri and Lahore served as imperial capitals as their rulers kept shifting the centre of power from time to time. Fatehpur Sikri built by emperor Akbar in the 16th century was the first planned city under the Mughals; unfortunately it had to be abandoned on account of lack of water supply to support the residents.

During the Mughal rule, the emperor continued to be the head of the administration, combining in himself the roles of law maker, commander-in-chief and dispenser of justice. For effective administration, the empire was divided into *subhas* and further subdivided into *sarkars*, *parganas* and *grams*. Akbar introduced the *Mansabdari* system (Mughal nobility) which was responsible for the administration of the state (*Mansab* was a grant to enjoy a *jagir* given to every official). There were four major departments and four officers in charge of each of them. The *Diwan*, who was the chief minister with overall responsibility of the administration including revenues and finance (sounds like present day chief ministers of many states in India who also handle the Finance portfolio), *Mir Bakshi* in charge of military pay and accounts, *Mir Samar*, responsible for maintenance of records and stores and Sadr was head of religious donations and education.

The structure of the provincial administration under the Mughals consisted of provincial units headed by the Governor (*Sipar Nazim*). *Subhadar* appointed by the emperor looked after civil and military affairs of a *Subha*. A *subha* was divided into *Sarkars* at the local level and a *Faujdar* executed the royal decrees, an *Amalgunar* collected revenue, *Muqaddam* was the village head assisted by a *Patwari* who took care of village records.

Sher Shah Suri, founder of the Sur empire in Bihar, who took control of the Mughal empire for a brief period (1540 to 1545) during the regime of Humayun introduced several innovative administrative reforms. He reorganised the empire and set up a new economic and military administration. His contributions include standardising the currency by introducing silver, gold and copper coins and naming it Rupee (which continues till this day), organising a postal system for the entire sub-continent, extending the Grand Trunk Road from Chittagong in Bengal to Kabul in Afghanistan, with *caravan serais* (inns) built along the highway and trees planted on both sides. He is also credited with reviving the historical city of Pataliputra (Burn, 1937).

On the whole, the rise and decline of pre-industrial and pre-colonial towns or urban settlements in India were closely linked to the political regime of the times. The religious and commercial activities played a role in limiting the impact of political vicissitudes, but the will of the ruler and the needs of the kingdom or empire, such as defence, were at the core. In Europe too, the origin of towns during the medieval times is attributed primarily to defence and trade considerations.

Chapter
2

The Colonial Roots of Urban Governance

> The history of India might be a record of invasions, of the rise and fall of dynasties, of the instability of the state, but social conditions remained unaffected by changes of rulers because their divine origin placed them, generally speaking, outside political control. Indeed, the stability of the Hindu social order was reinforced by the instability of the political system...The majority of the people—the cultivators of the land—took no part in wars or political upheavals. *Their real interest was not in who governed, but in how they governed*; is essentially the incidence of taxation, and the absence of interference in religion and customs.
>
> (Michael Edwards, 1967)

Beginnings of Colonisation

The colonial roots of British governance in India are generally traced to the ruthless exploitation of the country's rich resources—natural resources, raw materials and the skill and labour of its people—as much as to their military and political power of consolidation. Writing in 1901 about the economic conditions in the later nineteenth century, R.C. Dutt, a distinguished civil servant and economic historian, notes painfully but eloquently:

> "The poverty of the Indian population at the present day is unparalleled in any civilised country; the famines which have desolated India within the last quarter of the 19th century are unexampled in their extent and intensity in the history of ancient or modern times. By a moderate calculation, the famines of 1877 and 1878, of 1889 and 1892, of 1897 and 1900, have carried fifteen million people. The population of a fair-sized European country has been swept away from India within twenty-five years. A population equal to half of that of England has perished in India within a period which men and women still in middle age can remember."
>
> (Dutt, 1902, p. viii)

The colonisation of modern India began in early sixteenth century, soon after Vasco da Gama set foot on Indian soil in 1498. The pioneering and adventurous Portuguese navigator opened the sea route to the subcontinent which became a trading ground for the European nations. The Portuguese were quick to recognise the value of a sheltered harbour site in one of the islands on the west coast which they named Bombain or Boavida ('lucky harbour' in Portuguese), which later became Bombay. In 1510, Alfonso de Albuquerque captured Goa, the picturesque town and the surrounding region on the western coast which became the Portuguese base of their long and uninterrupted rule for a period of four and a half centuries till 1961.

The sixteenth and seventeenth centuries witnessed the Dutch, the French, and the British vying with each other to establish their overseas empires, of which India happened to be the largest. Ultimately, the British, more ambitious and enterprising, succeeded in expanding their footprint across the sub-continent. The East India Company (EIC), setting foot on Indian soil in 1600, after securing the grant of a monopoly of trading rights in India and Asia by Queen Elizabeth, played a key role in establishing the British hegemony in India. Bombay soon passed into their hands when the Portuguese decided to part with this coastal town as dowry to King Charles II who married the Portuguese princess Catherine of Braganza in 1661. In turn, it was leased to the East India Company for a measly sum of 10 pounds a year. In due course, Bombay not only became the major harbour site to develop trade for the Company but served as the nucleus for the British empire in western India. The Company shifted its base from Surat, the first trading post it had set up in the sub-continent, to Bombay.

Spreading its wings to the south-east, the British secured a foothold in a small fishing village called Madras or Madraspatam, and in 1687, King James II of England delegated to the East India Company the power to establish a Corporation and a Mayor's Court. Accordingly, under the Charter of 1687, a corporation called the Mayor, Aldermen and Burgesses (councillors of the present-day) of the town of Fort St. George and Madraspatam was established in 1688. Thus, Madras became the first city corporation established in India. On lines similar to Madras, in the north-east, the Calcutta Municipal government with a mayor and nine Aldermen was set up in 1727 under a Royal Charter.

With the onset of colonisation in the seventeenth century, urbanisation in India took a new form. The growth of modern towns in Europe was based on the forces unleashed by the industrial revolution in the 18th century. In 1800, the population of the continent was 175 million, of which only 1.6 per cent lived in 20 cities with a population of 1,00,000 or more. However, this figure rose to 120 by 1890 on account of the impact of industrialisation. The change from mere trading to manufacturing and the development of transport, particularly the railways, accelerated the growth of industrial centres in Europe. This had an influence on the growth of towns outside Europe and the Third World countries inherited their modern economic infrastructure from an era of colonisation (McGee, 1971). The introduction of railways in India in the 1850s contributed greatly to urban and economic growth of the country. Its impact, particularly since 1931, was profound, as evidenced by the fact that the number of cities with populations of 1,00,000 or more, which numbered 49 in 1931, rose to 2,500, along the railway lines.

The advent of the British also marked the beginning of what may be called 'modern urbanism' in India. The first Census of India of 1872 listed 16 one lakh cities. It is interesting to note that all of them happened to be trading centres and India served as the main market for British goods, as England had become the major industrial centre of the world. The European colonial powers sourced raw materials

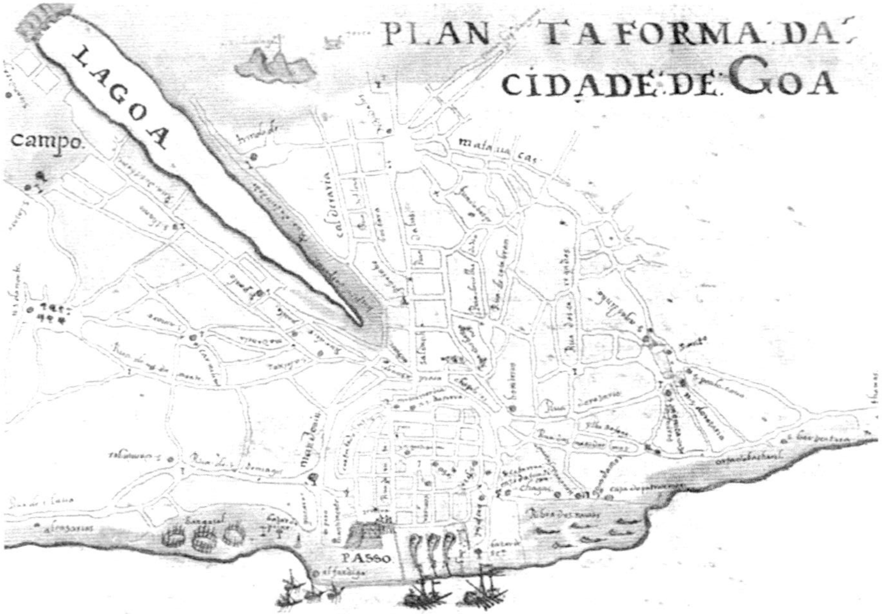

Fig. 2.1: An artist's impression of the plan of Goa in 1620; Goa was one of the most important colonial cities in the sub-continent at the time.

Source: Manuel Godinho de Heredia.

from India to feed their factories. Their economic policies proved detrimental to the smaller traditional towns, although major cities like Bombay, Calcutta, Madras and Delhi witnessed a growth of nearly 10 per cent in their population compared to 1800. Some historians opine that medieval towns like Agra, Ahmedabad, Baroda, Indore, Tanjore and Lucknow lost their importance due to the negative approach adopted by them in dealing with the colonial powers in matters relating to traditional industries such as handicrafts and cotton textiles. Mirzapur, famous for its copper and brassware industry, came to be called a 'sick town' at the beginning of the twentieth century.

The Geography: Mapping of the Subcontinent

One of the most significant events associated with the British rule was the establishment of The Survey of India in 1767, which has evolved over the years and emerged as the country's principal mapping agency. The initial efforts to launch the surveying work began in the southern cities of Madras and Bangalore. The first Government Survey School came up in Madras in 1834 and later developed into a civil engineering college. Even before surveying, mapping was undertaken. Encouraged by Thomas Pitt, the Governor of Madras, the earliest reliable map of the city, known as the Pitt Map was prepared in 1710-11.

In 1763, James Rennell, a young commander of a British ship, started surveying the Coromandel coast and mapped its southern reaches. Taking note of this, Robert Clive, the first British Governor of Bengal Presidency ordered Rennell to begin a general survey of Bengal and with it began "the Survey of India story in 1765" (S. Muthiah, 1987). Rennell's work resulted in the well known Bengal Atlas. Unable to adjust to the climatic conditions in India, Rennell returned to England but continued to supervise the work of surveyors in India for a long time and came to be famously known as the 'Father of Indian Geography'.

It was left to two remarkable persons, Colin Mackenzie and William Lambton, to launch the marathon work of surveying the sub-continet. Mackenzie began by carrying out a survey of the Deccan and later in Mysore. In 1806, Lambton began his project in Bangalore to realise a 'grand meridian line' for India, reaching Cape Comorin in 1808 (Mathur & Da Cunha, 2006). The survey aimed to link the

Coromandel coast with the Malabar coast and this project marked the beginning of The Great Trigonometrical Survey of India. From Bangalore once again in 1808, Lambton extended his arc north. Appointed Superintendent of this project in 1818, Lambton pushed forward enthusiastically to central India with the final goal of reaching the Himalayas. Unfortunately, he died in 1826 in a survey tent near Nagpur. The work, however, continued with his assistant, George Everest, taking over as Superintendent of the project and relentlessly marching along the line which came to be known as The Great Indian Arc of the Meridian and eventually capturing the highest peak of the Himalayan mountain range. Calculated as Peak XV in 1852, it was named after its pioneering conqueror as Mount Everest. Traversing a long distance of 2250 kms, this wonderful feat was described by Clements Markham, a renowned English geographer and explorer as "one of the most stupendous works in the whole history of science" (Mathur & Da Cunha, 2006).

From the urban governance perspective, the importance of city surveys cannot be overemphasized. From measurement of land parcels, big or small to fixing boundaries of cities or land development projects or individual properties, they play a crucial role. Unfortunately, city surveys have not received the attention they deserve and municipal authorities are handicapped by lack of accurate data pertaining to their own properties and those of encroachers of public property. This problem was experienced in Bengaluru recently during the heavy rains and floods, when it came to notice that flooding was caused on account of several unauthorized constructions. When BBMP started demolishing such structures, the occupants claimed their ownership, but the civic authority was unable to provide any evidence of ownership of the properties in the absence of survey maps.

Local Self-Governance in the Colonial Era

Lord Ripon, known as 'a true liberal of Gladstonian era' and considered the 'father of local self-government' in India, took the initial steps towards liberalising the administration and laid the foundation of representative institutions in the country. Ripon's Resolution of 1882 recommended setting up local boards, introducing a system of elections for members of the boards, and empowering the boards to manage local sources of revenue. The resolution recognised that local self-government served as an 'instrument of political and popular education', stating, "The task of administration is yearly becoming more onerous as the country progresses in civilisation and material prosperity...Under these circumstances, ... the only reasonable plan open to the Government is to induce the people themselves to undertake, as far as may be, the management of their own affairs; and to develop or create, if need be, a capacity for self-help...". Ripon's resolution was widely welcomed in India, Justice Ranade claiming that "a State paper more liberal, life-inspiring and instinct with true statesmanship can hardly be conceived and has certainly not been seen for many years in India".

Interestingly, British officials resisted attempts to free local authorities from the control of the district administration, much like Indian officials in independent India. Senior British officials like Sir J. Fergusson in Bombay and R. Thomson in Bengal expressed themselves against it, arguing that it would adversely affect efficiency. Similarly, much like today, provincial governments showed little interest in implementing the reforms. This was borne out by the fact that the system of nomination, instead of election, was continued for a long time. As Hugh Tinker, the British historian, put it, "the Viceroy was almost alone in his liberalism; the majority of local Anglo-Indian officials were conservatives, supporters of paternal administration so that reforms projected by Ripon were attenuated, or even ignored by the provincial governments and district officers who were responsible for putting them into practice' (Tinker, 1954, pp. 43-33).

In 1907, the British government constituted the Royal Commission on Decentralisation in India under the chairmanship of Sir Henry William Primrose to 'inquire into the possibility of decentralising some powers of the Government of India'. The Commission submitted its report in 1909, but unfortunately, it came into conflict with the India Office, the Government of India (GoI) and the provincial governments, each of whom had their own views, as did Indian nationalists and the native press. As a result, little came out of the report. Nearly a decade later, based on the Montagu-Chelmsford Reforms, the Resolution of 1918 articulated the basic principles of local democracy thus, stating that,

> "the object of local self-government is to train the people in the management of their own local affairs and that political education of this sort, must, in the main, take precedence of considerations of departmental efficiency. It follows from this that local bodies should be as representative as possible of the people whose affairs they are called on to administer, that their authority in the matters entrusted to them should be real and not nominal, and that they should not be subjected to unnecessary control, but should learn by making mistakes and profiting by them. The general policy, therefore, one of the gradual removal of unnecessary government control and differentiating the spheres of action appropriate for government and for local bodies respectively."
>
> [Venkatarangaiya M. & M. Pattabhiram (eds), *op. cit*].

Significantly, this time, many of the directions of the resolution were implemented by the provincial governments such as the election of Chairmen of Boards, financial flexibility and freedom from control. In August 1917, the British government made a declaration 'promising responsible government to India through the gradual development of self-governing institutions'. To fulfil the promise, a new legislation called the Government of India Act, 1919, was passed. This law introduced the system of 'dyarchy' and subjects such as local self-government, agriculture and cooperation were transferred to the provinces, enabling popularly elected ministers to exercise their authority.

The Statutory Commission, also known as the Simon Commission, appointed in 1927 to recommend measures to further liberalise the government, examined the functioning of local self-government. It observed that local self-governance in India did not exactly resemble the British pattern, which was more decentralised, and local bodies could formulate and execute their own policies. Instead, it resembled more the continental system of 'deconcentration', where the chief executive officer of the local government was appointed by the government, whose will he carried out instead of that of the local leaders (Pinto, 2000).

Nearly a century later, the power of appointing the commissioner of the municipal body continues to vest with the state government, making this observation still relevant and contemporary.

Decentralisation: Threat to or Consolidation of Union?

The measures taken by the government to decentralise power from the central to lower levels of administration may not have been motivated by a genuine desire to vest decision-making power in the people, but rather by the larger goal of strengthening the empire. This is evident from the statement made by the Secretary of State for India, Samuel Montagu, in the House of Commons on August 27, 1917. Before laying out his vision for self-governance in India, he recalled what Sir Thomas Monroe, British soldier and statesman, who had served as Governor of Madras in the early 19th century, had said:

> "What is to be the final result of our arrangements on the character of the people?. . Are we to be satisfied with merely securing our power and protecting the inhabitants, or are we to endeavour to raise their character, to render them worthy of filling higher stations in the management of their country and devising plans for their improvement?. . . We should look on India not as a temporary possession, but as one which is to be maintained permanently, until the natives shall in some future age have abandoned most of their superstitions and prejudices, and become sufficiently enlightened to frame a regular government for themselves, and to conduct and preserve it".

Montagu presented his own vision of self-governance, stating that "Indians must be enabled, in so far as they attain responsibility, to determine for themselves what they want done. The process will begin in local affairs which we have long since intended and promised to make over to them... As power is given to the people of a province or of a dominion to manage their own local affairs, their attachment becomes stronger to the Empire which comprehends them all in a common bond of union. The existence of national feeling or the love of and pride in a national culture need not conflict with, and may indeed strengthen the sense of membership in a wider commonwealth". (quoted in Deepak, 2021).

However, the intent of giving power to the people to 'manage their own local affairs' was intertwined with the ultimate aim of strengthening the colonial hold of the Empire over the people of the country. The Government of India Act of 1919 that followed, based on the Montagu Report, contained the seeds of the future constitution of India, incorporating key provisions such as the creation of central and provincial legislatures (Parliament and state legislatures) and the corresponding lists of subjects they could legislate on, as well as matters relating to the Indian Civil Service.

Significantly, it contained no provision pertaining to local government, and this decision to exclude the subject of local governance (urban and rural), consciously or otherwise, seems to have coloured the vision of the post-independence Indian constitution makers. The Indian Constitution of 1950 ignored the 'local'.

Impact of Colonisation on the Indian Economy

It is generally believed, as noted earlier, that the decline of India as an economic power started after the British set foot on Indian soil, the East India Company (EIC) and the Raj being responsible for draining the country of its wealth and resources (Darlymple, 2019). In the 18th century, the two Asian countries of China and India commanded major shares in global trade. Kidwai (1991) opines that the urban atrophy in India was caused by colonial urbanisation in terms of "diminution of population size and stagnation in productive economic activities in urban areas manifested through the interrelated sub-processes of de-urbanisation, urban de-industrialisation and spurious tertiarisation of the urban economy". By end of the 17th century, the level of urbanisation in India was noticed to be higher than at the end of the 19th. Habib (1963) believes that based on the data available, there was a very high ratio of urban to the total population of the country and it is unlikely that this was exceeded till very recent times.

Roy (2000), in his recent edition of *An Economic History of India, 1707-1857*, provides a different perspective. He has argued that the colonial government was a tiny part of the economy and its remittances abroad were offset by the silver that entered India through its trade surplus. The decline of the Indian economy had started even before the British rule. The empire in India was not the result of a violent conquest as the myth goes, Indians not wanting to be subjugated went down fighting. It happened because "they did not trust other Indians, wanted the British to secure power. They preferred British rule over indigenous alternatives and helped the Company form a state...The Company came to rule India because many Indians wanted it to rule India". The British Empire emerged from the alliances it formed with Indian rulers than grabbing their land by force.

In a historical context, it may be said that the process of urbanisation in India, as in many other colonial countries, began with the development of port cities. According to Sposito (1998), the first colonial cities emerged as ports destined to evacuate the riches extracted from the colony to the mother country. Over time, they began to have multiple functions as the colonisers settled in these port cities. The Industrial Revolution accelerated the process of urbanisation in Europe as people began to move from rural to urban areas. From this process, industrialists began to dictate their own spaces for housing, giving emphasis and notoriety in socio-spatial inequalities (Leite, 2014). The development of capitalism contributed significantly to the increase in the process of world urbanisation, especially in the European historical context because it was the European territory that constituted the central space for the capitalist mode of production (Sposito, 1998). Roy holds that the East India Company presided over "the start of a process that would see a firmer integration...of maritime trade with overland trade, of trade with production, of land with sea, integrating markets for commodities, capital, knowledge, enterprise and labour. If an integrated market is a marker of modern capitalism, the eighteenth century initiated that process in India. The process of modernisation under the British rule created one of the most impressive episodes of industrialisation outside Europe". The EIC facilitated India to establish itself as a major trading partner.

Chapter

3

Colonial and Princely Capitals

The three colonial cities of Bombay in the west, Madras in the south and Calcutta in the east served as strategic port cities and developed as major centres of industry, commerce, education and administration during British colonial rule. They constituted the colonial capital of the empire and emerged as India's first metropolitan cities, performing multiple functions and making significant contributions to the socio-economic development of the country. They also served as the provincial capitals of the eastern, western and southern regions, known as presidencies, while Delhi served as the capital of the northern region and also became the national capital in 1912. The municipal organisations that developed in the four metropolises served as models of urban governance for other parts of the country. The development of each of these three colonial capitals presents an interesting picture.

Madras, Bombay and Calcutta: Centres of Colonial Capital

Madras

Madras is considered to be the first city of modern India because it was where the first municipal corporation in the country was established because it is where the British Indian army first birthed. "It is in fact from the Madras Presidency that the first native revolt (known as the Vellore Mutiny) against British rule took place, preceding the 1857 revolt by a few decades" (Muthiah, 2008). In 1639, Sri Ranga Raya VI, the then king of the Vijayanagara Empire, granted a piece of land to Francis Day of the East India Company (EIC). The latter chose an area called Madraspatnam, which later came to be known as Fort St. George as it developed into a secure British settlement because it provided security; at the same time, rumours were rife that the main reason for this choice was his mistress lived in the vicinity (Pinto, 2000).

The transformation from Madraspatnam, described as 'a city of villages' to Madras, occurred fairly rapidly due to the inflow of people from neighbouring villages, especially the merchants who wanted to trade with the EIC. Workers came from other states too, partly sought by the British and partly on their own, especially those who wanted to avoid the arbitrary rule of the sultans of Golconda. The town, however, witnessed a division of social spaces into 'Black Town' and White Town, with the latter being reserved for the small number of Europeans.

Fort St. George area, with the White Town within and Black Town beyond began to develop into an urban agglomeration, absorbing within its fold the neighbouring villages, and eventually transformed into a metropolis. From the end of the seventeenth century to the last quarter of the eighteenth century (when Calcutta became the capital in 1774), Madras continued to be the principal settlement of the British in India. In the eighteenth century, the French, led by Dupleix, captured Fort St. George in 1746. However, within three years, in 1749, the British, led by Robert Clive, took it back. During the rest of the eighteenth century, with Madras as the base, the British consolidated their position and expanded their empire in India.

Between the last quarter of the 19th century and mid-20th century, Madras witnessed a number of developmental activities. Work on the harbour was completed in 1896. Railway lines were laid, initially connecting the city centre to the north, west and south. Later, the first electrified line connected Madras Beach to Tambaram in the south. Iconic buildings like the Madras High Court, Connemara Public Library and Moore Market were built during this period. Efforts were undertaken to clean up and beautify the beach, the 'pride of Madras' Governor Grant Duff who gave shape to the project said, "We have greatly benefited Madras by turning the rather dismal beach of five years ago into one of the most beautiful promenades in the world". No wonder, Madras quickly developed into the capital of a provincial Presidency.

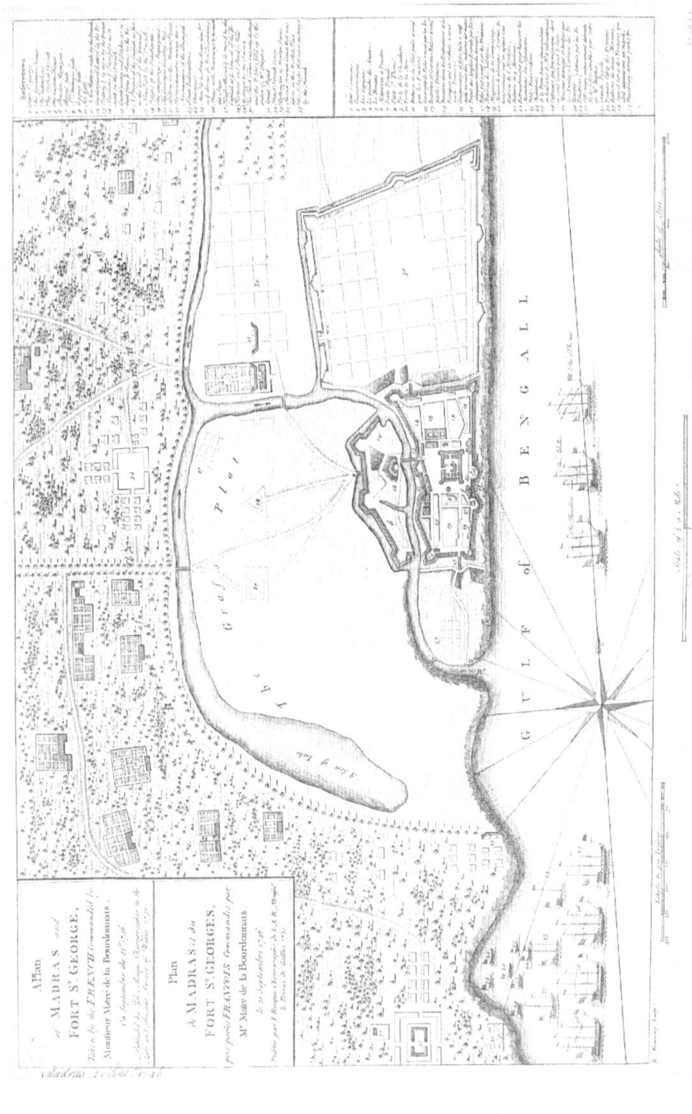

Fig. 3.1: An artist's impression of the plan of Madras in 1746.

Bombay

> The soft city of illusion, myth, aspiration, nightmare, is as real, maybe more real, than the hard city one can locate on maps, in statistics, in monographs on urban sociology and demography and architecture.
>
> (Raban, 1974, p. 4)

> The city is full of people claiming what's not theirs. Tenants claim ownership by virtue of having squatted on the property. Mill workers demand mills be kept open at a loss to provide them with employment. Slum dwellers demand water and power connections for illegal constructions on public land. Government employees demand to keep working long past when they are needed, at taxpayers' expense. Commuters demand further subsidies for train fares, which are already the lowest in the world. Moviegoers demand that the government freeze their ticket prices. The Indian government has long believed in the unreality of supply and demand; what you pay for an item, for a food or for a service has no relation to what it costs the producer.
>
> (Mehta, 2004, p. 128)

There are two kinds of cities, best captured by the two writers—one, the city that lives in our imagination and the other, the physical city where we live—in an apartment or a chawl, a luxury villa or a congested middle class locality, experiencing its beauty and filth, jostling our way through the jammed traffic to reach the workplace or coffee shop, the cinema hall or a theatre. No other city better represents this duality of city life than Mumbai or the Bombay of earlier eras. It was and continues to be the 'mythic city' of India, as described by Gyan Prakash, Professor of History at Princeton University, in his engaging book, *Mumbai Fables*; the harsh reality of city life in a large metropolis is vividly portrayed by Suketu Mehta, the renowned novelist. People go to this Maximum City from all parts of India in search of work to earn their livelihoods, to do business and become millionaires and billionaires, and with dreams of becoming a film actor, rich and famous.

What happened to be a group of seven islands under Portuguese control in the beginning of the 17th century, developed as a prominent port city after it passed into British hands and served as a major centre through which raw materials like cotton and opium passed. It is, however, important to note that the first trading post of the EIC was Surat, now in Gujarat, and was subsequently shifted to Bombay. After the British defeated the Marathas in the Anglo-Maratha war in 1819, trade and business expanded rapidly. In 1853, the Bombay-Thana rail link was built; subsequently, rail links were established with other cities like Nagpur and Raichur to the east, Baroda and Jabalpur to the north. The establishment of the first textile mill in 1854 saw an influx of migrants—artisans, traders, businessmen—into the city. The number of textile mills which numbered one in mid-19th century grew to 85 by 1921 with 1,46,000 workers, of which, significantly, 23 per cent were women. A prominent centre of textile industry, a maritime trading power and a junction of two major railways, no wonder, Bombay emerged as the leading industrial city of India, attracting people from all parts of the country.

As most of the population lived in chawls, Bombay's growth was unplanned. It was only after the epidemic of 1898 that city planning received close attention. Unfortunately, the poor became the first victims of planning; they were cleared out of the city centre due to congested and unsanitary conditions. Faced with a housing crisis, in 1918, the government brought in the Rent Act in 1918 with a view to keep rents at a reasonable level. Much earlier, in 1864, land reclamation work had been taken up by the Bombay Reclamation Company which won the right to reclaim the western foreshore from the tip of Malabar Hill to Colaba. During the years of the First World War (1914-18), the Bombay Port Trust executed a reclamation project which resulted in the creation of Ballard Estate and the development of the iconic Marine Drive. In early 20th century, Bombay also emerged as an international centre of pearl industry and a number of Gulf Arab merchants settled here and are supposed to have made a fortune (Ahmed, 2018).

Fig. 3.2: One of the options for developing the reclamation area in Bombay. This plan, with its capital complex layout and architecture, was eventually not implemented.

Calcutta

> Find, if you can, a more uninviting spot than Calcutta... it unites every kind of a perfectly unhealthy situation. The place is so bad by nature that human efforts could do little to make it worse; but that little has been done faithfully and assiduously. (Sir George Trevlyan, 1863)

> Imagine everything that was glorious in nature combined with all that is beautiful in architecture, and you can faintly picture to yourself what Calcutta is.
>
> Geoffrey Moorhouse, *Calcutta: The City Revealed*, 1971

In the mid-19th century, there emerged two contradictory opinions about Calcutta: the first by Sir George Trevelyan, British author and statesman, as a 'city of despair', and the second by William Hunter, his junior contemporary and a new recruit to ICS, as a 'city of joy'. Calcutta was considered to be founded by Job Charnock, an agent of the EIC, after he bought the three villages of Sutanuti, Kalikata and Gobindapur from a local landlord.[1] The site was used by the British first to build a factory, then a fort, and then expanded into a commercial and administrative centre, all before it came into their full possession after the Battle of Plassey in 1757. Developed as a presidency city, Calcutta emerged as the first capital of India under British rule in 1772. With industrialisation, the city started growing.

Starting primarily as port cities, the three colonial capitals developed as prominent centres for business, banking and administration. Alongside building factories and mercantile offices, the EIC fortified the towns to ensure the security and protection of people and goods. As the population grew with the inflow of migrant workers, the spatial pattern of the cities came to be influenced by the presence of a large native population and a small colonial elite, with the residential areas being segregated between the 'whites' and the 'natives'. The colonial settler population lived near the Fort in Bombay, in Fort William in Calcutta and in Fort St. George in Madras, while native Indians lived outside the forts in their own settlements. The native town was painted as chaotic and filthy, whereas the white town symbolised hygiene and cleanliness. The social segregation in these colonial cities was quite stark:

> Each community had its own space with a burying ground. The most basic division of space was that between Black

1. The founding of the city remains controversial after the High Court of Calcutta ruled in 2003 that Charnock cannot be called its founder as the three villages he supposedly 'found' were already in existence.

Fig. 3.3: Billboards at the corner of Harrison Street (Burra Bazar) and Strand Road in 1945-46.

Source: Clyde Waddell.

Town and White Town, which was reserved for Europeans. Workers such as weavers were actively sought after by the town's governor, but others came by themselves to avoid the arbitrary rule of the sultanas of Golconda....The English population of Madras was very small: under 200 at the end of 1699 CE with 30 servants of the East India Company, 35 free merchants and 38 seafaring men. There were 14 widows, 10 single young women and 22 wives. The "native population" of the Presidency was however estimated at 3,00,000 and their influx for work made Madras a rapidly expanding town. The street names reflect the very active commerce in cloths: Comatee is the Telugu for trader, and Chittee was a member of any one of the trading castes in southern India (Smith, 2018).

Delhi: Battleground to National Capital

In Delhi, we observe the good and bad of India. It is a gem with many facets, some bright, others darkened with

> the passage of time; even its stones whisper of the bygone ages...graveyard of many empires, it is the nursery of a new republic.
>
> (Nehru, 1991)

Believed to have been founded by the Pandavas of *Mahabharata* as far back as 10th century BCE—then known as Indraprastha and said to be the area between Purana Qila and Humayun's Tomb—Delhi has been a political and military battleground ever since. The nomenclature of Delhi, or Dilli, owes its origin to one Raja Dillu of the Maurya dynasty who is said to have founded a new city in the vicinity of the Qutub Minar. During the reign of Alauddin Khilji in the early 13th century, Delhi became the political capital. The efforts of Muhammad bin Tughluq to shift the capital from Delhi to Daulatabad in the Deccan ended in a fiasco on account of severe water scarcity. The capital was shifted back to Delhi after seven years in 1334, and it continued to be the undisputed capital during the time of the Mughals. When Ibn Battuta, a noted Muslim scholar and traveller from Morocco, visited Delhi in the 14th century at the time of Tughluq's rule, he was ecstatic: "What a vast and magnificent city... the largest city in India, nay the largest of all the cities of Islam in the East". Delhi's marketplace drew scholars, scientists, artists and poets from all over the Islamic world (Dunn, 1986).

In the context of governance, it may be noted that during the Sultanate and the Mughal periods, Delhi was part of an Islamic empire, wherein the primary duty of every ruler was to observe the laws of *Shariat* in his administration. As such, all people residing in the empire's territory were also subject to the same law.

In the northern part of India, the Mughals who had established a strong empire had made Delhi their capital. After the death of Aurangzeb in 1707, the territory became a battleground between different rulers. The British had to wait till 1803 to capture the city of Delhi from the Marathas. A Resident Chief Commissioner was appointed to take care of the administration of the area. After a period of nearly thirty years, in 1832, the territory of Delhi was handed over to the East India Company. Post-1858, when India came under the direct rule of the British Crown, Delhi was transferred to the Punjab, a newly formed unit, to be administered by a Lieutenant Governor.

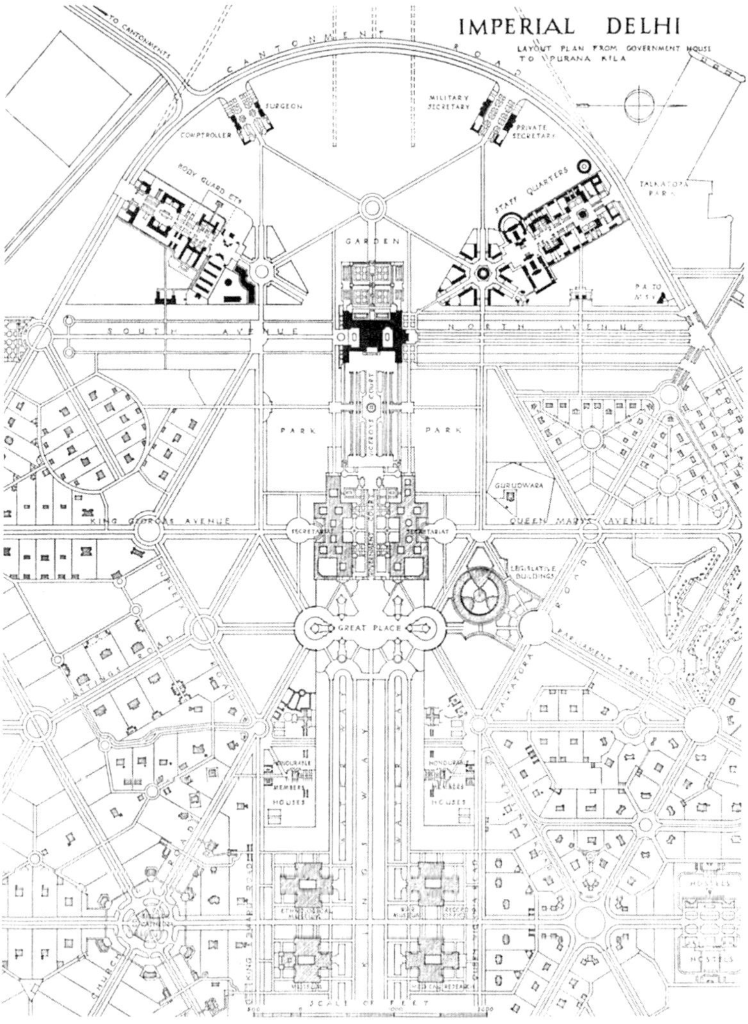

Fig. 3.4: Lutyen's 'Imperial Plan' for Delhi, 1912 to 1930s.

The industrial and commercial activities of Delhi received a boost with the advent of the railways, especially with eight railways entering the city. The city became a converging point for several trade routes, national and international; it also began serving as a key distribution centre for north and north-western India. After the national capital was shifted from Calcutta to Delhi in 1911, it started growing in political and economic importance. However, two different cities took shape, one, the Old Delhi, and the other, Lutyen's Delhi or what is now called New Delhi. The division also created two different cultures, the former identified with the Muslim population and the latter with other sections of society, including the elite. The partition of India in 1947, followed by heavy influx of refugees, the capital city was confronted with serious problems of rehabilitation and ensuring communal harmony.

While the three Presidency cities were developed by the British based on the European model, Delhi's municipal administration came to be based more on the Mughal tradition and associated with the 'mohalla' (neighbourhood), although under British influence, it followed the model of a 'native city' and a military 'cantonment' along with separate 'civil lines'. In 1863, a Delhi Municipal Committee, instead of a Municipal Corporation as in three Presidency cities was formed to perform the municipal functions. The Committee comprised 21 nominated members, of whom six were government officials and the remaining 15 consisting of non-officials included three Europeans, six Hindus and six Muslims. This system of nominated members continued till 1885, when elections were held on the basis of adult franchise; 12 were elected members, five nominated members and four were government officials, with the Deputy Commissioner of Delhi happened to be the ex-officio President of the Committee. The territory of Delhi, however, was administered directly by the Governor-General, 'acting to such extent as he thinks fit through a Chief Commissioner to be appointed in his discretion'.

Architecture, Culture and Society in Colonial Cities

During the colonial period, European styles of town planning and architecture started to emerge in cities and towns in India under British control. Notably, the Dutch pioneers of municipal governance in India established the Fort Kochi Municipality in 1664 before the Madras Municipal Corporation came into existence, but it had to be dissolved in the eighteenth century when Dutch authority became weak.

Although the British pattern predominantly influenced the architecture of the cities, the Portuguese and French also left their marks in Goa and Pondicherry, respectively. Meanwhile, old cities like

Kashi (Benares) in the north and Kancheepuram in the south retained their traditional styles of architecture and civic life.

The British-controlled cities exhibited a dual form: the modern and the traditional. The British part of the cities comprised cantonments designed to meet the requirements of their armed forces, large bungalows for the senior officers and barracks for the soldiers. Additionally, there were railway colonies with quarters for railway officers, clubs that catered to the leisure activities of the British elite while rigidly restricting admission to native Indians. The commercial areas were flanked by parks and European-style buildings such as administrative offices, educational institutions offering English education, and modern hospitals. The streets, buildings, institutions, and prominent areas were named after 'eminent' Englishmen who ruled India, including Cubbon Road and Bowring Hospital in Bangalore, Crawford Market and Albert Museum in Bombay; Dalhousie Square and Victoria Memorial Hall in Calcutta, and Ripon Building, Connamera Library in Madras.

In contrast, the local, traditional part of the cities consisted of narrow roads, congested, mixed land uses catering to the needs of the native population. It had its bazaars and temples and old-style buildings.

In the late nineteenth century, the British, who were accustomed to the cool climate of the northern hemisphere and unable to bear the heat of the tropics, built a new class of towns in the hills, which came to be called hill stations. Their choices were regionally well-distributed, with Simla, Mussoorie, and Nainital in the north near Delhi, Darjeeling and Shillong in the east near Calcutta, Mahabaleshwar in the west near Bombay, and Nilgiris and Kodaikanal in the south near Madras.

The framework for the administration of towns and cities in modern India was provided during the British rule. In 1870, Lord Mayo's resolution emphasised the need to decentralise financial and administrative powers to local governments. "Local interest, supervision and care are necessary to success in the management of funds devoted to Education, Sanitation, Medical Charity and Local Public Works. The operation of this Resolution, in its meaning and integrity, will afford opportunities for the development of Self-

Government, for strengthening Municipal Institutions, and for the association of Natives and Europeans, to a greater extent than heretofore, in the administration of affairs" (Venkatarangaiya & Pattabhiram, 1969).

Fig. 3.5: Shimla 'lower bazaar' around 1880, the market that was meant for the Indians.

Source: Brown and Shepherd, Calcutta.

Along with architecture, town planning and public health, it is also essential to take note of the social and cultural changes that were taking shape in colonial India, thanks to the influence of new communication technologies. One of the most transformative influences in the life of the Indian people was the **coming of cinema.** Bombay became the first film city of India, with its first film studio set up by Dadasaheb Phalke, producer-director and the 'Father of Indian Cinema' produced the first Indian movie, *Raja Harischchandra*, the story of a great legendary king, who was prepared to sacrifice everything to uphold the truth, in 1913. Though a silent movie, it marked the beginning of a new form of entertainment that captured the minds and hearts of all classes of city dwellers—the poor, the middle class and the rich, the ignorant and the educated. Mass entertainment in the true sense of the term, it soon spread its wings to other parts of the country. The Gemini Studio came up in Madras to produce films in Tamil and Telugu languages, and the New Studio in Calcutta for Bengali films, while Bombay movies were produced in Hindi for a wider audience.

As more films were produced, the film industry became an important part of the urban economy, generating employment for actors, artists, musicians, fashion designers, other skilled and unskilled workers and with more cinema theatres being built in cities to cater to more audiences. Apart from entertainment, what impacted the people more were the film songs, especially those that became classics.

Another activity that gained popularity during the colonial rule was **sport**, particularly the team games that had their origin in Europe, like football, hockey and cricket, games that tested individual skills like tennis and badminton, field sports like athletics. One game where Indians excelled their colonial masters after learning it from them was hockey in which they went to become Olympic champions. This boosted the country's prestige and even attracted the attention of Hitler, the German dictator, who it is believed, tried to win over the legend of Indian Hockey players, Dhyan Chand to the German side, but failed. Another sport, which began as a privileged game of imperial Britain, more specifically England, that gained popularity in India was Cricket. Initially confined to a privileged few, it gradually rose to dominate all other forms of sport. Cinema and Cricket have emerged as the biggest entertainment industry, generating considerable revenue to the state and central governments and becoming an essential part of city life.

The greatest impact of the British rule in India and other colonial countries lies in the introduction of **English education** and the learning of English language by Indians. Though confined mostly to the larger cities to begin with and to a minority, its influence is beyond sheer numbers and has spread across the country. True, it has had a negative effect of dividing society and creating inequalities, but English education has acted as the chief instrument of modernisation of India, especially in the learning of modern sciences and liberal arts and in enhancing our standing in the international arena. Much as Metcalfe's Minute of 1853 on English education has been subject to criticism as an imposition on Indians, it should not be forgotten that some great

Indian reformers of the 19th century like Raja Ram Mohan Roy had also played a crucial role in its promotion.

Cities developed by Princely States

Two-fifths of the subcontinent's territory and close to a quarter of its population came under the jurisdiction of the princely states. Most studies of Indian history restrict themselves to British-ruled India, excluding this large slice of Indian-ruled India, an approach that eclipses the experience of imperialism for millions who resided in these states and their political evolution (Pillai, 2021). In fact, states like Mysore and Cochin were educationally and industrially progressive and the two capital cities were considered models of town planning.

Fig. 3.6: Mysore Palace, built by the Wadiyars.

Source: Muhammad Mahdi Karim and Wikimedia Commons under GNU Free Documentation License.

In the 18th century, South India was a region of many mid-sized towns, unlike the Gangetic plain which was characterised by a few large towns and many small, well served by a transport network of rail and river; the southern towns being Bangalore, Mysore and Srirangapatnam in the old Mysore state and Hosur, Salem, Madurai, Tiruchirapalli, Erode, Dindigul, Thanjavur and Kanchi in Madras Presidency. "Classical Tamil rejoices in the city, in its design, in its architecture, its culture. (*ibid.*). A distinctive feature of most of them was they were also temple towns, some of them like Kanchi, Thanjavur and Tirupathi attracting a large number of pilgrims. It is important to add that churches and mosques also dotted these urban centres, lending them a multi-religious character. Bangalore and Thanjavur, where people from different regions of India, speaking different languages came to live acquired a cosmopolitan character.

History of Mysore and the Development of Bangalore

The history of Mysore and the development of Bangalore provide some interesting insights into the governance aspects of the British and the local rulers of the state. The rulers of Mysore were initially subordinate to the Vijayanagar emperors; they began their sovereign rule in the 16th century with control over large parts of Karnataka and some neighbouring regions of the south. Raja Odeyar, the first notable ruler of the Yadava (Wadiyars) dynasty was followed by a succession of dynastic rulers, until Nanjarajayya who squandered the state's resources pledged part of the kingdom to the Marathas. His inability to repay the dues resulted in the invasion of Mysore by the Marathas in 1758. Hyder Ali, a brave commander in the Mysore army, showed his prowess by defeating the Marathas and subsequently asserting his power and finally taking over as ruler of Mysore in 1761.

Hyder Ali and his son, Tipu Sultan, together ruled Mysore for nearly four decades (1761-1799). They boldly resisted the onslaughts of the British army, waging four wars, until Tipu Sultan was finally killed in the Fourth Mysore War in 1799. They were not only intrepid soldiers but paid attention to the administration and welfare of the people. Hyder Ali created the Lal Bagh in Bangalore, which has developed into one of the finest botanical gardens in India and attracts a large number of visitors. Tipu Sultan introduced the cultivation of mulberry and developed sericulture and today Karnataka is one of the leading silk producing states.

The British, after their conquest in 1799, handed over the throne to royal family of Mysore. As the heir to the throne, Krishnaraja Wadiyar III was a lad of five years, administration was entrusted to Dewan Purnaiya who had served as a minister under Hyder Ali and Tipu Sultan. An able and efficient administrator, he reorganized the administrative system, creating three departments—civil, revenue and miscellaneous, raised revenues by levying duty on goods, liquor and tobacco, apart from land, gave loans to peasants for cultivation and improved tanks and canals in the state. Governor General Wellesley was effusive in his praise of Purnaiya: "The Dewan seems to pursue the wisest and the most benevolent course for the promotion of industry and opulence, the protection of property and the maintenance of internal tranquility and order in Mysore". (Hettne, 1978)

When the king attained the age of 16, Purnaiya retired and the royalty regained the throne. However, the king's reign saw the collapse of revenue administration, leading to peasant unrest and an insurrection. The East India Company quickly annexed the kingdom and decided to appoint Commissioners to run the administration. Sir Mark Cubbon was appointed the first Chief Commissioner of Mysore in 1834. He introduced a number of reforms; divided the state into four divisions including a separate division for Bangalore and reorganized the judicial system, creating 85 taluk courts and eight munsiff courts. The most important change was shifting of the state capital from Mysore to Bangalore.

Cubbon was followed by Levin Bowring in 1862, whose tenure witnessed significant development activities. Nearly 1600 miles of new roads and 365 miles of telegraph lines were laid, Bangalore was connected to Jalarpet by Railways, education was encouraged by opening schools in villages, a public hospital was built in Bangalore (Bowring Hospital, a premier medical centre today) and coffee plantations were started. The state was divided into three divisions and eight districts. A Commissioner was appointed to administer a division and a Deputy Commissioner was made head of the district. It is noteworthy that this system of territorial administration continues till this day.

The measures taken by Cubbon and Bowring laid the foundations for the modernisation of Mysore. Bowring was followed by three other not so significant Commissioners. In 1881, the British decided to restore power to the king and Chamaraja Odeyar who had succeeded Krishnaraja Odeyar assumed the throne. The post of Commissioner was abolished and a British Resident was appointed. A new post of Dewan was created to head the administration.

The appointment of Dewans of Mysore who happened to be Indians opened a new chapter in the governance of Mysore state and Bangalore city. Able, devoted and industrious, they strove for the all-round progress of the state. Dewan Rangacharlu, the first Dewan took the first major step of introducing a democratic element in administration by establishing a Representative Assembly comprising leading merchants, planters and agriculturists. Though not a statutory body, policies of the government and a statement of expenses were brought to its notice. The first of its kind in India, it was conspicuously absent in British presidencies. Rangacharlu was succeeded by the highly talented Seshadri Iyer. He further strengthened the Representative Assembly by bringing in members who were elected for a period of three years. A major reform he undertook to put administration on a solid footing was introduction of the Mysore Civil Services Examination to recruit civil servants on the basis of merit. The most transforming moment during his time came when electricity was supplied for the first time anywhere in India to KGF (Kolar Gold Mines), the town where the first gold mining was undertaken in 1902 and equally significant, the first electricity line was laid between Bangalore and KGF, covering a distance of about 90 kms and Bangalore became the first city to be electrified in India in 1905.

A change in the royalty came when Krishnaraja Odeyar IV became the Maharaja whose period came to be called the 'golden age of Mysore'. A farsighted, enlightened and empathetic ruler who was ably assisted by Dewans such as the brilliant engineer-statesman, Sir M. Visvesvaraya and the popular Sir Mirza Ismail, ushered in changes of far reaching importance. Visvesvaraya was chiefly responsible for laying strong foundations for the economic, industrial and educational progress of Mysore. A number of public sector industries were started in Bangalore: the Government Soap Factory, the Metal Factory, Chrome Tanning Factory and so on. The Iron Works (now called Visvesvaraya Iron & Steel Ltd.) was set up in Bhadravati which developed into an industrial township. A builder of institutions, he established the Government Engineering College, the Mysore University, a Technological Institute, an Agricultural School and the Mysore Economic Conference.

Sir Mirza Ismail, who succeeded Visvesvaraya, continued the excellent work of his predecessor. He established new factories to manufacture items such as glass, porcelain, chemicals and fertilizers. A lover of gardens and parks, he was largely responsible for making

Bangalore the garden city of India. Mirza Ismail resigned in 1941 and the Dewan rule continued till 1947 when India achieved independence and the British rule came to an end.

The evolution of the governance of Bengaluru has an interesting history. Unlike the three coastal cities of Bombay, Calcutta and Madras which had the stamp of British colonialism in their early development, Bengaluru's growth had a local flavour. Founded by Kempe Gowda, I a local ruler of Yelahanka Nadu (near the present international airport, named after its founder) in the 16th century (1537), its urbanisation took place in more congenial surroundings. A great visionary, Kempe Gowda, during one of his sojourns, dreamt of building a city and took the initial step of erecting a mud fort (near the present-day Victoria Hospital). He also undertook welfare measures such as construction of tanks for supply of water, (some of which have now given way to urban uses like bus stand and stadium), and encouraging gardening. Realising the importance of promoting trade and commerce, he invited people from neighbouring regions to Bangalore, thus paving the way to development of a cosmopolitan culture with which the city has come to be identified. Trade-wise businesses began to develop in a concentrated block called pete (market) (present Avenue Road and Chickpet area) where people could live and carry on their business. It was also an example of integrated land use planning which provided for residence and work at the same place, as distinct from the segregated land uses of present-day master plans. A number of petes sprang up, each associated with a particular trade, such as Akkipet (rice business), Balepet (bangles), Cottonpet and so on. Thus Kempe Gowda, along with his son, Kempe Gowda, II who continued the good work of his father, can be said to have laid the foundation of the local economic development of Bangalore.

The Kempe Gowdas' rule was followed by the sporadic invasion of Marathas, rule of the Mysore royalty, Hyder Ali and Tipu Sultan and the British foray (noted above), after which the growth of Bangalore took a different turn. The urban local government of Bangalore featured an interesting case of One City-Two Municipalities. In 1862, two Municipal Boards were constituted, one for the old city, and another for the cantonment area, called the Civil and Military (C&M) Station; they were reconstituted in 1881 as the Bangalore City

Municipality and the Bangalore C&M Municipal Commission. The former was governed by the Bangalore Town Municipal Regulation of 1871 and the latter by the Madras Municipal Act, 1887, thus making a clear distinction between the local and the British jurisdictions. For the City Municipality, the Deputy Commissioner of Bangalore district was made the President while the Cantonment had the District Magistrate as President. It was only in 1949, two years after independence, that the two entities were merged under the City of Bangalore Municipal Corporation Act, which for the first time provided for the introduction of local democracy. The city was divided into 50 divisions and 50 municipal councillors were elected to constitute a democratically elected Municipal Corporation in 1951.

Meanwhile, as the city started expanding, it became necessary to regulate its urban growth and hence, Bangalore City Improvement Trust Board was constituted in 1945. The Board was entrusted with the task of developing planned housing and industrial layouts beyond the municipal limits. The Board continued to function till the present Bangalore Development Authority was constituted in 1976.

Chapter
4

Town and Country

Movement from Country to Town

Urbanisation is a process that involves population shift from rural to urban areas and occupational shift from agricultural to non-agricultural activities. It also involves concentration of the population at densities higher than those associated with agricultural populations (Rao, 1983). This is followed by changes in land use from agricultural to urban. About a century ago, the British economist Alfred Marshall enunciated three traits of cities: pools of settled labour consideration, the number and kind of people living in the town, and the places where they worked and lived.

The turn of the 20th century marked a transition in urban policy and planning. In the UK and other Western countries, the industrial cities of the 19th century, dictated by private, industrial concerns and thereby ignoring the needs of the working class, began to give way to the creation of cities with emphasis on the needs of the community. New concepts of town planning emerged as urban scholars turned their attention to critical issues of urban life such as housing, health and environment. Ebenezer Howard (1898), considered the first urban planning theorist propounded the 'garden city' model which he described as a city complete with housing, industry, educational, recreational and shopping facilities, surrounded by an agricultural belt. His highly influential work *Tomorrow: A Peaceful Path to Real Reform* received great acclaim and led to the building of the new garden cities of Letchworth and Welwyn in the proximity of London. He visualised planned cities with self-contained communities. Howard's work highlighted the importance of including the countryside or the rural/agricultural surroundings in the planning of a city. Years later, when plans were prepared for cities in India, the 'agricultural zone' or 'green belt' came to be recognised as part of the master plan. In North America, Clarence Stein, an urban planner and architect, carried forward the garden city movement and propounded the 'neighbourhood unit' model of development.

Fig. 4.1: Ebenezer Howard's conception of the Three Magnets: Town, Country and Town-Country that built a framework for economic planners to try and understand where people would go.

Town Planning in India

The origin of modern town planning in India can be traced to the utterly poor sanitary conditions in its cities. The setting up of sanitary commissions in each of the three presidencies of Bengal, Bombay and Madras can be considered to have provided the basis towards further developments in town planning. Up to the early 20th century, the development of towns and cities in India was guided more by the military and political requirements of British rule and the concerns of public health and sanitation. Sanitising crowded settlements was accorded priority. With the rapid urbanisation of Bombay caused by the growth of textile industry, town planning gathered momentum.

In 1914, Patrick Geddes, a Scottish biologist, sociologist, geographer and pioneering town planner, was invited to visit India to advise on town planning issues. In 1915, he visited a number of cities across the country, including Bombay, Ahmedabad, Jaipur, Agra, Delhi, Lucknow, Calcutta, and Madras. Between 1915 and 1922, he produced perceptive town planning reports as a result of these visits. He viewed the town not as inanimate things like roads and buildings, but a living organism that included the people. He felt that the urban planning practices prevalent at that time were divorced from Indian tradition and legacy, and advocated a more humanistic approach to the Indian city. Geddes introduced the concept of the 'region' and pointed out that a town cannot be planned independently without taking into account its regional setting. He also highlighted the relationship between social issues and town planning. The first Town Planning Act enacted in the UK in 1909 aimed at providing for 'the home healthy, the house beautiful, the town pleasant, the city dignified and the suburb salubrious' (Housing, Town Planning, etc., Bill, 1908). This ideal could not, however, be achieved as urban growth was accompanied by other problems, especially those caused by the two world wars. The UK government set up three commissions to study these problems and based on their recommendations, a new Town and Country Planning Act was enacted in 1947. Thus 'country' came to be included as a part of planning for the town and the city.

In India, the concept of town planning acquired a statutory basis with the enactment of the Bombay Town Planning Act in 1915.

However, earlier, following the outbreak of plague in 1896, the Bombay City Improvement Trust was set up with the objective of improving sanitary conditions in the city. The government and the city municipal corporation handed over all vacant lands to the trust, which implemented a number of measures like widening of roads in the central and crowded parts of Bombay to relieve congestion. It also planned the formation of suburbs. Similar trusts were set up in other major cities of India, like the Calcutta Improvement Trust in 1911, Hyderabad in 1912, Lucknow in 1919 and Delhi in 1937. Interestingly, much before these, in 1903, a City Improvement Trust came into being in Mysore, a non-presidency city under the administration of the Maharaja of Mysore and in Baroda, another princely city, in 1910. Bangalore had to wait till 1945 to get its own Improvement Trust Board.

The concept of the master plan aimed at planned, time-bound growth emerged during this time. Town planning legislations were enacted in different states. The Bombay Town Planning Act of 1915 was followed by the Madras Town Planning Act of 1920, while the princely states of Hyderabad and Mysore had put in place their town planning laws in 1916 and 1917 respectively. The Hyderabad drainage plans, formulated around 1909, attracted special interest thanks to two Indians, Sir Mirza Ismail, then Dewan of Hyderabad (1946-1947) and Sir M. Visvesvaraya, a brilliant engineer, both of whom had also served as dewans of Mysore state. The plan took into account the natural water courses of the area as a key input for growth and also to take care of emergency situations.

At this juncture, it is important to recall the contribution of Europeans like Otto Konigsberger, who served as the chief architect and planner of Mysore State between 1939 and 1948, at the invitation of the Maharaja of Mysore, Krishnaraja Wodeyar IV. Unfortunately ignored and forgotten, this German architect designed several buildings, public and private, including the Victory Hall (now Bal Bhavan) in Cubbon Park, the TB Sanatorium and Bangalore Bus City Terminus (now demolished). He is also credited with designing the Aeronautics Department, the Metallurgy Department, the dining hall and the auditorium at the Indian Institute of Science (IISc) in Bangalore.

Fig. 4.2: Sir Mirza Ismail road in Pink City in Jaipur, Rajasthan. Sir Ismail served as the Diwan (Prime Minister) of Jaipur, Mysore and Hyderabad.

Source: Chainwit and Wikipedia under CC-BY-SA 4.0 licence.

Another German who played a stellar role in developing Bangalore as a garden city and premier city of horticulture was Gustav Hermann Krumbiegel, who at the invitation of Krishnaraja Wodeyar IV, served as Superintendent of Government Gardens and later as the first full-fledged Director of Horticulture of Mysore State. Recognising the economic importance of horticulture that yielded better returns than food crops in improving the standard of living of horticulturists who depended on it, 'Krumbiegel introduced the economic garden into which he introduced economic plants yielding industrial products like fibres, resin gums, dyes, tans, aromatic oils, timber, rubber, fruits, flowers and fodder' (Jagadeesh, 2016). He also set up the Bureau of Economic Botany which had a unique system of indexing horticultural information. Apart from being a horticulturist, Krumbiegel was a town planner and designed the town squares in Mysore city and remodelled the Silver Jubilee Park and NR Square in Bangalore.

Earlier, between 1910 and 1930, the British architect Edward Lutyens undertook the task of designing the new capital of India when it was shifted from Calcutta to Delhi in 1912. Intended to symbolise the imperial power of Britain, New Delhi, or Lutyens' Delhi as it was called, was inspired by the European Renaissance style and followed the urban planning standards of Paris, Rome and Washington. The prominent features of New Delhi, alien to Indian styles, continue till this day. There is a central axis with a vast rectangular mall, surrounded by government offices, with the then Viceroy's house (now Rashtrapati Bhavan) as the crown, broad tree-lined streets and vast open spaces. A makeover of the area is in the offing, with a plan for a new parliament building.

Public Health and Town Planning

At a time when we are facing a serious public health crisis, still nursing the wounds of COVID-19, it is instructive to understand how the public health system has evolved in India. The colonial period saw the advent of infectious diseases as well as the development of tropical medicine and a modern public health system. Along with the East India Company officials who landed in 1600 on our shores came the first set of British medical officers, more as surgeons of the ship that brought them. But it was only in the second half of the 18th century, after the company's rule was established firmly on Indian soil that civil and military medical services were started. In 1785, medical departments were set up in the three presidencies of Bengal, Bombay and Madras. More than a century earlier, the first general hospital was established in Madras in 1679, and a second one another century later in Calcutta in 1796. Later, in 1835, the first medical college was started in Calcutta.

All the medical departments in British India were under the control of the central government until the Montagu-Chelmsford Reforms of 1919, when subjects relating to public health, sanitation and vital statistics were transferred to the provinces. This was followed by the Municipality and Local Boards Act, 1920-21 which provided a legal basis for the development of public health services.

The history of sanitation in India began with the appointment of a Commission of Public Health in each of the three British provinces, based on the recommendations of the Royal Commission in 1859.

The actual sanitary work was started in the cantonments established in certain cities where the military had a considerable presence under the Military Cantonments Act of 1864. A Sanitary Police Force was formed with a view to improve what was called 'military hygiene'. Separate sanitation boards were constituted to improve the civil sanitary conditions. These boards also functioned as municipalities in certain industrial areas and were later converted as notified areas. After the 1885 Act came into force, the responsibility for sanitation at the local level was transferred to the local bodies.

The outbreak of the the bubonic plague reportedly came to notice in 1812 in Kutch and then spread to other parts of Gujarat and Sind. However, the first official recorded incidence of plague was in 1896 initially in Bombay, Calcutta and Karachi which quickly spread to other parts of India and lasted till 1899. It was estimated that the deadly epidemic consumed the lives of about two million people.

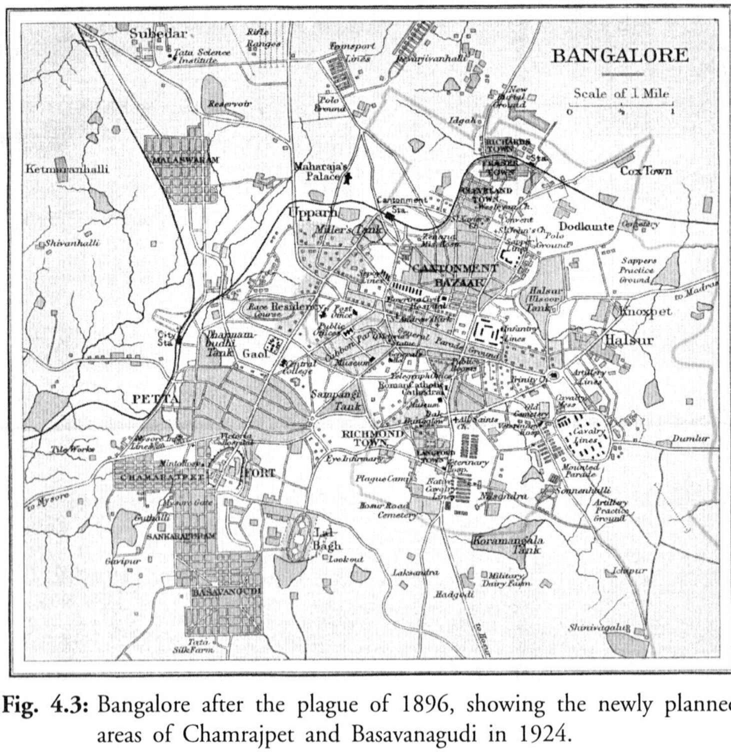

Fig. 4.3: Bangalore after the plague of 1896, showing the newly planned areas of Chamrajpet and Basavanagudi in 1924.

The plague brought to light the importance of sanitation in cities and how it is central to town planning. Based on a report of the Plague Commission of 1896, a number of measures were initiated to control epidemic diseases. Planning new areas for extension of cities where people could live came to be based on the principles of sanitation. In Bangalore, for instance, the new areas of Chamarajpet and Basavangudi were planned extensions following the outbreak of plague in the city in 1896-97.

Under the Epidemic Diseases Act, 1897, the Governor General bestowed special powers to local authorities to control epidemic diseases. This was followed by the Lepers Act of 1898, which led to the establishment of leper asylums and segregation of lepers. Earlier, in 1868, there was an outbreak of another deadly epidemic, cholera, that appeared more frequently at fairs and religious festivals. Malaria proved to be another leading cause of deaths in India following the establishment of the railways and irrigation networks without efficient drainage systems. This led to floods and stagnation of rainwater which proved to be breeding grounds for mosquitoes. Interestingly and distressingly, the mosquito menace continues till today along with inadequate drainage systems in our cities. It was the great scientist Sir Ronald Ross who joined the Indian Medical Services in 1881, who after painstaking research, demonstrated the life of a malarial parasite, leading to programmes for eradication of malaria. He was awarded the Nobel Prize for Medicine in 1902.

Cities, therefore, developed in the Indian sub-continent in diverse ways, supported by a range of monarchical, colonial and proto-democratic institutions. They were centres of trade, commerce, education, culture and the military. As they grew, newer concerns around planning and public health added more layers to their trajectories. Even by the time of Indian independence, it was being acknowledged that the urban is a vast and multidisciplinary area of governance, and newer modes of thinking would have to be instituted in order to maintain and enhance them.

SUMMING UP

The Urban Legacy of India

This brief survey of the cycle of growth, decay and rise of Indian towns and cities, beginning with the Harappan Civilisation, tracing the rise and fall of empires and their cities, passing through various phases of foreign invasions, internal conflicts and colonial rule up to the mid-20th century serves as a backdrop to understand the struggles of the postcolonial, politically independent but economically interdependent, semi-urban civilisation of India. In a predominantly rural, agrarian society, heavily reliant on agriculture for its sustenance and agricultural land for public revenues, the role of the 'urban' might appear small, but was, nevertheless, significant.

Cities, big or small, were capitals from where kings and emperors ruled; that's where they built their palaces and forts; that's where buildings of splendor and temples of grandeur came up, for that's where people came for trade and commerce. Architecture, culture and society thrived in these cities, whether they were planned and made by the princely states or eventually, by the colonial powers. During the much-loathed colonial times, the much-derided imperial powers built new towns and cities, set up schools, colleges and hospitals; where Indian entrepreneurs built industries, and our trade and commerce started expanding, laying foundations for the country's economic prosperity. There was significant movement from 'country' loosely defined as the rural countryside to these new urban centres, leading to initiatives and new thinking on 'planning' urban areas. Several Indian and European thinkers developed various modes and methods to approach planning, with a chief concern around public health, after epidemics of various infectious diseases ravaged these concentrated centres of population.

The British no doubt left behind a divided and impoverished nation, but the colonial era also laid the foundations of modern progress, particularly during the latter half of 19th and the first half of 20th centuries. The four metropolitan cities of Bombay, Calcutta, Madras and Delhi that developed during this period became the nodal centres of the four regions of the country providing connectivity and the required impetus for industrialisation and urbanisation for the rest of the country. The displacement of 10-20 million people following the partition of the country had a huge demographic impact. With a large Muslim population leaving Delhi and about 5,00,000 Hindu and Sikh refugees pouring in from across the borders, the population of Delhi, for example, doubled literally overnight.

In such a situation, the primary tasks before the new government were therefore to attend to the post-partition issues of restoring law and order, rehabilitation of the refugees and other matters concerning building a new nation—consolidating over 600 states and provinces into a single political entity, writing a new constitution to establish the framework for governance, and initiating socio-economic development measures.

The colonial rule left behind enormous challenges, and our leaders began the hard task of rebuilding the nation, thinking and planning from the national capital, Delhi, and the other capital cities of the states. There were other towns and cities spread across the length and breadth of India, and their numbers and their inhabitants were also increasing.

Part II
Urban India: 1950-2000

Chapter

5

Lost in Transition

Urban Policy and Planning

Urban Development in the Five-Year Plans: Misguided Priorities

The First Five-Year Plan (FYP) for the planned development of India took nearly four years to take shape after Independence. The FYPs aimed to eliminate poverty and advance socio-economic development, in keeping with the objectives of economic growth, self-reliance, equity, social justice, full employment, and modernisation.

The priority sectors of the FYPs, which varied from agriculture and energy planning industry and housing, reveal a fragmented approach to development. During the plan period spanning over 60 years from the early fifties, urban policy and planning did not figure prominently in the agenda of the planners and took a backseat in the planning processes of the country. As the country was predominantly rural, with over 80 per cent of its population living in villages at that time, the focus of the First FYP (1951-1956) was to achieve agricultural development and food security, apart from the rehabilitation of refugees from the Partition. It did, however, refer to the need for a National Town and Country Planning Act.

The Second FYP (1956-1961) went one step further and called for the enactment of such legislation in all states, along with preparation of master plans for important cities. It also drew attention to the problem of housing shortage and the proliferation of slums in the country. The Third FYP (1961-1966) took note of the growth of urban areas in India and the cost of providing basic services like housing, water supply and sanitation. The central government provided financial assistance to the states by setting up town planning departments for the preparation of comprehensive master plans for fast-growing cities. In contrast, the Fourth FYP (1969-1974) advocated the need to decongest large cities and limit further growth of the urban population. It also pointed out the need for legal provisions for the implementation of regional plans. The Town and Country Planning Organisation (TCPO) prepared a model law, which provided a framework for the states to formulate their own town planning legislations.

'Urban Development' as a chapter appeared only in the Fifth FYP (1974-1979). Until then, housing, which included rural housing, received greater attention. The plan emphasised the need to formulate a National Urbanisation Policy, National Human Settlement Policy and National Population Policy, along with developing policy instruments to deal with the critical issue of urban land. Further, the plan provided for implementation programmes for environmental improvement of slums, construction of housing colonies and augmentation of civic services. The Sixth FYP (1980-1985) once again mentioned the need to devise a National Urbanisation Policy and introduced a scheme for the Integrated Development of Small & Medium Towns (IDSMT) with a view to provide adequate infrastructure for these towns. The Seventh FYP (1985-1990) referred to the Industrial Location Policy and how it should subserve the needs of regional and urban planning. The policy also intended to strengthen the capabilities of urban local bodies (ULBs). The Eighth FYP (1992-1997) developed an integrated planning framework across a hierarchy of rural and urban settlements and the associated spatial development of small and medium towns. It also drew attention to the need for an enabling environment to achieve the goal of ensuring housing for all. The Ninth FYP (1997-2002) dealt with the broader issue of developing urban areas as 'economically efficient, socially equitable and environmentally sustainable entities'. The plan highlighted the importance of energy planning in the transport sector. It also referred to other programmes like Urban Basic Services for the Poor (UBSP) and Prime Minister's Integrated Urban Poverty Eradication Programme (PMIUPEP).

The Tenth FYP (2002-2007) spoke about improving the quality of life in urban areas and stressed the importance of benchmarking service standards, public-private partnerships and urban public transport. By the Eleventh FYP (2007-2012), the planners had realised that the concept of a master plan was not well-suited for rapidly growing Indian cities. It once again called for the formulation of a National Urbanisation Policy and the interlinking of the planning frameworks at various levels. The Twelfth and the last FYP (2012-2017) re-emphasised the deficiencies of master plans by pointing out that it was barely linked to any financial or operation strategy. It also proposed the setting up of five Institutes of Urban Management to enhance the capacity of personnel to manage cities but they failed to take shape.

On the whole, the FYPs lacked consistency in addressing issues related to urban development, with the same themes being repeated time and again in different plans. The emphasis was more on programmes such as the development of small and medium towns, slum improvement, housing, and basic services like water supply. Budgetary allocations were provided for such programmes, though not adequately.

There are several reasons for why urban development did not receive the importance it deserved by the Planning Commission for well over half a century after Independence. Firstly, as mentioned before, in the initial phase of planning in the 1950s, India's population—and thus, its voters—was predominantly rural, with agriculture being the main occupation of the people. Naturally, the focus was on increasing food production and reducing poverty. Conjecturally, it may be added that Mahatma Gandhi's idea of village republics could have influenced the political decision makers and planners, in contradistinction to Dr. B.R. Ambedkar's description of the village as 'a sink of localism, a den of ignorance, narrow-mindedness and communalism' (Dr. B.R. Ambedkar, Constituent Assembly Speech, 1949).

Secondly, urban development does not constitute a single sector like agriculture, industry or education; it is multisectoral and multidisciplinary. In fact, there was no separate ministry for urban development until 1985. There was only a Ministry of Works, Housing and Supply which paid little attention to urban issues. In the absence of a single nodal agency, urban development lacked a champion to advocate its case to the Planning Commission.

It was in the Eleventh FYP that substantial funds were allocated to a large programme like the Jawaharlal Nehru National Urban Renewal Mission (JNNURM), though it was more an independently conceived Mission focusing on urban infrastructure development and urban reforms, rather than an outcome of the planning process. In short, the approach to urbanisation and urban development turned out to be piecemeal and ad hoc.

The town planning laws of states declared grand aims and objectives. For example, the Statement of the Objects and Reasons for the Karnataka Town and Country Planning Act, 1961 states that a uniform town planning law is necessary for

> "the regulation of planned growth of land use and development and for the making and executing of town planning schemes in the State. Physical planning has to precede economic planning as otherwise cities, towns and villages of our country will grow to unmanageable sizes without proper planning resulting in unhealthy surroundings. Physical planning with coordinated effort on a large scale is necessary if the people are to live in a better, healthier and happier environment. The proposed is expected to solve the Town Planning problems". (p. 53)
>
> (Karnataka Town and Country Planning Act, 1961)

More than 60 years after the town and country planning Acts were enacted, we are far from achieving their objectives. Instead, the fear about cities growing to 'unmanageable sizes without proper planning resulting in unhealthy surroundings' has come true. The Task Force on Planning for Urban Development, set up by the Government of India in 1983, observed that the policies and programmes of the FYPs had been 'half-hearted and loosely coordinated. Spatial considerations have never received adequate attention' (Task Force on Planning for Urban Development, 1983). Town planning problems, far from being solved, have only multiplied. The urban environment has deteriorated, posing great risks to the health and well-being of people and the safety of the planet. With hardly any action taken on the recommendations made by the task force, the government was quick to set up the National Commission on Urbanisation (NCU) under the chairmanship of renowned architect Charles Correa in 1987. The commission carried out a detailed study of the various dimensions of urbanisation and arrived at a comprehensive set of 78 recommendations, including a programme of state interventions 'to direct and modify the course of urbanisation in future' [Ministry of Urban Development (MoUD), 1988].

Thus, the pattern of urbanisation that emerged in post-Independence India was disjointed and carried a colonial character, marked by low incomes, inadequate levels of food consumption and a high degree of informality. This was typical not only of Asia but all developing countries (Berry, 1973). Unlike the high-income countries of the West, the nascent cities of India, particularly the Presidency cities under British India—Bombay, Calcutta and Madras—stood out as 'conclaves' of development poles with a sharp decay in the levels of development in proportion to the distance from their centres (Rao, 1983). This trend continued post-1950 with the emergence of new metropolitan cities like Bangalore and Hyderabad, and further expanded to cities like Pune and Ahmedabad. MoUD (1998) pointed out that 'the urban situation in India is one of deep crisis' and that the task of tackling the various issues was 'one of extraordinary complexity'. It called for measures 'analogous to those used when a house is on fire, or there is a citywide epidemic'. Unfortunately, we failed to act in time and seem to have waited in anticipation of not just a citywide epidemic, but a worldwide pandemic. The urban crisis continues and has only worsened. The status of urbanisation in India today has been aptly summed up by the latest State of the Cities India Report as follows: "There exists today multiple narratives of urbanisation—it is said to be rapid, moderate, slow, messy, and hidden, all at the same time" (Mathur *et al.*, 2021, p. 2).

How India Urbanised: Slow, Unplanned, Unregulated

In the beginning of the twentieth century, the urban population of the world was only 13 per cent of the total population; by 1950, it had reached nearly 30 per cent. Correspondingly, the level of India's urbanisation was 10 per cent and just under 20 per cent respectively

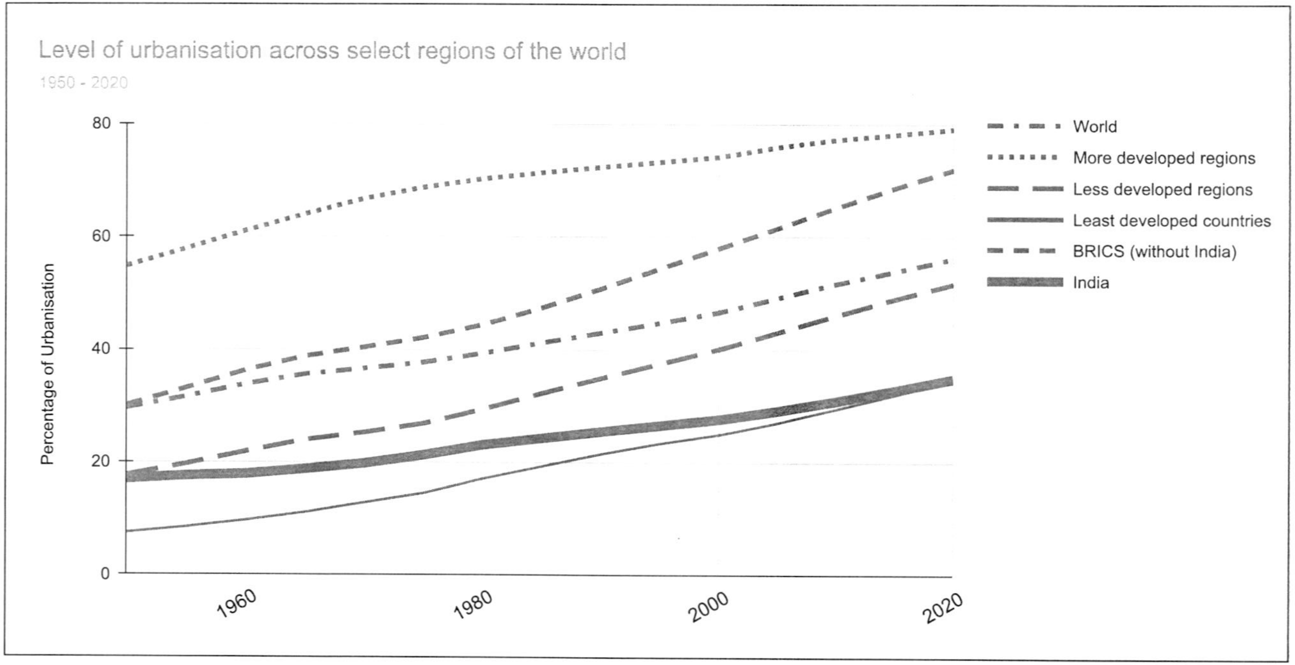

Fig. 5.1: India's level of urbanisation, 1950 to 2020, in comparison with other regions of the world, India's level of urbanisation is substantially lower than comparable countries such as in BRICS. Data are from "World urbanisation prospects: The 2018 revision", by United Nations, 2019. Copyright 2019 by United Nations.

(United Nations, 2019). The urban growth in India in the period of 1950-2000 has been far slower than the world average.[1]

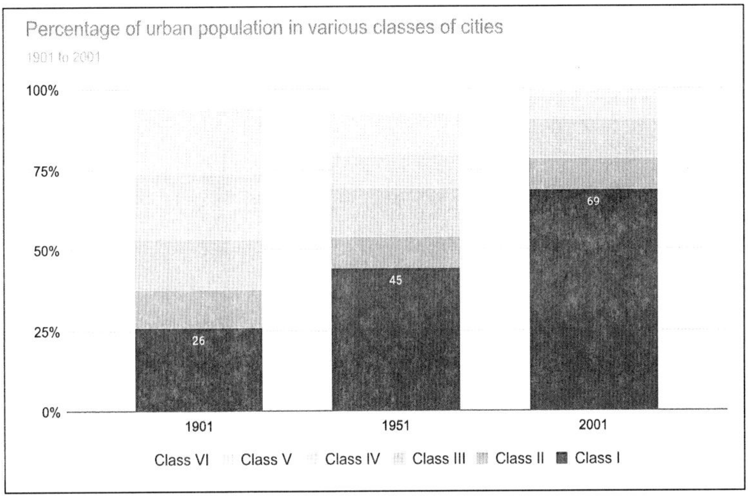

Fig. 5.2: Percentage of the urban population in India in various classes of cities: 1901 to 2001.

An analysis of decadal urban population growth in India reveals the following features. The total number of urban settlements went up from 3,035 in 1951 to 7,933 in 2001, an increase of more than two times over half-a-century (Mathur, *et al.*, 2021, p. 21). At the same time, the proportion of the total urban population living in Class I towns went up from 26 per cent in 1901 to 45 per cent in 1951 and then 69 per cent in 2001, revealing the dominant role of large cities in India's urbanisation.

In recent years, the discourse on urbanisation has given rise to the question 'what is urban?' There is no one universal definition of the 'urban'; indeed there are many. The Census of India (2011) has classified urban areas into two categories: statutory towns and census towns. Statutory towns refer to administrative units defined by the states as 'urban' like municipal corporations, municipalities, nagara palikas and so forth. Census towns are administrative units that meet

1. Although Part II of this book covers the period 1950 to 2000, data up to 2011 and official projections till 2031 have been referenced in order to maintain continuity in the narrative.

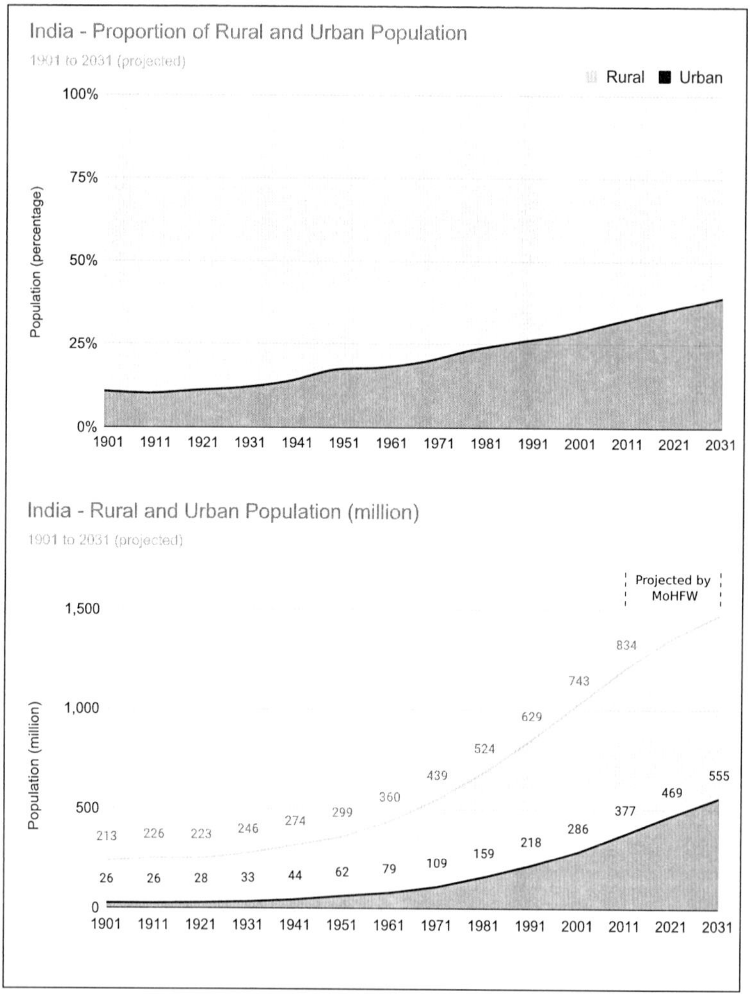

Fig. 5.3: Proportion of rural-urban population and growth in rural and urban populations, from 1901 to 2031 (projected). Data sourced from Ministry of Health and Family Welfare, Government of India (2022). *Report of the Technical Group on Population Projections.*

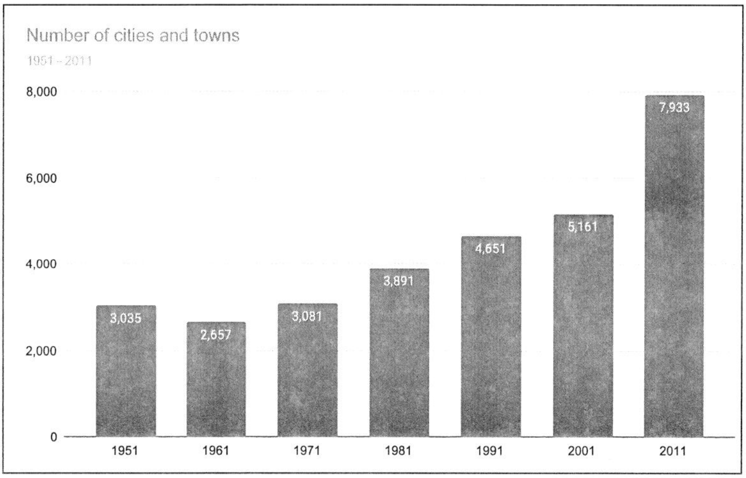

Fig. 5.4: Number of cities and towns in India from 1951 to 2011. *Source:* Census of India 2011.

the following three criteria: (a) a minimum population of 5,000 persons; (b) at least 75 per cent of the male population being engaged in non-agricultural pursuits; and (c) population density of at least 400 persons per sq. km. According to the Census of 2011, 84.5 per cent of the urban population of India lives in statutory towns, 1.1 per cent in

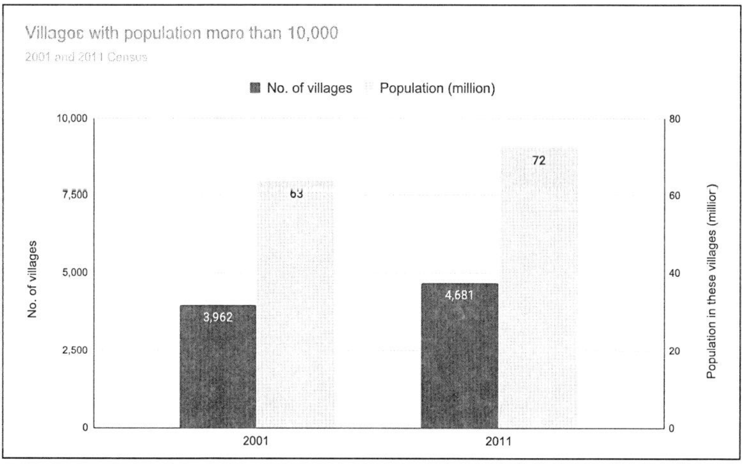

Fig. 5.5: Number of villages with population more than 10,000 and their population in 2001 and 2011. Data sourced from Government of India (2011) Census of India, 2011.

their outgrowths and 14.4 per cent in census towns. Overall, the level of urbanisation in India is 31.16 per cent according to the last census.

It is interesting to note that the 2011 Census recorded 4,681 villages with a population of over 10,000, with a total population of 79 million. As the census is the main source of data on various aspects of urbanisation in India, and the work of the census for 2021 is yet to begin, we are handicapped by the lack of recent data.

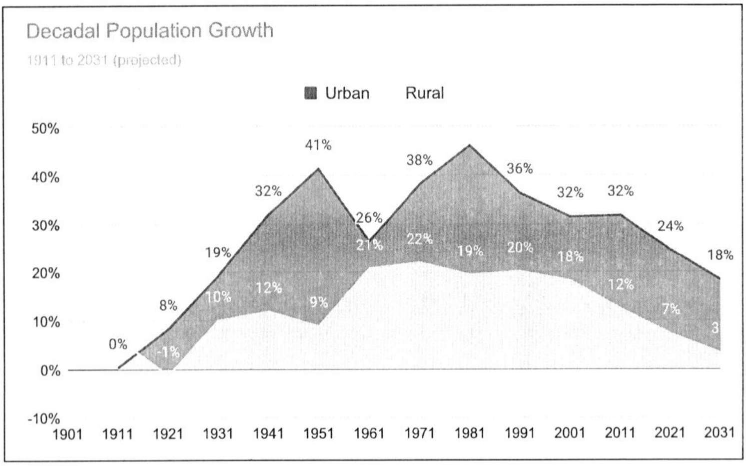

Fig. 5.6: Decadal population growth in urban and rural areas in India, 1911 to 2031 (projected). Rural population growth is expected to taper out to nil over the coming decades, while the urban population will continue to grow at a fast, even if declining pace. Data sourced from Ministry of Health and Family Welfare, Government of India (2022). *Report of the Technical Group on Population Projections.*

Urbanisation occurs on account of four factors: natural increase in population; migration of people from rural to urban areas; reorganisation of existing physical boundaries of a town or city by inclusion of new areas; and reclassification of villages or rural settlements as urban.

The characteristics of change are therefore bound to vary from decade to decade. Overall, natural increase has been a major contributor to urbanisation, followed by rural-urban migration and reclassification of rural settlements as urban. The trends in migration reveal that in 2011, the number of rural-urban migrants was 80 million, urban-urban migrants was also 80 million, and urban-rural migrants was 30 million. However, the number of rural-rural migrants was far higher at 210 million. It is also important to take note of the fact that intra-state migration was much higher at 396 million, compared to inter-state migration which was only 54 million. What is significant is the relatively low contribution of rural-urban migration to urban population growth at just around 20 per cent over the last few decades, making India an outlier among fast-growing, emerging and developing economies (Mohan, 2021). The decade 2001-11 witnessed a significant decline in natural increase of the population to 43.3 per cent from 60.9 per cent between 1991-2001, a normal rate of 22.8 per cent in rural-urban migration, but a huge rise in the population counted in census towns at 31.2 per cent (Mathur *et al.*, 2021).

This is how the World Development Report (World Bank, 2009, p. 163) had commented on India's rural-urban migration:

> The economic benefits of migration are not always recognised by policy makers. Two forms of policy have been attempted to counter migration in India. The first response has been to increase rural employment, in an attempt to stem movement out of rural areas. The second policy response is implicit. Because of the perceived negative effects, local governments remain hostile towards migrants, while employers routinely disregard laws to protect rights and needs.

The official census figure of urbanisation in 2011 is 31.2 per cent (377 million); this figure has, however, been challenged by the World Bank estimate, which shows that it is far higher at 55.3 per cent based on satellite night lights data. This includes the people living in urban-like density or 'agglomeration index', which is the globally used alternative measure of urban concentration in the absence of consistent cross-country census figures. This methodology may be questioned but the World Bank's explanation is that population growth occurs in the fringes outside cities, a part of which is recorded in official statistics as 'outgrowths'. According to UN estimates, India's rural population will begin to decline in absolute numbers around the year 2027. Thereafter, population increase in India will be wholly urban (Mathur *et al.*, 2021; United Nations, 2019).

Forms of Urbanisation

The forms of urbanisation have been continuously changing, evolving into patterns difficult to define. Schmid (2014) has captured these changes realistically:

> The process of urbanisation has changed fundamentally in recent years. For more than a century, the dominant form of urbanisation was concentric, with suburbs arranged like belts around an urban core. This is how the large agglomerations of the 20th century emerged. Around the end of the twentieth century, however, the urban growth pattern began to change as manifested in a wide variety of places: the process of urbanisation has become undirected; existing urban forms are beginning to dissolve; centrality is becoming polymorphous. Overarching polycentric urban regions are taking shape. Extremely heterogeneous in structure, they include old city centres as well as the once peripheral areas. (p. 67)

The city structure is a complex phenomenon that comprises different entities such as land, infrastructure, objects and beings that are independent or interacting with their environment. The Indian city, as it evolved during the British period and transitioned into the post-Independence phase, was dual-structured, like all colonial cities in developing countries, with their 'indigenous and anglicised' (Smailes, 1969) characteristics co-existing as much as the 'bazaar-peasant economy' and 'firm-typed capitalist economy' (McGee, 1971). It has been called a 'collection of period pieces' (Jones, 1966) and a city of 'pre-industrial society' living in a 'post-industrial city' (Ginsberg, 1970). Cities with rich histories such as Delhi, Hyderabad and Varanasi have more complicated structures as they have inherited political, economic and cultural systems from different historic periods. Broadly, the following patterns and scales can be identified in the process of urbanisation in India:

Fig. 5.7: A map of Rourkela, Odisha. The steel plant is clearly visible as the most dominant element. The planned nature of the rest of the city is also visible.

Source: openstreetmap.org

- **Commercial urbanisation.** Market towns of medium size exhibiting many commercial activities, particularly retail and wholesale trade, with a regional resource base. Examples are Vijayawada in Andhra Pradesh and Gangavati in Karnataka.
- **Industrial urbanisation.** Emanating from national economic policies, industrial towns and cities have developed in different states. Bhilai in present-day Chhattisgarh, Rourkela in Odisha and Durgapur in West Bengal emerged as new townships as a result of the construction of steel plants in these places. Lignite Corporation emerged in Neyveli and another township in Tamil Nadu. Old industrial towns include Jamshedpur, where Tata Steel Company is based, and Bhadravati, another steel-based town in Karnataka.
- **Metropolitanisation.** With the growth of urban agglomerations, urban areas with a population of more than a million came to be called metropolitan cities. They are characterised by an industrial and tertiary economic base, urban sprawl with scattered built-up areas, and villages and small towns in the proximity. They enjoy wide communication networks and well-connected national and regional transport routes. Due to the large scale of flow of people, goods and services, there is also large-scale consumption.
- **Peripheral urbanisation.** The expansion of the city beyond agglomeration into the rural tract has led to the conceptualisation of the urban periphery or the urban fringe; it may be considered an extension of the metropolis but more complex to define and manage. It has lacked a single definition but may be described as a semi-urban or peri-urban area which is in the process of transformation. Pointing out that no single theory or model adequately explains activities in the rural-urban fringes, the Department for International Development Report (1999) sums up a peri-urban area as 'an interface, a transitory zone of mixed rural and urban economic, social, cultural, and natural resource uses at the periphery of cities in developing nations' (p. ix).

(Master) Planning Indian Cities

The major policy interventions in urban planning in India have taken place through the instrument of the master plan which is "a dynamic long-term planning document that provides a conceptual framework to guide future growth and development...making the connection between buildings, social settings and their surrounding environments" (Amirtahmasebi *et al.*, 2016, p. 18). The first such intervention came in the form of the Delhi Master Plan, which was formulated with technical assistance from the Ford Foundation (including professionals from the United States of America and United Kingdom) in 1962. Interestingly, it received the personal attention of the first Prime Minister of India, Jawaharlal Nehru. The visionary leader then set his eyes on building a modern city that would reflect the spirit of a new India and invited French architect Le Corbusier to design a new capital for the state of Punjab. Thus came into being the city of Chandigarh.

From Delhi, the Ford Foundation turned its attention to Calcutta where, thanks to the efforts of the first Chief Minister of West Bengal, B.C. Roy, the exercise for the preparation of a master plan was set in motion. Here, the approach differed from that of Delhi, which was considered rather rigid. The result was the Basic Development Plan of Calcutta in 1956 which was regarded "a thoughtful and feasible plan to deal with the formidable economic, infrastructure, and social challenges confronting a developing country's metropolis". The Development Plan for Greater Bombay had been prepared in 1964 but, as it had precipitated haphazard development in the periphery, a regional approach was adopted and a Bombay Metropolitan Region Plan was brought out in 1970.

Following town planning legislations in states, the state governments undertook preparation of master plans initially only for the larger cities. Bangalore prepared an Outline Development Plan (ODP) in 1972 which was followed by a Comprehensive Development Plan (CDP) in 1984, a Revised CDP in 1995, and a Master Plan in 2007 which is currently in force. A revised Master Plan with a time horizon of 2031 (13 years) was prepared by the Bangalore Development Authority (BDA) (the city's planning authority) and sent to the state government for approval in 2018. As it was still under consideration of the government for over three years, the new chairman of the BDA decided to scrap the plan and prepare a new master plan in 2022; the appointment of consultants for the purpose is said to be under progress.

Urban Planning in Bangalore

My first brush with preparation of the Master Plan came as soon as I assumed office as the Secretary of Housing and Urban Development (HUD) department in 1983. Chief Minister (CM) Ramakrishna Hegde called me and said that Bangalore lacked a master plan and it must be prepared as early as possible. Hegde was a man with a vision and he was responsible for ushering in decentralisation in Panchayati Raj institutions in Karnataka. While he did not undertake a similar exercise in urban areas, he had a vision for Bangalore city and used to occasionally share his ideas with me. After the CM's mandate, I called a meeting with the concerned BDA officials, which was the statutory city planning authority responsible for preparing master plans. I was informed that under the Karnataka town planning legislation, there was no provision for a master plan. Instead, a two-stage process had been prescribed for preparing a city plan and an Outline Development Plan (ODP) which was to be followed by a Comprehensive Development Plan (CDP). An ODP for Bangalore had been prepared for a period of 15 years from 1961-76. The CDP should have been ready by 1976, but it did not see the light of day even seven years later in 1983.

My attempt to understand the processes behind the preparation of a plan for a city, be it the master plan, the ODP or the CDP, was the beginning of my exploration of the 'urban' world. I started understanding how cities evolved, their growth and decay over the years, the process of urbanisation, planning of towns, development of infrastructure, and the governance of cities. My curiosity about the causes of the long delay in the preparation of the CDP, much to the annoyance of town planners and others involved, led me to believe that the preparation of a plan requires two processes: the governance process and the planning process. The former consisted of the political and administrative aspects and the latter comprised the technical aspects including the content and the methodology. Both processes are important but in a broader context of setting goals, mobilising resources, and delivering and implementing outcomes, I felt that the governance process was critical. This was where our failures seemed more pronounced. Though this view was tentative at the time, it has only been strengthened over the last four decades, not only with regard to planning but other urban matters as well.

After deliberations on various issues pertaining to both technical and governance aspects, we arrived at a timeline for the completion of the CDP. The town planners wanted a year's time as a number of surveys were to be conducted for the plan, but the CM was in a hurry and wanted it completed in three months. Finally, they agreed to a six-month period, which got extended to eight months, as the law required that comments from the public had to be invited on the draft plan and only after due consideration of these comments could the plan be finalised. The entire process actually took nine months and the first Comprehensive Development Plan of Bangalore was published in 1984.

Although the commitment to the CM was fulfilled belatedly, I was not satisfied with the document. I felt that it was not a development plan in the true sense of the term, let alone a comprehensive one. The CDP turned out to be primarily a land use plan that showed the existing land use conditions at the time of the field survey and the land uses (classified as residential, commercial, industrial, public, semi-public, transportation, and agricultural including the green belt) that are likely to prevail after a period of 15 years. An important part of the land use plan pertains to zoning regulations which attract considerable attention, particularly of builders and architects because all buildings in the city have to conform to the zoning regulations.

The development part of the plan included the requirements of infrastructure such as water supply, housing, roads and transportation based on population projections. They were rough estimates and not based on credible data. I also discovered that most public comments pertained to land use issues rather than development matters. Landowners, including some politicians, were more interested in knowing if their lands were likely to be acquired for the purpose of development at a future date, and if so, whether that could be deleted from the plan. I may add that there was no proactive approach on the part of the BDA to give wide publicity to the draft plan or involve people's participation.

The CDP's time-frame was 15 years, up to the year 2000. However, after about 10 years, considering the rapid growth of the city, the government felt the need to revise the 1984 plan, leading to a Revised Comprehensive Plan being prepared in 1995. I was not associated with its preparation as I was outside the urban sector at that time. However, I found the revised plan more or less similar to the earlier one of 1984, except that the conurbation area (earmarked for development) had increased and the area under the green belt had decreased, indicating the rising demand for building space. It also implied that the decision-makers were yielding to pressures to reduce green spaces. I was shocked by the callous approach of the BDA town planners in determining land use, the most glaring example being the one pertaining to Electronic City, established in 1980, and two other industrial estates in areas that were shown as green belt, exposing the distortions in the process of planning and weaknesses in governance.

Apart from Bangalore city, as the Secretary of Urban Development, I had to deal with urban planning of all towns and cities of the state of Karnataka in the 1980s, which numbered a little over 200. At that time, urban planning meant little more than the preparation of the master plan. But, who was responsible for the preparation of the plan? And why had there been so much delay?

In the entire urban planning process, several questions regarding governance arise. Who makes the decisions and who implements them? Are all the stakeholders involved in the preparation and implementation of a plan? Are the right people, with the necessary qualifications and adequate experience, assigned the right tasks? Are adequate resources made available for its undertaking? Is there a proper monitoring mechanism to track progress and hold authorities accountable?

Often, the primary decision-makers are the chief minister (the political leadership), the secretary (the bureaucratic leadership) and the head of the department (the technical leadership), who may be assisted by their own officials. In practice, I found that some of the technical officers (town planners in this case) wield considerable political influence and render advice to the minister directly, overlooking the secretary. I noticed this particularly while effecting some changes in land use, contrary to planning norms. The implementers include head of the field organisation, head of the technical wing and those working under them. The final results on the ground depend on them and they can be subjected to pressure from politicians or other stakeholders. This meant that there was hardly any consultative process in plan preparation, except calling for written comments. In recent years, however, with an active civil society, consultations do take place but there is no guarantee that the suggestions of the public or even experts will be taken into consideration.

Delegation of tasks to the right people depends on two factors: (a) availability of such persons, and (b) the choice made by the decision-maker. Sometimes, these factors fall in place and other times, they do not. Of late, the appointment of external consultants has helped to a great extent. However, there is still an overall dearth of financial resources at the state level. This is reflected in allocations, depending on the priority attached to a particular plan or project. There are also cases where despite availability of funds, implementation has suffered.

Further, there are several deficiencies in the monitoring system, which accounts for poor results in many areas. Review meetings mostly turn out to be routine, and hardly anyone is held accountable for failures. Also, a lot depends on who conducts the monitoring exercise and how serious they are about it.

Under the Town and Country Planning Acts, it was mandatory for all cities to prepare a master plan. It is important to note that only some Indian towns and cities have master plans. Table 5.1summarises how many statutory towns and census towns actually had master plans in 2021.

Table 5.1: Status of Master Planning in Indian cities in 2021

Town Category	Total Towns in Category	Approved Master Plan	Under Preparation
Statutory Towns	4,041	1,566 (39%)	359
Census Towns	3,892	650 (17%)	268
Total Cities and Towns	7,933	2216 (28%)	627

Source: Ministry of Housing and Urban Affairs, 2021.

Master planning in India has been subjected to criticism by planners, urban experts, and the general public. While the master plan aimed to regulate the physical and spatial growth of the city, the absence of a clear policy to control the unabated growth of large metro cities and the development of second and third order cities has resulted in a skewed urban pattern. Basic services like water supply, sanitation and road maintenance have always been in the municipal domain, but the cash-strapped municipal bodies had been unable to take up large infrastructure projects. Hence, state governments had to provide financial assistance through grants and loans to the ULBs. Some states created parastatal organisations to provide water supply and sewerage networks. The first centrally sponsored scheme for urban areas came in the form of the Integrated Urban Development Programme (IUDP) for medium sized and large cities and the Integrated Development Programme for Small and Medium Towns (IDSMT). These schemes met with little success and failed to create the desired impact.

Attempts to Influence Trends in Urbanisation and Building New Cities

As noted earlier, there are mainly two factors driving urbanisation in Indian states: natural increase in population and migration. The first accounts for a major share of urban growth, mostly in northern states like Bihar, Uttar Pradesh (UP), Madhya Pradesh (MP), Punjab and

Rajasthan, and the second is observed predominantly in states such as Maharashtra, Gujarat and Delhi (Mathur, *et al.*, 2022). While we have under-urbanised states like Bihar and Odisha, two states, Tamil Nadu and Kerala, are on the threshold of crossing the half-way mark of 50 per cent, and Maharashtra is getting close too. India, as a whole, is under-urbanised and is expected to cross 50 per cent before 2050 (Census, 2011).

Is it possible to direct and modify the future course of urbanisation in a region? Analysing the wide spectrum of urbanisation conditions in 422 districts of India in the late 1980s, the NCU noted that there were districts which were 100 per cent urban and those which were 100 per cent rural. In 109 districts, over 90 per cent of the total population was rural; they were also poor and backward and had the highest potential for migration to urban areas.

One of the policies adopted by the state governments has been to encourage industries to set up base in backward areas by offering incentives. For instance, Karnataka, in its successive industrial policies, has classified talukas into categories that are provided incentives based on their backwardness. In order to discourage more industries in Bengaluru city, it has been declared a no-incentive zone. This approach of incentivising backward areas to promote industrialisation did not find favour with the NCU (1988) which observed that "propping up backward no-industry districts by giving incentives to entrepreneurs will not by itself help either the process of industrialisation or of rural development". The experience of Karnataka is instructive. Attractive incentives (such as tax concessions, land at cheaper rates, etc.) offered to backward areas in consecutive Industrial Policies from 1996 to 2019 have failed to achieve any policy objectives. Except for large manufacturing and polluting industries, entrepreneurs have always preferred Bangalore over other areas despite the lack of incentives for obvious reasons like better infrastructure, connectivity, educational, health and entertainment facilities. As a result, Bangalore has continued to grow, adding to its traffic congestion and infrastructure woes. There is also an anomaly in the selection of areas for incentives. For instance, in Karnataka, Anekal taluk has been declared as eligible for concessions, even though it is a part of the Bangalore Metropolitan Region and close to Hosur, a thriving industrial township located in Tamil Nadu. This has actually nullified the very purpose of the industrial location policy. In this context, it is pertinent to refer to the lack of coordination between urban and industrial policies and planning. Industrial development has taken place without taking into account the spatial requirements of the planned development of a region. This has led to distorted urban development on one hand and delayed provision of infrastructure and services needed for the industry on the other. The development of a region depends on the effective functioning of all sectors of the economy and hence the need for integration of economic and spatial planning.

In order to cope with the rapid urbanisation of India, some urbanists argue for building new cities instead of investing large amounts to improve the existing ones, while others believe that building new cities is time-consuming, highly capital-intensive, and unlikely to yield the desired results. It would be useful to look at the experience of some newly-built cities and their present condition. The first new city post Independence was Chandigarh, a product of the vision of Jawaharlal Nehru and the urban design of Le Corbusier, intended to be a symbol of modern urban India. Then came Gandhinagar, the new capital of Gujarat; Bhubaneswar, the new capital of Odisha; Naya Raipur, capital of the newly created state of Chhattisgarh; and the most recent one is Amaravati, the capital of the newly formed Andhra Pradesh.

The idea of 'new towns' was conceived in England to deal with the problem of high population densities in cities. The first such town to be built was Milton Keynes, about 40 km from London. Historically, Asian cities have always had high population densities. About two decades ago, the World Bank advised strongly against such cities, after studying a new town proposal of Kabul, the capital of Afghanistan. It contended that the infrastructure for any town must be developed much in advance of its actual occupation, which means heavy capital and transportation investment, causing negative cash flows for many years. This would be hard to justify when 80 per cent of Kabul's existing population lacked adequate access to infrastructure.

This question was examined recently by the Indian Institute for Human Settlements (IIHS) (Revi *et al.*, 2020) while submitting its recommendations to the 15th Finance Commission. It concluded that,

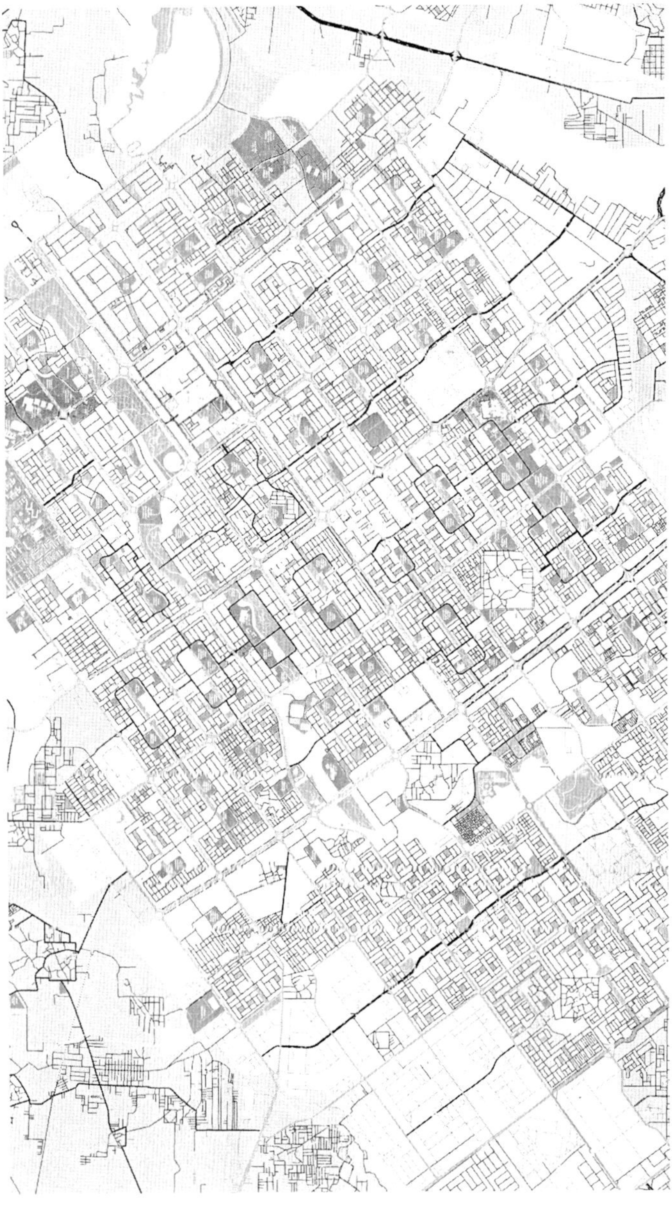

Fig. 5.8: A map of Chandigarh. The city was planned in a classic grid pattern with provisions for social infrastructure, institutional areas and housing for different economic classes in each sector, as far as possible.

Source: openstreetmap.org

contrary to popular perception, new towns and cities have contributed marginally to the share of India's urban population (less than 2%) and number of settlements (less than 0.1%) over the twentieth century. They have taken 30-50 years to reach critical economic mass and a population size of one million. "They have been more expensive to plan and build and have typically overshot their initial budgets by significant amounts, due to delays in execution and inflation. New towns have a limited impact on India's economic landscape, disproportionate to their imagination in policy". Hence, it is not prudent to create new towns, owing to their "long gestation period, medium-term impact, and resource intensity". The 15th Finance Commission has ignored this and recommended a grant of Rs. 8,000 crores to incubate eight new cities across the country, and the central government has accepted this proposal in totality, while no further details have been put out.

Lack of Urban Policy Perspective

In India, urban planning has more often followed urban development instead of guiding it according to a pre-designed plan. Cities have grown and developed in a spontaneous manner, dictated more by market forces than well-conceived and cohesive policies. Both the Task Force on Urbanisation and the NCU have commented strongly about the lack of spatial concern in the planning process of the country.

> Policy is uncoordinated in as much as national planning tends to be in terms of sectoral outlays while the urban planning has been mainly linked with physical outlays.
>
> (Task Force on Urbanisation, 1983)
>
> Spatial planning must become an integral part of the national economic planning process. The objective of spatial planning is to generate a process of spatial development which optimises utilisation of resources, reduces regional, spatial and economic imbalances, strengthens rural and urban interrelationships, improve the quality of life of majority of the people, protects the environment and maintains an ecological balance.
>
> (NCU, 1988)

> The haphazard growth of cities in India has resulted partly from a lack of a framework for urban policy, both at national and state levels. While migration and industrialisation naturally contribute to urbanisation, policy intervention does provide some direction to the future urban growth.
>
> (NCU, 1988)

Unfortunately, these well-meaning recommendations were ignored and no attempt was made to formulate any policy to guide urban development. In the absence of a national urban policy, states had also shown reluctance in framing policies at the state level. Karnataka was one of the exceptions. As far back as 1984, when I was Secretary to the State Government at the Department of Housing and Urban Development (HUD), we prepared a comprehensive paper on Urban Policy and placed it before the Economic and Social Council of the state, headed by the CM. The Vice Chairman was the renowned architect Charles Correa who appreciated the effort. There was extensive discussion on the paper and some useful suggestions were made. In 2009, when I was an Advisor to the CM, we brought out the Urban Development Policy of Karnataka, which was later adopted by the state with some modifications.

Chapter
6

Urban Poverty and Inequality

> *"Any city, however small, is in fact divided into two, one the city of the poor, the other of the rich"*
>
> (Plato, 360 AD, p. 141).

As the famous Greek philosopher predicted, most modern cities mirror ancient Greece in this respect. The growing urban-urban divide has attracted serious debate not only in poor and developing countries, but in rich countries as well.

The Urban Economy and Unequal Society

It is well established that there are strong linkages between urbanisation and economic development. The contribution of cities to the national economy far exceeds that of the rural sector and continues to increase by the day. To say that cities are the engines of economic growth has become a cliché now. In India, however, urban development has not received the recognition it deserves in macro-economic policies or the national planning process. In fact, as noted earlier, there was an attempt to slow down the pace of urbanisation by checking migration from rural to urban areas. The economic reforms of the 1990s did not percolate down to the city level and the liberalisation measures undertaken at the macro level were not reflected at the local level. Even the 74th Amendment of the Constitution, which aimed to decentralise authority to ULBs, did not spur reforms to empower the urban local government to promote economic development which continued to be in the domain of the state. Deprived of any decision-making power in shaping the urban economy, the ULBs continue to exhibit their colonial character, and urban governance has taken a backseat.

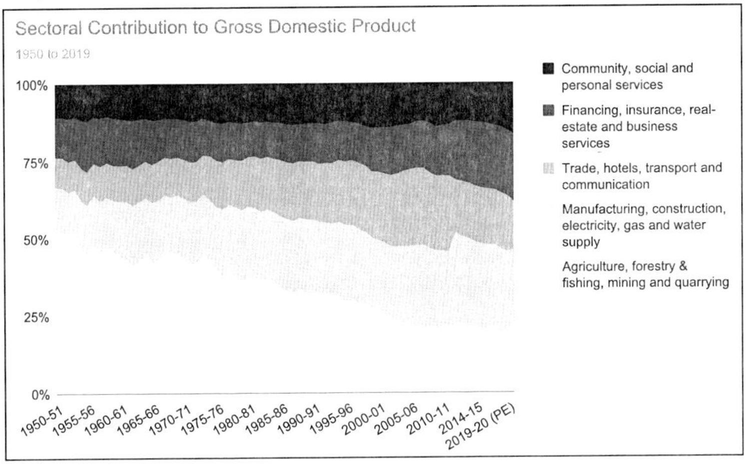

Fig. 6.1: The changing relative contributions of India's production sectors, 1950 to 2021.

Source: Economic Survey 2021.

Why is the urban economy so important? For one, people are continuously moving to cities. Between 1950 and 1980, across the globe, more than a billion people migrated from rural areas to cities (United Nations, 2004). This is not just a demographic shift but also an economic shift. People move to urban centres for education, employment and entertainment, all of which have tremendous economic significance and social relevance. The sectoral contribution to India's GDP shows the rising share of the urban sector, from 29 per cent in 1951-52 to 52.3 per cent in 2011-12[1], although the urban workforce (27%) is far less than the rural one (47%) (Mathur, *et al.*, 2021). The structural shift in the economy indicates a rising trend of the secondary and tertiary sectors (manufacturing and services), which are predominant in urban areas, and decline of the primary sector (agriculture and allied services), which are confined mostly to rural areas. Another indicator of urban economic growth is the urban-rural per capita GDP ratio which increased from 1.96 in 1951 to 2.7 in

1. This is significantly lower than 60 per cent, which is ubiquitously perceived to be the urban share of the GDP (Mathur, *et al.*, 2021).

2004-05, but declined to 2.4 in 2011-12. Increasing investments in cities, whether domestic or foreign, are making cities more prosperous. The changing lifestyle of the middle classes, now marked by a higher consumption expenditure, holds out as proof.

Secondly, it is important to take note of the inequities on account of urban growth. The benefits of economic development and urbanisation are not equally or equitably distributed between the urban and rural areas or across different segments of the urban population. Indian urbanisation, like that in other countries, has its pitfalls. The unequal economic gains of higher productivity, the process of accumulation of surplus capital in land and housing, inadequate mass transportation services and insufficient drinking water and sanitation are manifestations of poverty of not only the population but also the urban governments (Mathur, 1999). Poverty, unemployment, slums and squatter settlements are symbols of socio-economic inequalities and wide disparities in urban India. The result is an urban-urban divide caused primarily by the distorted allocation of resources by the state and the private sector on one hand, and the failure in governance to invest the economic gains in the public good on the other hand. This is reflected in the lack of ULBs' capacity to provide adequate infrastructure and services to the growing urban population.

Economic policy decisions have also led to distortions in the market, particularly the urban land market, adversely affecting access to housing and basic amenities by the urban poor and the migrant population. Subsidies on essential services like water and electricity have increased the burden on infrastructure, with public agencies unable to recover even the cost of supply. Ironically, the rich also become beneficiaries of such subsidies. The industrial location policy, aimed at promoting industries in backward regions, has actually helped the big industries who prefer strategic location and occupation of valuable urban land to subsidies.

Industrialisation in post-Independence India engineered economic growth and created new types of jobs. Initially, national industrial policies prioritized the large-scale manufacture of capital goods, established large public sector units in different cities across the country, and also created new industrial townships. Bangalore, for instance, became the centre to manufacture telephones (ITI Ltd.), machine tools (Hindustan Machine Tools or HMT), electronic goods

(Bharat Electronics Ltd., or BEL), and earth movers (Bharat Earth Movers Ltd., or BEML). Together with the aircraft industry, which had been set up in the 1940s, these large industrial units generated thousands of jobs from the shop floor to the top management level. The same was the case with other industries like Bharat Heavy Electricals Limited (BHEL) manufacturing heavy electricals in Bhopal, Heavy Engineering Corporation Limited (HECL) producing capital equipment and machinery in Ranchi, and Cochin Shipyard building and repairing ships in Cochin. The steel industry gave birth to new towns such as Bhilai (in present-day Chhattisgarh), Durgapur (West Bengal), and Rourkela (Odisha). Alongside large industries, small and medium industries started coming up in almost all states with encouragement from state governments, mainly in the form of incentives and subsidies. New industries were also being set up in the private sector to manufacture a wide range of goods including materials for construction (bricks, cement, steel, floor tiles and furniture) as well as consumer goods (textiles, food products, soaps, household items, drugs, etc.). Traditional industries such as handicrafts, handlooms, and jewellery continued with private enterprise, with some encouragement from the state through public sector corporations and boards. The states also provided land and infrastructure for small and medium industries in newly built industrial townships.

The types of jobs that emerged in post-Independence industrialising and urbanising India ranged from unskilled and semi-skilled apprenticeships at the shop floor to professional engineers, managers and office staff in finance and administration departments. A large number of jobs were created in the tertiary sector like tourism, travel services, hotel industry, retail and other support services. The education and health sectors registered steep growth with the multiplication of schools, colleges and hospitals. From the urban development point of view, more industrialisation and services meant more urbanisation, which also resulted in a large informal economy in the cities. The urban economy in India thus presents a contrasting picture of economic growth with a predominantly informal economy and deepening inequalities, peopled by a large number of poor, though the poverty ratio is declining.

Poverty and Inequality Indices

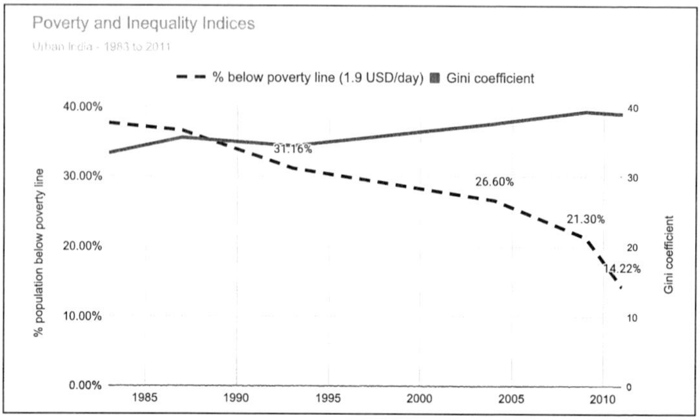

Fig. 6.2: India: urban gini coefficient 1990 to 2010.

Source: World Bank PovCalNet & Dykstra *et al.,* (2014).

The number of people living below the poverty line in Indian cities is shown to have reduced continuously from nearly 40 per cent in 1985 to just under 15 per cent in 2010. However, one must also consider that this poverty line is debatable as it is very low at USD 1.90 per day. At the same time, inequality as assessed through possession of wealth and assets, in the form of a gini coefficient, has unfortunately steadily increased in the last few decades.

The understanding of urban poverty during the planning era was somewhat misplaced. Dandekar and Rath (1971) had observed: "The urban poor are only an overflow of rural poor into the urban area". This concept is no longer valid and the definition of urban poverty has gone beyond merely consumption expenditure or per capita income. The definition is now more inclusive and takes into account several vulnerabilities of the poor—social, spatial and economic—due to precarious employment.

Slums and Informal Settlements

> Slums are a physical and spatial manifestation of urban poverty and intra-city inequality. However, slums do not accommodate all of the urban poor, nor are all slum dwellers always poor.
>
> (UN-Habitat, 2003, p. xxvi)

Housing conditions in cities reflect all the characteristics of poverty, inequality and informality in urban India. On one side, there are slums with very inadequate and huddled accommodation and on the other side lie sprawling gated communities with luxury housing, with a vast array of medium-sized and quality houses in the middle. This is a common sight in large cities across the country. The urban housing shortage is estimated to be 18.78 million units (Technical Group on Estimating Housing Shortage, 2012-17, 2018). While almost all people have a roof over their heads, it is the adequacy and quality of housing that impacts the quality of living. Slums, in particular, have been a blot on our cities.

Dandeli, 1967

My first encounter with slums was not in the big city of Bangalore where I grew up, but in the small industrial town of Dandeli in the North Kanara (now Uttara Kannada) district of Karnataka. As Assistant Commissioner of Karwar, I also happened to be the Chairman of the Dandeli Notified Area Committee (NAC), a government constituted body in place of an elected municipal council to manage civic affairs of the urban area. There were two private industries in the town, the Dandeli Paper Mills Ltd. and The Indian Plywood Company. Most of their workers lived in slums. When I first visited a slum where workers of the paper mill lived, I was appalled at their living conditions—filthy surroundings, lack of sanitation and leaky huts. I wondered how they managed to live in that environment. In my youthful enthusiasm, I thought I would transform the slum, but in my two-year stay in the district and my visits to Dandeli at periodic intervals (my headquarters was about 100 km away), all that I could manage was a marginal improvement in sanitation and replacement of some leaky roofs. That was the first big lesson in my career—the deflation of the ego.

The origin of slums goes back to the Industrial Revolution in England when people moved from villages to cities like London and Manchester to find jobs in the newly built factories. The factory owners exploited their labour by neither paying them adequate wages nor providing them a decent shelter. So, they squatted wherever land was available and these huddled settlements grew into slums.

This phenomenon was replicated in other colonised countries where factories were built. In India, the first slums were noticed in Bombay and Calcutta.

Fig. 6.3: Slum map of Mumbai, 2017.

Source: Slum Rehabilitation Authority, Mumbai.

Post-Independence, the state paid little attention to the growth of slums, as our planning model turned out to be exclusionary. While the well-developed high- and middle-income housing colonies were designated as 'formal', as they conformed to the requirements of the master plan, slums and squatter settlements came to be considered 'informal', and therefore 'illegal'. Indian master planning failed to take into account the shelter needs of the poor. With continuous migration, the result was a housing shortage, particularly for the poor and vulnerable sections, further leading to the proliferation of slums. UN-Habitat (2009) summed up the situation aptly:

> The most obvious problem with master planning and modern urbanism is that they completely fail to accommodate the way of life of the majority of inhabitants in rapidly growing, largely poor and informal cities. The possibility that people living in such circumstances could comply with zoning ordinances designed for European towns is extremely unlikely. Inappropriate zoning ordinances are instrumental in creating informal settlements and peri-urban sprawl. It could be argued that city governments are producing social and spatial exclusion as well as environmental hazards, as a result of the laws and regulations which they adopt. (pp. 5-6)

In a broader context, the housing sector is a significant contributor to the national economy because of its linkages with other sectors providing goods and support services. The national income from housing sector rose from Rs. 9.15 billion in 1960 to Rs. 16 billion in 1977 (National Buildings Organisation, 1987). The housing sector is expected to contribute 11 per cent of the GDP by 2020 (99 acres, 2018). Housing, being a labour-intensive process, generates a high degree of employment; about one per cent of the total workers were involved in the construction sector until 1970s, of which almost 60 per cent were engaged in house construction (*ibid*). However, the poor and low-income groups cannot afford house ownership due to the high land prices in cities. In the 1950s and 1960s, the government took some measures to build houses for the disadvantaged sections, but they were inadequate and built at a slow pace. It was followed by a Slum Improvement Programme in select cities, which again met with limited success. In the 1980s, the government, with the assistance of the World Bank, launched the Sites and Services programme, which helped in providing basic infrastructure and security of tenure to the slum dwellers. It achieved considerable success in the states of Andhra Pradesh and Tamil Nadu where the programme empowered slum dwellers with a secure tenure and the opportunity to design and construct a house of their choice (Gulyani, 2016).

It was only in 1992, with the new economic policy of liberalisation, when the government announced a National Housing Policy, shifting its approach from a 'provider' of housing to an 'enabler', drawing private home builders into the redevelopment of slums instead of merely improving them. "The government has to create a facilitating environment for growth of housing activity rather than itself taking on the task of building" (National Housing Policy, 1992). The concept of affordable housing was introduced and incentives were offered to encourage the private sector to take up construction of houses for the low-income groups. In 1998, a revised policy called National Habitat and Human Settlement Policy was brought out, calling for a 'housing revolution'. Its main features included optimisation of land use, repeal of the Urban Land (Ceiling and Regulation) Act, 1976, amendment to rent control legislations to stimulate investment in rental housing, and modification of planning regulations that can help checking the growth of slums. In spite of these policies and other efforts, the policy goal of ensuring "the basic need of 'Shelter for All' and a better quality of life to all citizens by harnessing the unused potential in the public, private and household sectors", has remained unfulfilled till now.

Experience of Slum Rehabilitation

As Commissioner of Bangalore City Corporation (BCC) in the late 1980s, I was associated with the Association for Voluntary Action and Service (AVAS), an NGO engaged in the rehabilitation of the residents of Lakshmipuram slum in the Indiranagar area of Bangalore. Comprising mostly women and headed by the highly committed Anita Reddy, AVAS had prepared a project report to build houses for 127 families residing in the slum. Somehow, the project was not taking off. One day, Anita met me and explained the details of the project and the problems they were facing in its implementation. I was impressed by the innovative concept where the poor households themselves designed, planned and executed their housing needs. I told her that the project would be fully supported by the BBMP.

I visited the slum adjoining the main road connecting Ulsoor, a busy middle-class area populated mostly by Tamilians, with Indiranagar, an upcoming cosmopolitan middle class extension. The people were mostly service providers such as construction labourers, vegetable vendors, auto drivers, domestic workers and the like. They told me that while they were able to earn their livelihoods, their existence in the place was shaky as they faced threats of eviction and demolition of their huts. When I asked how they would build houses on their own, they expressed confidence that they would be able to do so with the strong support they were receiving from AVAS including loans to finance the construction.

Building a new management system

The Bangalore City Corporation is infusing a new blood of professionals into its cadres and a touch of management in its system.

Disclosing this, the new Corporation Commissioner Mr. Ravindra said, "The Corporation does not even have a architectural design cell though we do have lot of construction programmes. On the same lines we should have a few computer professionals who can evolve suitable softwares to utilise our computer to the maximum. What is needed is introduction of a management concept in the Corporation working and we are shortly going to arrive at it."

The Corporation has also acquired a Rs. 4.3 lakh computer. The micro 32 computer supplied by the Electronics Corporation of India Limited (ECIL) is however lying unused. It is presently being utilised only for pay roll preparations covering only two ranges of the staff.

Mr. Ravindra informed that skilled staff were being recruited to handle the computer and utilise it to the maximum. Preparation of software will also be developed for handling property tax, tenders and other accounts.

Among the management changes to take place is decentralisation of the commissioner's power. Four deputy commissioners are to be made incharge of four zones into which the Bangalore city has been divided for effective and speedy redressal of public grievances and other day-to-day affairs.

The Corporation also has new plans and projects up its sleeves. Two major ones are the slum development programme of Lakshmipuram and the building of a modern council hall near the present Corporation office.

Corporation commissioner A Ravindra

Referring to the slum programme Mr. Ravindra said, "With the assistance of HUDCO, the City Corporation is taking up this development programme. We have envisaged to build 122 tenaments in Lakshmipuram slum opposite the grave yard near Adarsha Theatre, Ulsoor. Some of these tenaments wil have a first floor and others only the ground floor. The vacant space being created in this slum will be utilised for civic amenities like park, milk booth etc."

Mr. Ravindra added "We are also building 500 to 600 tenaments near Koramangala for the economically weaker sections of the society. This project after completion will be mainly utilised to shift slum dwellers to this site and clear the slums as far as possible. "The Koramangala project, envisaged at a cost of 240 lakhs will be providing shelter for nearly 1,500 families. HUDCO is financing 70 per cent of the cost of this project.

Mr. Ravindra explained "There are over 200 slums identified in Bangalore of which 60 comes under the Corporation area. The balance are covered under BDA and the Slum Development Board."

He lauded the activities of AVAS, a social service organisation headed by Ms. Anitha Reddy. Due to this society's efforts the slum dwellers at Lakshmipuram were convinced of the corporation motives and they have agreed to make arrangements to shift temporarily to enable construction activities. Mr. Ravindra added "If any social service organisation come up with such schemes the City Corporation will only be too happy to launch a housing scheme in such slums".

The Corporation is also all set to commence the construction of a Council hall at a cost of Rs. 186 lakhs. The foundation stone was laid by Prime Minister Rajiv Gandhi on Jan 7, 1987.

Tenders called by the Corporation has been finalised and M/s. Consulting Engineering Services (I) Pvt. Ltd., of New Delhi is likely to bag the tender as they have quoted the lowest. Other firms which participated in the tender are M/s. Premnath Associates, Bombay (who have built the planetorium in the city), M/s. Karekar Sundaram, Bangalore and M/s A A Architects.

The council hall spreads over 6,682 square metres of build up area and will have two floors.

The basement will accommodate a parking lot and the reception hall. The first floor will house the Archives, Standing Committee Chairman's rooms totalling four nos., two mini meeting halls, the council hall, the mayor and his deputy's office, and the commissioner office. The top floor will have only library.

The council hall will house 150 council members and public gallery with a capacity to house 150 persons.

The council hall will be air-conditioned. Concealed desk top mikes are a speciality.

— B.G. Siddesh

The City Tab, July 26 -Aug 1, 1987

Fig. 6.4: A newspaper report from August 1, 1987, reporting on the slum Lakshmipuram slum development project.

Source: AVAS.

Then began the ordeal. It was not as simple as I had imagined. Firstly, there were a number of forces operating in the 'interests' of the poor slum dwellers. Their real interest was in the land whose value was high and rising. Secondly, the proposed in situ rehabilitation posed serious problems as we had to find an appropriate space for temporary shelter during the time of construction. Third, there were internal problems among the stakeholders such as the size of the house to be built, the norms for allocation of housing units to different families, preference for the floor they would like to occupy, and so on. This was anyway something they sorted out with the support of AVAS. BCC had to contend with the first two issues besides the crucial issue of grant of property title deeds. We had to adopt a participatory approach where all three parties, the slum community, AVAS, and BCC, engaged in discussion to resolve the issues arising from time to time.

Fig. 6.5: Consultation on the plans for the development of Lakshmipuram slum in Bangalore.

Source: AVAS.

Finally, the project was successfully executed and it went on to win the National Habitat Award for the first participatory people's housing scheme for the urban poor of Bangalore in 1995. For me, it was doubly satisfying as I was back in the corporation as Administrator. More importantly, it opened my eyes to the plight of people living in slums. I was convinced that with a collaborative approach between the community, a committed civil society organisation, and the government agencies, it is possible to overcome all odds in the planning and execution of any project. At the grassroots level, in issues involving people's interests, participatory governance is indeed the right way.

The housing sector also reflects the deep social and economic inequalities in Indian cities. The glaring contrast in the housing conditions and access to basic amenities of water supply, sanitation, electricity and transport between the slums/squatter settlements and the gated communities, is nothing less than appalling. Why is such a state of affairs continuing 75 years after Independence? Is it a governance failure or something more? These issues will be explored in more detail in Part III.

Emergence of the Urban Middle Class

Among the many changes that shaped the nineteenth century, the emergence of the middle class is salient. While the term may refer to different social entities elsewhere, in India it acquired a new valence through a history that encompasses colonialism, nationalism and the desire for upward social mobility (Joshi, 2017). Colonial India exposed many young people to Western education in schools and colleges established by the British, initially in prominent cities like Madras, Calcutta and Bombay, and later on in other urban centres; some of them travelled to the UK and USA to obtain degrees from Western universities. Influenced by European ideas and ideals, a new class emerged that questioned traditional religious beliefs, the caste system's injustices and gender discrimination. The freedom struggle was led by those influenced by the liberal ideologies of the West. Mahatma Gandhi, Jawaharlal Nehru, Sardar Vallabhai Patel and BR Ambedkar, the leading lights of the freedom struggle, were products of Western universities. Under the spell of these towering personalities, many young men and women joined the struggle. The new educated and rational class that emerged during the colonial era signalled the birth of modernity in India, which was closely associated with the 'urban'.

How do we define the middle class? Is it the class perched between the rich and the poor, the elite and the disadvantaged? Or is it a cultural construct that varies over time and context, as postulated by Sanjay Joshi? According to Joshi (2017), in colonial India, many young people, through exposure to colonial institutions, fashioned themselves as the Indian 'middle class'. Like their British counterparts, they sought to distance themselves from the 'decadence' of the elder elites, even as they disparaged the plebeian class, thus emerging as the harbinger of modernity.

Michal Kalecki, a distinguished Polish economist, who also served as an economic advisor to the Government of India, after a brief visit to India between 1959-60 (Mazurek, 2018), observed that Indian society was divided into three groups: the landlord and business classes at the top; the workers, the landless, and the poor peasants at the bottom; and the rich peasantry, small businesses, and the professional class in the middle. He further characterised the Indian state as an 'intermediate regime'—neither capitalist nor socialist but in the control of a middle class (Kalecki, 1999). In Indian democratic politics, it is these 'intermediate' classes that had access to power through the institutions of the state. The politicians and the permanent civil service belonging to different castes and regions were the middle class (Baru, 2021).

The generally accepted definition of middle class is in economic terms. Lawrence (2006), a British economist, in his study of the middle class in Great Britain in the mid-nineteenth century, arrived at the salary of £156 a year to identify the starting point of the middle class. Bhalla (2017) finds that 150 years later, our own definition of the middle class (US$12 a day on purchasing power parity basis) comes very close to that of Lawrence. He further points out that the middle class has benefited the most from economic growth and is therefore a supporter of economic reforms. "The middle class is a sense of values, an indicator of aspirations, a belief in 'law and order.'" It is a class that attaches great value to education and merit; a belief in merit may be the middle class' signature.

In India, the first two decades of the post-Independence era (1950-70) witnessed a slow growth in the urban population. From 17.3 per cent in 1951, the rate of urbanisation showed a marginal rise to 18 per cent in 1961. The next two decades registered a higher rate of growth with the urban population reaching 19.9 per cent in 1971 and 23.3 per cent by 1981, with the 1970s registering over 3 per cent growth. We notice a surge of urban growth in certain metropolitan areas such as Bangalore, recording a steep rise of 76 per cent in the 1970s and 41 per cent in the 1980s (various editions of the Census of India). As industrialisation began to gather pace and employment opportunities expanded, large cities became magnets for attracting immigrants and investments. With increasing incomes and good educational and health facilities, a new urban middle class began to emerge in India.

The rise of the middle class also signifies the rise of civil society in India. Non-governmental organisations (NGOs), Resident Welfare Associations (RWAs) and social justice activists began negotiating and bargaining for better civic amenities and delivery of services. They protested against actions of the government leading to environmental damage and its 'arbitrary' decisions against the interests of the people. The foundation for such protests had been laid down during the freedom struggle with Gandhi's non-cooperation and civil disobedience movements against the British. Social reform movements, led by religious and social organisations as well as eminent individuals against caste discrimination, superstitions and other social evils, along with the demand for political rights and representation in democratic or semi-democratic bodies created by the British, were mainly a middle-class phenomenon. The Indian National Congress (INC), which played a leading role in the freedom movement, was itself considered 'a middle class machine' (Ghose, 1973, p. 19).

The cultural renaissance witnessed during the second half of the twentieth century coincided with the urban transition from the colonial period to the politically free era of planning and development. This may be attributed in a substantial measure to the rise of the urban middle class. New forms of art and architecture and public and private spaces began to take shape, reflecting the aspirations of the middle class. New buildings to house the legislatures of state governments exhibited unique styles of architecture, reflecting the meeting of tradition and modernity. The Vidhana Soudha in Bangalore, perhaps the finest legislature building in India, with its dome carrying the four-faced lion, is an example.

Following the birth centenary celebrations of Rabindranath Tagore, the Nobel laureate and giant literary figure of the 20th century, new cultural centres came to be established in all state capitals of the country. The Rabindra Bhavans provided the much-needed platform for the development of diverse forms of art that India has been an heir to. The middle class has now come to occupy the highest positions in the political, bureaucratic and the business world. How did the Indian middle class manage to become hegemonic without any significant economic or social power? How did it end up playing a key role in the economic, social and cultural activities of India?

Chapter 7

The Political Economy of Urban Development

Post-Independence India has been marked by a peculiar kind of dualism, perhaps unwittingly created by the Indian Constitution. The opening words of this seminal document, 'India, that is Bharat' have come to be identified with two Indias—the 'India' of the urban, English-speaking, modern, and middle and upper classes, and the 'Bharat' of those who speak native tongues, belong to the lower middle class, and reside on the fringes and slums of urban and rural India (Deepak, 2021). In a broader sense, it also signifies the urban-rural divide. This binary has influenced the political, economic and social discourse of modern India as well as its economic growth trajectory and political dynamics. Economic decision-making is a political process and the resultant political economy shapes public policy. This has far-reaching consequences, which can be seen in the way our cities have grown and been governed.

A significant trend in the development process in India is the increasing concentration of economic and political power. The power, that was initially in the hands of the state and a few big businesses has begun to spread to other sections of society. With rising prosperity fuelled by urbanisation and economic liberalisation, new institutions of social, economic and cultural power have started to assert themselves. Baru (2021), a policy analyst and writer who was Advisor to former Prime Minister Manmohan Singh, in his recent book *India's Power Elite* delineated the dynamics of the political transition in post-

Independence India including the recent developments in the twenty-first century. He postulated that while political power continues to be exercised by the 'governing elite' (Pareto, 1916) comprising the politicians in power and higher-level bureaucracy, a 'non-governing elite' that includes the rich businessmen, public intellectuals and celebrities like film stars and sportspersons, who can influence or critique public policy, came into existence. This new elite is capable of wielding power through modern state institutions or traditional institutions like caste or a combination of both.

The formulation of public policy is influenced by political, economic and social considerations, which can be termed as 'political economy'. In practice, the operation of the political economy in India is marked by the capture of urban resources by the elite and the wealthy, mainly by gaining control over urban land; securing privileges in education, health and other services; and manipulation of the procurement process.

Urban Land: The Critical Issue

Growing urbanisation creates an increasing demand for land which is the basis for all human settlements. Being a finite commodity, the supply of land does not always keep pace with its demand. The use of urban land is contentious in all countries simply because the supply of surplus land is limited and subject to so many competing claims (Drabkin, 1977). Dissatisfaction with the emerging forms is almost universal. However, in developing countries, where towns and cities often double in area as well as population within a decade, these land problems are most critical (World Bank, 1983). Failure to provide enough land for urban expansion results in high land prices, exacerbates the creation of high-density slums and generally lowers urban productivity (Bertaud, 2010). The rapid expansion of cities is also eating into valuable agricultural land which is converted for urban uses.

Land Prices

The urban land problem arises mainly because of the high land prices in urban areas, especially in large cities. The price of serviced land (with all amenities like roads, water supply, sewerage, electricity etc.) is much higher. Coupled with speculation, owning a piece of land or a house in cities has become unaffordable for most people. The real estate and land market is described as a 'haven for black money' because the level of land prices and their rate of appreciation tend to be higher than in other goods and assets. This has resulted in non-availability of reasonably priced land for low-income groups, leading to the poor being driven into unsuitable outskirts and peripheries of the city. The supply of new urban land falls far short of the demand created by the rise in urban population, incomes, and economic and social activities.

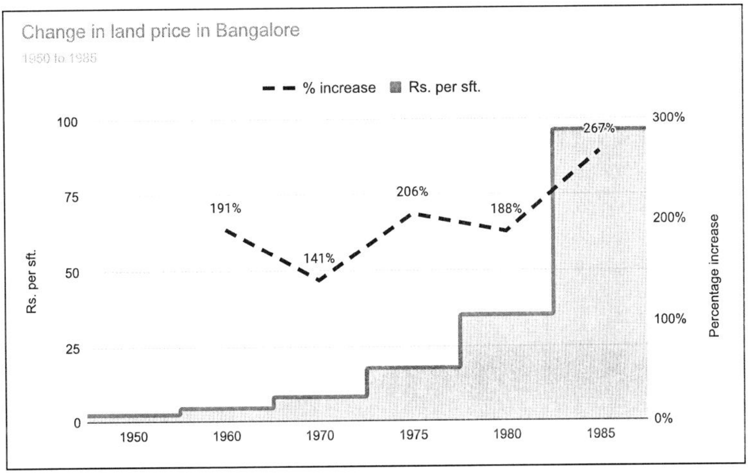

Fig. 7.1: Land price in Bangalore: 1950 to 1985.

Source: Dr. A. Ravindra (1996). *Urbal Land Policy*.

Data on land prices in metro cities like Mumbai, Delhi and Bengaluru shows a continuously rising trend in space and time. In a research study on land values in Bangalore, it was found that the average land value increased from 24.84 per sq. foot in 1976-77 to 96.23 in 1985-86, that is, a four-fold rise in a period of 10 years. With reference to the base year of 1950-51 (2.23 per sq. foot), the increase was a phenomenal 44 times (Ravindra, 1996), reflecting the scramble for a resource that was or was perceived to be in short supply.

Distorted Urban Land Market

In spite of various interventions by the government, the urban land market in India continues to present a distorted picture. The failure of public agencies like the planning and development authorities is reflected in: (a) the inadequate supply of public land for housing for different segments of the population, particularly the lower-income groups; and (b) the inability of the government in controlling or regulating land prices. The distortion caused by public policies becomes evident in the behaviour of the beneficiaries of publicly allotted lands who sell them after the lease period or even earlier through informal transactions in the open market, commanding a much higher price, and move to less expensive areas. This has also led to large-scale conversion of residential properties to commercial use, making a mockery of the land uses prescribed in the master plan. Bengaluru presents a vivid example of this phenomenon where entire areas earmarked for residential use have been changed to commercial use, transforming the very character of the city and adding to infrastructure and traffic problems. Well-planned and peaceful neighbourhoods have turned into commercial hubs with shopping centres, restaurants, pubs and bars, pushing up rental values.

Cities in India have been plagued not only by illegal constructions and encroachments, but by unauthorised land uses. There are other kinds of problems related to land such as land tenure, ownership rights, land transactions, registration of documents and so on. The urban land system in India has turned into a vicious circle, extending its arms across the economic, political and social dimensions, benefiting the rich and the powerful rather than common citizens. At the root of it lies the failure of the government to formulate a sound land policy and enforce regulations. In general, the way countries formulate policy is never completely coherent; there is no silver bullet to reduce supply constraints on urban land, neither complete laissez-faire nor a government monopoly on land development can by itself solve the problem (Bertaud, 2010). In India, this failure may be attributed, at least partly, to the supine indifference of the government to formulate the right kind of policy or to regulate the wrong kind of market behaviour.

The problem of urban land supply was recognised as early as the 1960s, when the Government of India constituted a Committee on Urban Land Policy in 1963 to examine the problems relating to urban land and make its recommendations. The Committee submitted its report in 1965 and outlined four basic objectives of the urban land policy: (a) optimum social use of urban land; (b) supply of adequate quantity of urban land at reasonable prices; (c) encouraging community effort for land development and housing; and (d) preventing concentration of land ownership (Prakash, 1965). The NCU, after studying the committee's report, added two more objectives: (a) encouraging socially and economically efficient allocation of urban land; and (b) promoting flexibility of land use in response to changes resulting from a growing city (NCU, undated).

The government did not formulate any urban land policy as such. Instead, it made interventions through the instruments of land acquisition and zoning regulations. The former was aimed at providing land for public purposes such as housing, setting up industry and infrastructure development, and the latter was intended to regulate land use in urban areas. The third intervention came through a new legislation called the Urban Land (Ceiling and Regulation) Act, 1976 in order to "prevent the concentration of urban land in the hands of a few persons and speculation and profiteering" (The Urban Land (Ceiling and Regulation) Act, 1976).

All these three policy instruments of public intervention, paved with good intentions and meant to serve public causes, also turned out to be political instruments for rent-seeking and bureaucratic corruption, which put the citizens at the mercy of the state. Let us see how they worked in practice.

Land Acquisition Laws

The Land Acquisition Act of 1894 enacted by the British provided the legal basis for the acquisition of private land for public purpose. Broadly speaking, 'public purpose' is the general interest of the community as opposed to the interests of private individuals. The state governments and the urban development authorities have been acquiring private land for the purpose of developing housing colonies, industrial estates and public works such as construction or widening of roads, flyovers, subways and other public transport requirements. Over the years, the supply of land thus acquired has greatly facilitated urban development and provision of housing.

The process of land acquisition has, however, posed serious problems such as inordinate procedural delays, issues relating to the compensation of landowners, litigation etc. This is illustrated by data pertaining to a few land acquisition cases in the BDA in the 1970s and 1980s. The time taken to complete acquisition proceedings ranged from 2-10 years. The land finally acquired falls far short of the land notified for acquisition, amounting to about 57 per cent of the total notified areas. Further, more than 270 cases were pending in courts, as recorded in 1988, with a majority being stuck for 3- 7 years and more than 10 per cent of the cases pending for over 7 years. Eventually, the courts also enhanced the compensation significantly, awarding on an average 3.5 times the compensation awarded by the BDA (Ravindra, 1996).

The consequences of the flaws in the land acquisition process are twofold: (a) heavy costs incurred by the acquiring body in terms of paying huge compensation to landowners and the delayed availability of land; and (b) suffering caused to landowners on account of the long wait in getting compensation after losing their property. Apart from these, there are certain hidden costs. Lands that are notified but have not been occupied or taken possession of for a long time get encroached. This is where political economy takes over. Attempts to remove encroachments meet with stiff resistance. It is a vicious circle: under-valuation of property to begin with, delays in acquisition and finally, unauthorised occupation of notified land.

It must be mentioned that some states like Gujarat have done a better job in land acquisition by adopting innovative methods such as negotiation and land sharing with landowners, which have speeded up the acquisition process. Other states like Karnataka are now adopting such methods too.

A new land acquisition law called the Right to Fair Compensation and Transparency in Land Acquisition, Rehabilitation and Resettlement Act, 2013 replaced the Land Acquisition Act of 1894. Its main objective is "to ensure, in consultation with institutions of local self-government and Gram Sabhas, a human, participative, informed and transparent process for land acquisition for industrialisation, development of essential infrastructural facilities and urbanisation with the least disturbance to the owners of the land and other affected families and provide just and fair compensation to the affected families and make adequate provision ...for their rehabilitation and resettlement".

(RFCTLARR Act, 2013)

Under this Act, the landowners are given priority in that their consent must be obtained before acquiring the land. The government, however, is exempted from this provision if the land is needed for developing public infrastructure. The new Act has been subject to much criticism. While it is important to safeguard the interest of the landowners, it is also necessary to simplify the procedures for land acquisition.

At this stage, it is necessary to refer to the issue relating to the acquisition or transfer of central government land to the states for infrastructure or any other public purpose. Defence land should be particularly mentioned, especially in cities where cantonments are situated. The Ministry of Defence insists on payment of compensation, equivalent to market price, before transferring such land to the state government. On the other hand, when the centre undertakes any infrastructure work, it often insists on the land belonging to the state to be transferred free of cost. The Tamil Nadu government has, in its Industrial Policy Note of 2022-23, suggested that as land forms the major portion of overall project cost, if the state transfers land free of cost to GoI, which subsequently monetises the infrastructure, the state should be entitled to a share of the gains.

Land Acquisition in Karwar and Bangalore

Let me recall my own experience in land acquisition matters. In my very first job as Assistant Commissioner (Sub Collector) in 1967 in Karwar, a quaint little town with beautiful natural landscape, on the western coast of Karnataka, I had to deal with a large land acquisition project for building a strategic sea port. The Government of India had launched a project to establish a military naval base at Karwar which required a vast parcel of land. The Assistant Commissioner was designated as the Land Acquisition Officer and I had to deliver the land within the prescribed time limit.

The Land Acquisition Act, 1894 prescribed a transparent but lengthy process for the acquisition of private land. First, a preliminary notification had to be issued, declaring the intent and purpose of acquisition, the specific lands to be acquired, the names of the landowners and a call for objections, if any, to the acquisition.

This had to be followed up by a personal hearing of the parties and then the issue of final notification, mentioning the details of lands to be acquired where objections did not sustain. The landowners are then asked to file their claims for compensation and finally an 'award' is passed for acquisition of the land along with compensation.

The issues I faced were threefold. The first related to litigation. The people of Karwar were a highly litigant lot and a good number of cases used to land up in courts. More frustrating were the stay orders and injunctions from the courts, putting a break on the acquisition process till the disposal of the case, which resulted in further delays. Secondly, the amount of compensation fixed would invariably be challenged under a provision of the Land Acquisition Act called 'reference to the civil court'. This would take an unduly long time as it involved examination of witnesses. I had the experience of being summoned by the civil court at Karwar to give evidence long after I had ceased to be the Assistant Commissioner. In most cases, I found that the court would enhance the compensation fixed by the Land Acquisition Officer on the ground that the market value was higher than the amount awarded. Finally, I must point out that the North Kanara district, being mostly covered by forest, had very small land holdings and the agricultural land acquired from the farmers not only render them landless, but also deprived them of their livelihood without offering any alternative means. But public purpose takes precedence and my personal sympathy for the farmers who lost their land is supposed to have no place in the government's scheme of things. During my stay of two years at Karwar, I could acquire a substantial quantity of land for the expansion of the port and naval base project.

Let me now narrate a different sort of experience in land acquisition in Bangalore when I was chairman of the BDA in the mid-1990s. As the public agency for providing housing and infrastructure facilities in the capital city, the BDA had been acquiring large extents of land in the outskirts of the city. After a review of the status of land acquisition and distribution of house sites, I discovered that a considerable area of land was available for allotment of sites, but was lying vacant with no justifiable reason. Dissatisfied with the replies given by the staff, I decided to go and see things for myself. On inspection of the area, I found that the land was littered with small structures with no occupants. On enquiry, I learnt that they were unauthorised and the landowners (or land grabbers) were preventing the BDA staff from going ahead with their work.

It was nothing but an open encroachment of public land and I told the concerned officials that the unauthorised structures had to be removed and the site distribution work must commence. So, we planned what was to be a 'secret operation' for dismantling all the unauthorised structures and re-possessing the land. On the day fixed for the operation, I got a call from the CM in the early hours of the morning to go and meet him later in the day and till such time, no action was to be taken to demolish the structures in question. I knew what was in store and dutifully went and met the CM and explained to him the situation. After listening to me, he explained that while he appreciated my stand, there seemed to be genuine hardship for some landowners and that I should wait for 'further instructions', a favourite euphemism in the government lingo for an indefinite wait. I waited and never got any instructions as long I was chairman of the BDA.

The CM, who generally never interfered in my work, was obviously under heavy pressure from those with vested interests. All my efforts to meet and convince him about the genuineness of government interest in the case were in vain. I was thoroughly disappointed because it was a case of land acquired by the BDA that was being grabbed and it is needless to elaborate further on the strength of the land mafia in the IT capital of the country.

The contrast between the cases of Karwar and Bangalore is instructive. In the small town, the ordinary and poor farmers followed the law and lost their lands for a 'public purpose' and in the large metropolis, the land acquired for a similar purpose was surrendered by the government to land grabbers!

Land Zoning Regulations

Regulation of land use is done through zoning regulations, which are part of the master plan. Urban land in the planning area, including the city as well as the periphery, is normally classified into six zones—residential, commercial, industrial, public/semi-public, parks and other recreational areas, and agricultural. Spatially, an urban area is expected to develop in conformity with the land use plan. Any person intending to put their land to a use other than what is prescribed must seek permission for 'change of land use' from the relevant authority. This power to grant change of land use, often exercised in a discretionary manner, is another source of corruption. For example, between 1981 and 1987, the BDA allowed 301 land use changes officially, while at the same time, there is no record of the number of illegal changes made by people themselves. This number is, however, misleading as in practice, many more variations (or deviations) from the prescribed uses have taken place, which are 'unauthorised' (Ravindra, 1996).

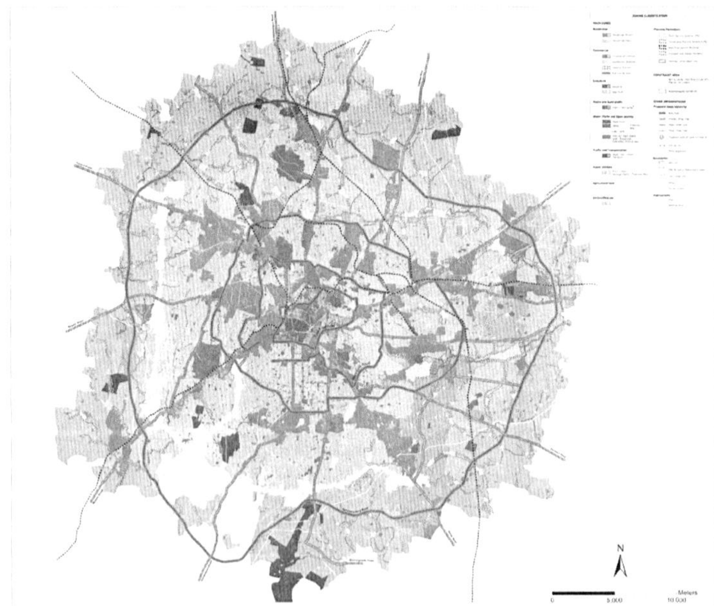

Fig. 7.2: The Comprehensive Development Plan for Bangalore 2015. Various land uses allowed on particular parcels of land are represented by various colours on the plan.

Source: Bangalore Development Authority.

Illegal Constructions and Developments

One of the most ticklish problems confronting city administrators pertains to illegal constructions and encroachments on public lands. Bangalore is far from being free from this malaise as it is acute here. When I was the Administrator of Bangalore City Corporation, one of the serious problems that came to my notice was parking of vehicles on roads and footpaths, thus obstructing free flow of motor and pedestrian traffic. One of the reasons that caused parking violations, I discovered, was buildings, constructed or used in violation of the law. In particular, I found that many commercial buildings were putting their basement floors to commercial use, even though they were meant for providing parking facilities as prescribed under the building regulations, resulting in increased roadside parking. My discussions with the concerned officials of the corporation revealed that notices had been issued to the owners of such buildings for violating the law but neither had they taken action to restore the basement space for parking, nor was any punitive action taken by the officials; in fact, there seemed to be collusion for the continuation of status quo. So, something drastic had to be done to deal with the problem.

A team of trusted officials in the corporation and the police department was put together to carry out a secret operation. In the early hours of a morning in July 1995, the assigned people swooped down on the basements of specific commercial buildings in a central locality of Bangalore, St. Marks Road and demolished the unauthorized structures. The event created a huge sensation, was widely reported in the media, and welcomed by the people at large. It was the first time any such action was taken to deal with illegal constructions in Bangalore. Similar action was taken in other parts of the city before the courts intervened by issuing stay orders. It was disappointing that the judiciary came in the way of an effort to curb the spread of illegal constructions.

In the short term, the action taken had a tremendous impact. Those who had indulged in flagrant violation of building regulations had received a jolt. Interestingly, while notices had been issued to about 200 errant builders, over 300 stay orders were received from the courts. The most positive impact was the awareness it created among builders and the public. Many of builders, particularly the bigger ones, started providing for parking space in basements henceforth.

Unfortunately, the problem of illegal constructions continues unabated and is only getting worse, with 80-90 per cent of buildings in the city considered illegal in some form or the other. The situation has become so intractable that the government has made its intention clear by announcing its policy of regularisation, thus encouraging building activity in violation of the law, while some optimistic activists continue their legal battle.

"Few actions of the City Corporation have endeared it to the citizens of Bangalore than Saturday's demolition of unauthorized cellar level structures on the St. Mark's Road.

When the Corporation wielded the crowbar on the structures put up by the lawless builders who have turned St. Mark's Road, which till recent years was an exclusive residential area into another 'Avenue Road' it was exercising punitive powers which it had long forgotten. For long, it was a story of the Corporation harassing the middle and lower middle class in the name of building bylaws and allowing the monied builder to go ahead with violations with impunity. It was the general opinion that the building bylaws existed to extract bribes from the prospective builders....

It is noteworthy that the Corporation has acted when it is under an Administrator and is without an elected Council adopting resolution after resolution to please the members and the Corporation engineers sanctioning building licenses after the usual queries....

The Corporation Administrator, Dr. A. Ravindra has said that the Corporation had issued notices to many owners and developers of high rise and commercial complexes who had misused the space especially used for parking. They had decided to take strict action against such violations."

From *The Hindu*, July 10, 1995, Front Page

There is hardly any city in India where developments have taken place strictly according to the master plan or zoning regulations. The responsibility for this must be shared by both the citizens and the authorities. In general, citizens show little respect for civic laws, which is reflected in numerous traffic violations, litter and garbage strewn across streets, encroachments, and violation of building regulations. The authorities, on their part, show little concern to scrutinise the applications for change of land use and communicate their decision in time, provoking more people to violate building regulations instead of waiting. What is curious is that they do not take legal action against violators of law, which has resulted in the mushrooming of illegal structures. This is, of course, deliberate as illegal buildings, trades and businesses constitute a big source of corruption. Regimes flexibly deploy law to tacitly allow, regulate and banish low-income group informal land uses (slums or street vending) while allowing or ex-post legalising the elite informal real estate projects that flout zoning laws or launder money (Varley, 2013).

Akrama-Sakrama: Legalising the Illegal

The Government of Karnataka conceived a novel scheme to deal with the insurmountable problem of the numerous illegal constructions and residential layouts (colonies) that had cropped up over the years in Bengaluru. It was extremely difficult to demolish them as it would render many poor people homeless and it would also be a waste of their housing investment. So, the remedy was to regularise these constructions. A law was passed in 1991 called the Regularisation of Unauthorised Constructions Act. This was challenged in the court. Later, another law, the Karnataka Town and Country Planning Act and Certain Other Laws (Amendment) Act was passed in 2004 for the same purpose.

The Act provided regularisation subject to certain conditions. On application by the property owners, violations to the extent of 50 per cent in case of residential and 25 per cent in case of commercial properties could be regularised after payment of the prescribed penalty. Violations pertained mainly to setbacks and floor area ratio that included exceeding the number of floors permitted. Rules were framed and time limits were set to complete the process. But the implementation was not easy as it meant appointment of competent officers to receive applications, scrutinising them, hearing the parties, and passing orders for regularisation or rejecting them if the conditions were not met. Even before this process could take off, the matter was caught up in litigation. PILs were filed and stay orders were issued, and the cases dragged on. Finally, the High Court of Karnataka upheld the validity of both the 2004 Amendment Act and the scheme to legalise the violations in January 2017. However, no action has been taken to initiate the process of regularisation till now, in spite of numerous announcements to this effect.

In the meantime, the matter has been subject to intense debate. Those opposed to regularisation contend that the scheme violates Article 14 (right to equality) and Article 21 (right to life) of the Constitution as it denies the right to a healthy and planned environment, which is an essential part of right to life. They also point to the judgment of the Supreme Court, which has held, on more than one occasion, that large-scale regularisation of illegal constructions would infringe upon the right to environment. The scheme further infringes on the right to equality under Article 14 as it favours those who violated the law while discriminating against those adhering to the law. On the other hand, those in favour of regularisation argue that there is no point in demolishing houses at this stage and it would cause severe hardship to the poor and middle classes in a city with very high land prices, especially when most of them have invested their life's savings to build a roof over their head.

The problem of illegal constructions is an endemic across large Indian cities. In Delhi, the Supreme Court took cognizance of the issue and constituted a monitoring committee in March 2006 to identify unauthorised structures and the causes of illegal building activities. The municipal corporations of Delhi were asked to seal illegal premises. As this was in progress, the Government of India set up a Special Task Force with powers to direct local bodies to provide necessary infrastructure and curb illegal constructions. This resulted in a tug-of-war between the court-appointed committee and the government created task force. The central government enacted the National Capital Territory of Delhi Laws (Special Provision) Amendment Act, 2006 with the intention "to protect certain forms of encroachments and unauthorized development from punitive action, viz., demolition, sealing, displacement etc." (NCTDLSPA Act, 2006). Those accused of unlawful construction were provided protection from penal action for a period of three years.

The core issue boils down to one of governance in the form of the failure of the state on two counts. Firstly, the state failed in enabling access to housing at the right time to the increasing population in an ever-growing city, and secondly, it allowed illegal constructions to mushroom without taking any action to prevent them or punishing the offenders. It is only some civil society organisations that have been fighting against illegal constructions and encroachments on public land, and it is only court intervention that propels action in some rare cases, the most recent example being the demolition of the 100-metre tall twin towers in Noida at the insistence of the local residents' association who had the patience to fight in the courts for nearly ten long years, with the Supreme Court finally ordering demolition in August 2021. Over a year earlier in January 2020, the apex court had similarly ordered demolition of four housing complexes in Maradu near Kochi for violation of Coastal Regulation Zone (CRZ). In 2019, the Bombay High Court authorised the Collector of Raigad district to pull down 24 bungalows illegally built along the Alibaug coast (Firstpost, 2018). In the same year, the Madras High Court ordered demolition of a sprawling bungalow built in Chennai at East Coast Road, for violating CRZ norms and building regulations.

On their part, those constructing the buildings without seeking prior permission and wantonly violating building regulations must share the responsibility for contributing to the chaotic state of affairs due to traffic congestion, parking problems, pollution and public inconvenience at large. It is clear that there is a collusion of interests at the cost of the city and its citizens. While a sympathetic view needs to be taken in the case of the poor, who struggle to get a piece of land and a roof on their head, the government, by extending protection to all offenders without discrimination, has become a party to encouragement of illegal constructions and the consequences thereof.

Urban Land Ceiling Law: A Failed Attempt at Urban Land Reform

The implementation of the Urban Land Ceiling Act, 1976 is a tale of good intentions gone awry and ending in total failure except enriching some politicians and bureaucrats. The Act aimed to achieve its objective of preventing concentration of land by first, imposing a ceiling on the quantum of vacant land a person can own in a city (ranging from 500 sq. m to 2,000 sq. m depending on the city size), and second, by placing restrictions on the transfer of urban property, which required obtaining prior permission from the competent authority. The implementation of the Act faced so many hurdles that its very purpose was defeated. Some of the provisions were self-defeating, the most glaring one being Section 20, pertaining to grant of exemption, under which a person could claim exemption from the acquisition of their surplus land on grounds of hardship. This enabled almost every person to seek exemption citing some reason for hardship, real or imaginary. For example, in Bengaluru between 1976 and 1987, about 77,548 acres were declared as surplus by landowners, the competent authority determined only 11,275 acres (about 15%) as surplus, and the area finally acquired was a mere 3,445 acres (less than a third determined by the authority). About 2,375 cases for exemption under the Act were filed in the same period, amounting to a total area of 6,521 acres. The surplus land acquired was eventually a tiny fraction of what would have been the actual surplus.

Land reform has been recognised as a key element in the governance of states in India since Independence. But this pertained to agricultural land in the rural areas where the pattern of land ownership played an important role in the life of the people and had an impact on the economy of the village and the state. Each state enacted land reform laws suited to its requirements with the objective of achieving equitable distribution of land. This primarily involved fixing a ceiling on the extent of land that can be owned by a person and ensuring a fair deal to the tenants. The degree of success varied from state to state.

There was no such law governing urban land. Though land is a state subject under the Constitution, the central government took the initiative to legislate on matters relating to ownership of urban land. This was during the period of Emergency (1975-77) and it was not difficult for the centre to get the consent of most of the states in order to legislate on a state subject. This is how the Urban Land (Ceiling and Regulation) Act, 1976 (ULC Act) was passed, which aimed at preventing the concentration of ownership, hoarding, and speculation of land and controlling the rising land prices in cities.

Implementing the Land Ceiling Act

I recall that dealing with matters relating to the ULC Act was an important part of the assignment when I was Secretary of Urban Development in Karnataka in the early 1980s. First, as it was a new law, we had to plan its implementation and it was not an easy task. Apart from the complex legal issues involved, it was not a popular measure as it would result not only in taking away immoveable property from the rich and the upper middle class, but also difficulties for ordinary people whose property transactions were held up for want of permission from the government. This also led to delays in inflow of revenue for the state government on account of delays in registration of documents under the Registration Acts of various States, as enacted by their legislatures in different years.

A large number of applications used to pour in every day seeking two kinds of permissions: one for exemption to hold or retain surplus land in the possession of a landowner under Section 20 of the Act; and two, for transfer of land or property by way of sale, mortgage or other means under Sections 26 and 27 of the Act. The scrutiny of applications in order to establish their genuineness and to determine whether exemption or permission for sale/mortgage is to be granted involved a huge amount of work and we had to create a separate organisation for the purpose. We then set up a separate office of Special Deputy Commissioner (Urban Land Ceiling) with supporting staff to attend exclusively to this work. This was of course the easier part in the effort to implement the law; the real problems surfaced in the actual operational part.

I was faced with the challenging task of dealing with applications for grant of exemption. The law provided for exemption on two grounds, namely, hardship and public interest. How does one determine hardship? The reasons cited included repayment of loans, celebrating daughter's marriage, medical expenses, and so on. Determining public interest in individual cases was a vague exercise. In short, the judgement was more subjective than based on objective criteria and this proved to be a god-sent opportunity to all those interested in making a fast buck. The power to grant exemption in particular came as a boon to the political bosses. In almost all cases where I would recommend rejection, the file would come back with the orders of the minister: 'Exemption granted'. Several officials involved in processing cases at the field level also benefited.

Things reached a stage where the government realised that it was not possible to achieve the socialist goals it had set for itself and took an unprecedented step of scrapping the Act. In 1999, the Parliament annulled the legislation and authorised the states to decide on similar lines. The states took their own time to repeal the Act (such as Tamil Nadu in 1999 itself and Maharashtra in 2007). The main reason for the failure of what would have been a revolutionary urban land reform measure was the practical difficulty in implementing the law. The ceiling limits were arbitrarily fixed, determination of surplus land was not easy, small landowners were genuinely affected, and seeking permission every time land was transferred amounted to nothing less than harassment. Moreover, the law placed too much reliance on the integrity of the government functionaries and citizens and vested too much discretionary power in the enforcing authorities, which was misused. It turned out be a lesson in how not to make a law.

The Public Procurement Process

Public procurement refers to the procurement or purchase of goods and services by the government for the execution of public projects or meeting the needs of the government. The procurement process is governed by rules and guidelines framed by the government. While there is no central law in India that governs the process, there is a Manual for Procurement of Goods, 2017 that contains guidelines for purchase of goods. States have their own rules and regulations. Karnataka, for instance, has a Karnataka Transparency in Public Procurement (KTPP) Act of 2000.

In view of the large volume and magnitude of public projects in India, the opportunities for companies or contractors who supply goods and services, including those who undertake construction works, have increased. Central projects like JNNURM, Atal Mission for Rejuvenation and Urban Transformation (AMRUT), Pradhan Mantri Awas Yojana (PMAY), Smart Cities Mission (SCM) and numerous programmes of state and local governments have opened up a huge market for the private sector. A sound procurement process is therefore crucial in ensuring delivery of efficient and quality public services. Normally, purchase of goods and services is done through a competitive bidding or tendering process. However, in cases of urgency or where the value of goods procured is very small, the procedure is waived or simplified by directly obtaining quotations from reputed suppliers.

The operation of the procurement system also constitutes a source of corruption where both parties, the giver and the taker, can collude, resulting in illegal gain and delivery of poor quality services, whether they are basic services like water supply, sanitation or housing for the poor, or building roads, flyovers, bridges or buildings for the benefit of the public at large. Where they meet the prescribed standards, excess costs are built into the tenders, thus causing losses to the public exchequer. The politician-bureaucrat-contractor/agent nexus operates quite efficiently and secretively till matters reach excessive levels at times.

A glaring case of 'excess' came to light recently in January 2022 when the Karnataka Contractors Association came out openly alleging that the authorities concerned (at city and state levels) were demanding 40 per cent premium (kickbacks) for approval of tenders. The wide publicity it received led to an uproar from the public and the opposition parties. The contractors threatened to stop all work until their problem was solved and complained to the Prime Minister. After several months, the matter rests in status quo.

There is another side to the contractors' story. One of their major complaints was that their bills remain unpaid for a long time even after completion of their work. A conversation by the author with the Commissioner of BBMP revealed that this was true and payments amounting to over Rs. 2,000 crores were pending for the last two years. He explained it by saying that there was a serious shortage of funds and it was not possible to pay the bills in time. But then, the question is how did such a situation arise? Every year, works are sanctioned in excess of the provision made in the budget on account of 'political pressure' and contractors are forced to execute them, resulting in half-completed or poor quality of works. Payment or 'clearance' of bills, as it is called, gets delayed and constitutes another source of corruption.

An Attempt to break a Nexus

In 1995, when I was serving as the Administrator of Bangalore City Corporation, a major problem that confronted me was the poor quality of roads in the city. Potholes were a common sight then, as they are now. After a quick survey of the city roads, I concluded that the fundamental problem was the absence of standard norms and procedures in the planning and execution of roads. With the assistance of a few technical consultants (working pro bono), tender documents were prepared incorporating the standards prescribed by the Indian Roads Congress and fresh bids were called for a set of roads.

To my utter surprise, and what I thought was strange at that time, there was not even a single response to the call for tenders. The local contractors found that conforming to the standards prescribed was beyond their capacity, and more importantly, they would not derive the expected profits. So, they all ganged up and decided to scuttle the new process that was designed to be transparent and made manipulation difficult.

A couple of years later, when I was back as Commissioner of the corporation (for the second time), wiser from the earlier experience, I adopted a different strategy to tackle the problem of ensuring quality roads in the city. Since good quality required huge investments, and the municipal body was short of funds, I decided to launch a Municipal Bonds Scheme with the objective of raising Rs. 100 crores for the purpose of improving road infrastructure. First, we engaged experts to carry out a scientific survey of the road conditions, and then prepared the bid documents.

We then had to go through an elaborate process of rating of the municipal corporation for its creditworthiness and obtain the creditworthiness certificate from a credit rating agency. Next, we had to obtain the approval of the corporation council and finally the state government. The procedures were completed, and we floated municipal bonds to raise an amount of Rs. 100 crores in October 1997. To our great satisfaction, the issue was oversubscribed and we succeeded in mobilising Rs. 125 crores (Reserve Bank of India, 2022). The time had come for Bangalore to see some good quality roads.

Then came the bigger challenge—getting approval from the municipal council. The same body which had willingly given its consent to launch the bonds, now dithered. Once they sensed that the contractors who were qualified to execute the work would not show favours or compromise on quality, they withheld their approval. The mayor called me for discussions and suggested that the works be re-tendered, as no bids were received from the 'right' people, namely, the local contractors. I responded politely that it would be difficult to do so, as we were bound by the commitments made under the bonds scheme, and there could be no compromise on the quality of works. The discussions prolonged for a few days but there was no meeting ground. I was faced with a choice, either compromise and dilute the procurement process or be prepared for a 'transfer', the weapon politicians generally wield to get rid of 'inconvenient' officers. I decided in favour of the latter, which did not take long to come.

While transfers are common in the civil service, I was left with a feeling of disappointment that I failed to convince the political decision-makers about a matter that was entirely in public interest.

New Privileges

Cities have become the nerve centres of all creative activity, but they are also creating deep divides within society with new forms of elitism and privilege influencing political decision-making. English education, an urban privilege, has been a huge differentiator not only between the rural and the urban, but between different classes of people in urban areas. Ram Manohar Lohia, a leading socialist politician of the twentieth century, famously said that India is divided not just on class and caste lines but the English speaking were also divided from the vernacular Indian. He identified three characteristics that distinguish India's ruling classes: 'high caste, English education, and wealth'. This holds good even today except that politics has opened the avenue for other castes to also join the ruling class. But all of them, including those representing rural areas, live in cities enjoying the privileges of the elite class. During the pandemic, most poor children were deprived of education as over 70 per cent of the government schools were closed and many could not be part of the online classes on account of lack of a smart phone or a tablet. In contrast, only less than 20 per cent of the private schools were shut during the same period.

Living comfortably in cities, more so in large metropolises, has its own set of demands. A lot depends on affordability and to what extent it can match one's aspirations, whether it is the type of house or locality one chooses to live in, or the school or college the children attend, or the means of transport one uses to travel and so on. The members of the ruling class and businessmen, through a mutually beneficial relationship, establish easy access to the best of things. People in power grant approvals to real estate developers for their projects and the latter oblige by providing luxury apartments and villas. Similar deals take place for other kinds of benefits: admission to high-end schools and colleges, shares in companies, and cuts in contracts for construction of infrastructure projects. At the core of such relationships lies the ability of the business classes to finance political activities, primarily for elections. Writing about the power elite in the US in the 1950s, the American sociologist, Wright Mills (1956) observed that 'mutual dependency' confers on business class the 'institutional powers of wealth'. "With the corporate world becoming more intricately involved in the political order, corporate leaders have become intimately associated with politicians and especially with key politicians who form the political directorate of the United States government" (p. 167).

The situation in India at present is not very different. Prior to economic liberalisation, the mutual dependency syndrome existed in one form; post-1991, it might have assumed other forms. Market economy might have done away with the 'license-permit raj' but it has been replaced by the 'regulation raj'. While it is necessary to regulate market behaviour, the regulation policies and the way they are operated ensure the continuation of state dominance in some way or the other. Different types of lobbies have exercised their power and influence at different points of time. For instance, in Karnataka, the liquor lobby was a dominant player during the decades of the 1960s to the 1980s, the education lobby (mainly engineering and medical) was highly influential during the 1970s to the 1990s, the real estate lobby assumed significant power from the 1980s and continues till now, and the Information Technology (IT) lobby from the 1990s. They are exercising increasing power, alongside accumulating immense wealth. The trends could vary from state to state, depending on which type of business thrives in a particular region, like the mining industry in Odisha, oil industry in the north-east, and the IT industry in Karnataka. Associations like Federation of Indian Chambers of Commerce and Industry (FICCI), Confederation of Indian Industry (CII), and the Associated Chambers of Commerce and Industry of India (ASSOCHAM), which represent industry and business, have come to wield considerable influence in determining the economic policies of the government.

The twenty-first century has seen the rise of the nouveau riche Indians figuring in the billionaires list. In May 2021, we had 140 of them, with India ranking third in the world, behind the US and China. Their wealth is splashed across the prominent metropolises of the world—London, New York, Delhi, and Mumbai. In terms of the urban economy, the crucial question that arises is not about the creation of wealth, which is essential for a nation's prosperity, but about how it is distributed. One view is that it is necessary to create a large number of billionaires who can contribute to production and employment generation and this might also lead to reduction of disparities.

The link between politics and business has assumed a new dimension, with the entry of businessmen into politics. Business magnates like KK Birla and Navin Jindal from the north and Murasoli Maran and Vijay Mallya from the south gained entry into the Rajya Sabha. Some others managed to win Lok Sabha seats. The royal family of Scindias have been full-time politicians. In the states too, those with money power are nominated to the Legislative Council and some others get elected to the Legislative Assembly, for example the Reddy brothers in Karnataka. As a corollary, individuals already well entrenched in politics venture into businesses, particularly into real estate, health services and education.

Chapter

8

Decade of the 1990s

The Reform Era

By an interesting coincidence, the decade of the 1990s was marked by three major reforms that had a significant impact on the economy, society, politics and urban governance in India. First, the economic liberalisation policies implemented by the Government of India, coinciding with the phenomenon of globalisation across the world; second, the 73rd and 74th Amendments to the Indian Constitution, heralding decentralisation of governance in the rural and urban areas of the country; and third, the growth of Information Technology (IT) impacting all spheres of human activity.

Economic Reforms of 1991

1991 proved to be a crucial year in the history of the economic development of modern India. First, India was faced with an unprecedented balance of payments crisis and it had to take the extraordinary decision to pledge the country's gold with the Bank of England. The crisis was also an opportunity to make radical changes in the economic policies that it had pursued hitherto as they had stifled economic growth. P.V. Narasimha Rao, who had just taken over as Prime Minister, realized that it was time to abandon the path of command and control and liberalise the economy. Structural reforms, which did away with industrial licensing and introduced trade liberalisation, opened up the doors to robust economic growth. In his first address to the nation after assuming office as Prime Minister in June 1991, Narasimha Rao spelt out the outlines of a reforms package:

> This government is committed to removing the cobwebs that come in the way of rapid industrialisation. We will work towards making India internationally competitive, taking full advantage of... opportunities offered by the evolving global economy. We also welcome foreign direct investment on a sizeable scale so as to accelerate the tempo of development... Obstacles that come in the way will be removed... A time-bound programme will be worked out to streamline our industrial policies and programmes to achieve the goal of a vibrant economy that rewards creativity, enterprise and innovativeness... Our vision is to create employment, eradicate poverty and reduce inequality.
>
> (Rao, 1991)

The reforms that provided the necessary thrust to industrialisation also accelerated urbanisation, attracting more investments into cities. It is axiomatic that industrialisation and urbanisation follow each other, and that's what started happening in India since the 1990s. I had the opportunity of working in the industrial sector in the early 1990s and as the Chairman and Managing Director of Karnataka State Industrial Investment & Development Corporation, I was directly involved in promoting investments. I could see a surge in the demand for financial assistance from entrepreneurs to set up new industries in Karnataka, particularly in Bangalore.

It was also the time the winds of globalisation were blowing across countries, promoting international travel, which essentially meant movement from cities in one country to cities in another. This necessitated creation of better urban infrastructure and generated a competition between cities to provide necessary facilities to attract more investments. I recall the efforts of Chandrababu Naidu, then CM of Andhra Pradesh, to make Hyderabad better than Bangalore in the late 1990s and it set off a healthy competition between him and Karnataka's CM S.M. Krishna. While Naidu succeeded in improving the infrastructure of Hyderabad, Bangalore continued to maintain its lead in the IT sector. Other cities like Gurgaon and Pune also started attracting investments. The acceleration of industrial development, as a result of a liberal economic policy, exerted a huge pressure on the state and local governments for reforms in urban governance.

Decentralisation: Local Democracy

Following the economic reforms of 1991 came the political reforms at the local level through the 73rd Amendment to empower the Panchayati Raj local bodies in 1993 and the 74th Amendment to empower Urban Local Bodies (ULBs) in 1994. Four decades after the constitution came into force, the parliament decided to decentralise the powers hitherto enjoyed by the states to the local bodies. However, as the subject of local bodies came under the State List, the amending law left it to the state governments to devolve powers to these units. While most of the states were quick to decentralise powers to the Panchayati Raj institutions, they showed no keenness to do so in respect of ULBs. Hence, the pace of urban decentralisation was rather slow.

Before looking at the features of the 74th Amendment, it would be useful to understand the municipal governance systems prevalent in the 1990s. Broadly, the following models of municipal institutions were prevalent in the country:

- An elected municipal local body (the council) comprising directly elected councillors from wards—municipal constituencies into which each town or city is territorially divided.
- A mayor and deputy mayor elected directly by the people or indirectly by the elected councillors.
- Standing committees comprising a specified number of councillors to deal with matters pertaining to finance and taxation, public works, public health, waste management and so on.
- A commissioner is appointed by the state government and acts as the head of the administration holding most of the executive powers of the municipal organisation.

The actual powers vested in different authorities may vary from state to state.

Broadly speaking, the legislative and policymaking powers are vested in the elected council and the executive powers are vested in the commissioner. The mayor has limited powers and, in most cases, is a ceremonial head (except in Kolkata where they enjoy substantial powers). The standing committees are entrusted with specific functions and powers, especially those relating to approval of projects subject to certain financial limits. Thus, there is a distribution of powers within the municipal body with checks and balances.

According to the 74th Amendment, there will be three categories of municipalities in every state: (a) a Nagar (Town) Panchayat for a transitional area (i.e., an area in transition from rural to urban); (b) a Municipal Council for a small urban area; and (c) a Municipal Corporation for a large urban area.

The classification of municipalities has to be done on the basis of certain criteria, such as population, density, revenue generated for local administration, the percentage of employment in non-agricultural activities and the economic importance of the area. A municipal area will be divided into territorial constituencies called 'wards' and the seats in a municipality will be filled by direction from these wards. The number of wards in a municipal area is determined by each state government in accordance with the principles of delimitation. It would be useful to understand the process of delimitation to appreciate the local election process.

Delimitation is governed by the Delimitation Act, 2002, a central law to fix the boundaries of the legislative assembly and Lok Sabha constituencies. This work is carried out by a Delimitation Commission set up by the Government of India and the demarcation of boundaries is based on Census data. The last delimitation was done in 2002; according to the criteria laid down under the Act, the constituencies must be geographically compact and delimited keeping in view physical features, boundaries of administrative units, communication facilities and public convenience. Importantly, every assembly constituency must fall wholly within a single parliamentary constituency.

The body of elected councillors from these wards constitutes the municipal council. Reservations are provided to Scheduled Castes (SCs) and Scheduled Tribes (STs); a state may also provide reservation to Other Backward Classes (OBCs). To ensure that elections to municipalities are conducted in a free and fair manner, the constitution has provided for the creation of an independent State Election Commission. Elections are to be held once in five years, coinciding with the term of the councillors.

The constitution has not prescribed any organisational structure for ULBs, but has listed the functions to be performed by them in the 12th Schedule. It has also provided a planning framework for cities. Metropolitan cities shall have a Metropolitan Planning Committee (MPC) which will be responsible for preparing a metropolitan development plan. While not prescribing any numbers, the character of membership has been defined. Two-thirds of the members shall be from amongst the elected members of the municipalities and chairpersons of the panchayats in the metropolitan area, and one-third may include representatives of government and other such organisations who are useful for ULBs to discharge their functions. At the district level, there will be a District Planning Committee (DPC) headed by the chairperson of the Zilla Panchayat, of which at least four-fifths of the members shall be elected members of panchayats and the municipalities in the district. The DPC has the responsibility of preparing a draft Development Plan for the district, which shall include rural and urban areas.

Each state had to pass a separate law or amend the existing municipal law to give effect to the provisions of the constitutional amendment. That they were in no hurry to do so is a telling commentary on the commitment of the state legislators and the government to local democracy. Little progress was achieved during the six years of the 1990s in implementing the constitutional mandate.

The Committee on Urban Management of Bangalore, 1997

Let me refer to the interest shown by the Karnataka government to bring about reforms in the governance of Bangalore when they set up an expert committee for the Urban Management of Bangalore in 1997 under my chairmanship. I also happened to be the Commissioner of the Bangalore Municipal Corporation at the time. Due to the city's unprecedented growth and urban degeneration, the committee's mandate was to suggest restructuring of the urban local government by recommending alternative models.

Along with discussions with various stakeholders, the committee visited Mumbai, Calcutta, Ahmedabad and Surat to understand their municipal corporations. They observed that Maharashtra and Gujarat have somewhat similar systems of municipal administration (both having been part of what was earlier the Bombay Presidency). Bombay is the richest municipal corporation in India and its finances were sound, but its large slum population, acute land and housing problems, and continuous flow of migrants to the city in search of jobs presented unique problems. Calcutta presented a different kind of scenario. With a mayor-in-council system, municipal governance was more democratic in character. The administration functioned at a slower pace compared to the other cities, but culturally, the city was more vibrant.

We were impressed by the performance of Surat's municipal corporation following the plague, which had reduced the city to near collapse. It was a virtual turn-around under the able leadership of the municipal commissioner, SR Rao, with municipal staff showing unusual zeal and commitment. Sanitation received high priority, encroachments occupying half the streets were removed, and the city was cleaned up. It was an example of how a city can be transformed by meticulously following the administrative rules of efficiency and motivating the staff (as told by Mr Rao). Support of the people and politicians played an important role in the successful execution of the programs. Ahmedabad city also showed a great deal of improvement by developing its infrastructure. On the whole, the cities of Gujarat showed better performance than the other two cities we visited.

The committee made far-reaching recommendations which were very well received by the public, but sadly not taken seriously by the government. From an overall perspective, it observed that the urban management of Bangalore should be based on the principles of decentralisation, rationalisation of functions between the state government and the ULB, unified administrative organisation, allocation of adequate resources, and capacity building for the efficient discharge of functions at various levels. The major recommendations included certain fundamental reforms in the structure and functioning of the BCC (now Bruhat Bengaluru Mahanagar Palike or BBMP) and some parastatal organisations.

In respect of the BCC, the suggestions were: (a) increasing the term of the mayor to two-and-a half years from the existing one year; (b) having only one standing committee in place of the existing four; (c) replacing first-past-the-post system of election of municipal councillors by proportional representation, which will be a more realistic reflection of the opinion of the electorate; (d) bringing all civic amenities like water supply and sewerage, slum improvement, environmental protection and so forth under the purview of the BCC; and (e) creating the post of Chief Commissioner in BCC who will take responsibility for planning and project management for the city as a whole, relieving them of day-to-day routine functions.

As part of administrative restructuring, a radical suggestion was made to wind up the BDA as it had not served much purpose in its existing form. Instead, a Bangalore Land and Housing Development Corporation was proposed to be set up as a joint sector body for land development and housing, which would operate on commercial lines. Its mandate would be to provide low-cost housing through cross-subsidisation or government grant-in-aid.

The Advent of Information Technology

The twentieth century was witness to major technology breakthroughs, which had a tremendous impact on the growth of industry and enabled use of new management tools, contributing to greater efficiencies in the functioning of institutions. This was true of the management of cities as well. The use of computers, internet and modern technology such as Geographic Information System (GIS) in urban planning and management facilitated more effective delivery of services.

The most striking feature of this period was the revolutionary change unleashed by the power of modern information and communication technology. The evolution of digital computers following the Second World War generated an entire subculture of research and development, applications, users and consumers of processed data, leading to the creation of intellectual fields dealing with information and its impact on organisations (Ellis *et al.*, 1999, as cited in Heitzman, 2004). By the end of the century, the Information

Age came into being, evolving through a three-stage process: from a data-processing era (1960-1980) through a micro-era (1980-1995) to a 'network era' (Nolan, 2000, as cited in Heitzman, 2004).

In India, initial steps towards building an information infrastructure were taken with the establishment of the National Informatics Centre in 1977 for the purpose of providing online access to information for the Planning Commission. Subsequently, it expanded its scope to computerisation of government offices, construction of databases and provision of electronic information. In 1987, it set up the Network Informatics Center Network (NICNET) that would include mini computers or local area networks at state capitals and microcomputers at district offices. In 1986, the Department of Electronics initiated the Education and Research Network (ERNET) with assistance from the United Nations Development Programme with the aim of networking research organisations and universities. The New Telecom Policy of 1994 created opportunities for corporate broadband communication and the National Telecom Policy of 1999 enabled private operators to access international gateways. All these measures helped to strengthen the human and technological capabilities for generating innovations and facilitating India's entry into the digital era of the twenty-first century.

SUMMING UP

Urban policy and planning in India has been characterized by a lack of clarity of vision and strategies to deal with the complex problems of growing urbanisation. The measures adopted by the government since Independence have not yielded the desired outcomes in governing urban India. Initially, in the post-independence period, urban development did not receive adequate attention in the macro-economic planning process and the five year plans. Even after it started gaining importance, the recommendations of a number of commissions and committees on urban planning and reforms were ignored. The 74th Amendment on decentralisation of powers to ULBs was an initiative of the central government, and its implementation has suffered due to the reluctance of states to empower ULBs. Further, the ULBs lack the capacity to meet the challenges of rapid urban growth in terms of financial resources, technical expertise and qualified personnel.

Over the years, the state has withdrawn somewhat from direct provision of services in urban areas, and has tended towards more project-based or financialized solutions as an 'enabler'. These approaches have led to new industrial towns and other attempts at controlling and managing forms of urbanisation. This approach too, cannot be said to have yielded better results. As of 2021, only 28 per cent of cities have an approved master plan, reflecting the fact that the state has limited inclination or capacity to govern rapidly growing urban centres.

The enormity of the task of development is not to be ignored. Urban development is multi-sectoral, and the various agencies involved in it, such as water supply, electricity, public transport and so on, often work in silos, resulting in a lack of coordination among them. Urban infrastructure and services also suffer from several deficiencies, such as land and housing, mobility and so forth. This has further implications for larger problems like poverty and climate change. Although poverty has been declining, inequality has been increasing, creating an urban-urban divide, between the rich and the urban 'middle' class on one side and the poor on the other. Poor air quality, loss of water bodies and farmlands in the urban periphery, excessive exploitation of groundwater, encroachments and illegal constructions have all contributed to environmental degradation.

Political economy has impacted life in cities more negatively than positively in meeting the challenges of urbanisation. The structure of urban governance continues to reflect a colonial character and there is a lack of political will to come to grips with the real issues and find realistic solutions. Most reforms and initiatives have been piecemeal and reactionary. Some far-reaching changes have been initiated since the economic reforms of the 1990s, which led to the liberalisation of the economy, constitutional changes to empower the local governments and thrust to modern technology. How have they impacted city growth and the issues relating to the new challenges of the twenty-first century are discussed in the next part.

Part III
The Urban Revolution and Its Discontents

Chapter
9

The 21st Century Urban Revolution

"Without cities we would all be poor".

(Jane Jacobs, 1969)

There is a low rate of urbanisation and per capita income in the regions of the Global South compared to those of the Global North. This has been articulated by the United Nations: "Cities make countries rich. Countries that are highly urbanised have higher incomes, more stable economies, stronger institutions, and are better able to withstand the volatility of the global economy than those with less urbanised populations" (UN-Habitat, 2006, p. 48). As more and more people migrate towards towns and cities, an urban revolution is taking shape. This brings with it new hopes and challenges.

The first two decades of the twenty-first century mark a significant shift in the demographic history of the world. In the year 2008, the global urban population crossed the threshold of 50 per cent, clocking 3.5 billion out of a total of 7 billion. By 2022 November, the world's population had grown to 8 billion, with 57 per cent (4.5 billion) living in urban areas. While the industrialised countries of the west and Latin America have achieved a high rate of urbanisation over 70-80 per cent, the developing countries of Asia and Africa have lagged at less than 50 per cent, some even lower than 30 per cent (see Figure 5.1 in part 2) (United Nations, Department of Economic and Social Affairs, Population Division, 2018). (World Urbanisation Prospects: The 2018 Revision, Online Edition). India belonged to the latter category with only 29 per cent of its population living in urban areas in 2001.

From the year 2001-2009, for the first time since independence, the absolute population added to urban areas exceeded that of rural areas—an increase of 96 million in urban areas as compared to 90.4 million in rural areas, from the previous census. Urbanisation crossed the 30 per cent mark in 2011, accounting for 31.1 per cent or 377 million people out of a total of 1.21. The decade of 2011-21 witnessed a further spurt in urban population which reached nearly 470 million or 35.4 per cent of the total estimated population of 1.4 billion (National Commission on Population, MoHFW, 2021).

While the share of the urban population continues to be low in India, there are clear signs of rapid urbanisation in a country which was predominantly rural. States in the southern and western parts of the country have exhibited an impressive urban growth—Goa, Kerala, Tamil Nadu and Maharashtra showing a decadal urbanisation rate of over 45 per cent. On the other hand, the northern and eastern states have fared poorly, with Bihar at an abysmally low 12 per cent and Assam at 14 per cent (National Commission on Population, Ministry of Health and Family Welfare, 2020).

According to the most recent district-wise analysis based on 2011 data (Mathur *et al.*, 2021), out of 640 districts in the country, 81 had over 50 per cent of their populations living in urban areas while the level of urbanisation in 268 districts (41% of the total districts accounting for 11% of the country's urban population) had not reached even the 1951 All-India level of urbanisation of 17.3 per cent. In 2011, only 181 districts had an urbanisation level in excess of the country-wide average of 31.3 per cent. "Not only are these districts under-urbanised, these are under-serviced as well in terms of access to water supply, electricity and toilets and present a formidable challenge to the process of urbanisation and economic growth" (p. 45).

Transition to New Forms of Urbanisation

We need to understand the process of urbanisation across states to gain an appreciation of the regional variations and how it impacts the process of socio-economic development of the country as a whole. The largest concentration of urban population is to be found in Maharashtra (51 million in 2011), while the lowest is in Himachal Pradesh (6.8 lakhs in 2011—excluding very small states like Arunachal

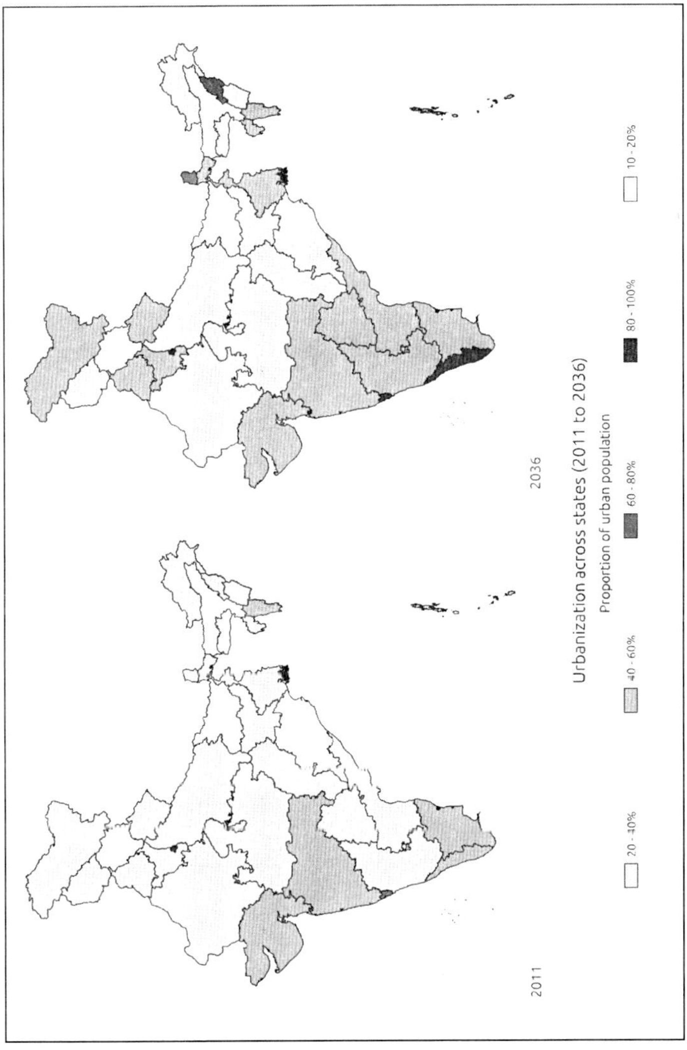

Fig. 9.1: Urbanisation across states, 2011 to 2036 (projected).

Source: MoHFW, 2021.

Pradesh and Meghalaya). In terms of share of urban to rural, Tamil Nadu tops with 48.4 per cent urban, excluding smaller states like Goa (62.17 %) and Mizoram (52.11%). District-wise urbanisation reveals that 81 districts have over 50 per cent urbanisation, while 268 have less than 17 per cent, which was the national level of urbanisation in 1951 (Mathur *et al.*, 2021; National Commission on Population, Ministry of Health and Family Welfare, 2020).

The patterns of urbanisation across states reveal some interesting features. States like Karnataka, Telangana and West Bengal are dominated by a primate city, while urbanisation in states such as Uttar Pradesh, Madhya Pradesh, Rajasthan and Gujarat is more evenly distributed. In Maharashtra, although Mumbai dominates the city status, there are four other heavily metropolitanised cities including Pune. Similarly, in Tamil Nadu, apart from Chennai, the premier city, there are six other million plus cities in the state. Kerala presents a unique picture of urban-rural continuum where one can hardly notice where a town ends and the village begins. Its largest city, Thiruvananthapuram, had not yet attained million+ status in 2011 and only two other cities, Kozhikode and Ernakulam had a population of above five lakhs.

Vaddiraju (2021) in his work on "Urban Governance and Local Democracy in South India" has made a comparative study of urban governance in the four southern states of Andhra Pradesh (united), Karnataka, Kerala, and Tamil Nadu. He argued that there has been urban concentration and a 'top heavy' process of urbanisation in the first two states while in the latter two, the pattern of urbanisation has been highly dispersed and not centred around the capital city. Urbanisation has been taking place mainly around Bengaluru in Karnataka and Hyderabad in Andhra Pradesh. It may be added that after Andhra Pradesh was divided into two states—Andhra Pradesh and Telangana, the pattern shows clear distinction between the two states. Andhra Pradesh does not have a primate city like Hyderabad. On the other hand, in Andhra Pradesh, the largest city of Vishakapatnam is the only million plus city with a population of 1.35 million (in 2011), followed by Vijayawada with a population of 0.9 million and Guntur of 0.5 million.

The New Capital of Andhra Pradesh—Amaravati

After the formation of the new state of Andhra Pradesh in 2014, the selection of its capital city presents an interesting story. Chandrababu Naidu, the Chief Minister of the state at that time, wanted to build a new capital and chose a site between Vijayawada and Guntur, a historical place called Amaravati. A controversial land acquisition process was initiated to acquire a vast area of 33,000 acres. Critics pointed out that the acquisition included fertile agricultural lands and would affect the livelihoods of a large number of farmers, apart from causing losses in agricultural production.

A number of committees were constituted to examine the proposal and suggest a suitable place for the location of the new capital. Prominent among them were the three committees headed by B.N. Srikrishna, K.C. Sivaramakrishnan, and G.N. Rao. Nevertheless, the Chief Minister, without taking into consideration their recommendations, went ahead with his plan for land acquisition of 33,000 acres.

In the 2019 assembly elections in Andhra Pradesh, the Telugu Desam Party (TDP) under C.B. Naidu lost and the Yuva Jan Shramika Rythu (YSR) Congress Party under the leadership of Y.S. Jaganmohan Reddy came to power. Call it a twist of fate, the new CM scrapped the Amaravati project and came up with an entirely new idea of having three capitals for the new state of Andhra Pradesh on the ground that building one mega-capital would lead to neglect of other regions of the state. With decentralisation as the theme, he proposed three new capitals—one at Amaravathi and the other two at Visakhapatnam and Kurnool. The first would be the legislative capital, the second, the executive capital and the third, the judicial capital. Accordingly, a new legislation, the Andhra Pradesh Decentralisation and Inclusive Development of All Regions Act, 2020 was enacted. This was challenged in the High Court of Andhra Pradesh, with more than a 100 writ petitions having been filed. However, in a sudden move, the Andhra Pradesh government withdrew the Act in 2021, perhaps sensing the strong opposition to the proposal. In a further twist to the story, in March 2022, the Andhra Pradesh High Court directed the state government to develop Amravati as the capital city of the state, as per the original plan, and the Chief Minister has responded in January 2023 by declaring that the city of Visakhapatnam will be made the capital of the state.

Primate cities

The growth of primate cities is another important feature of urbanisation in India as in other developing countries. As a generalisation at world level, high urban primacy is associated with countries with a small area, dense population, low per capita income, export-oriented and agricultural economies and a colonial history and rapid rates of population growth (Linsey, 1965). In India, Kolkata in West Bengal, Hyderabad in Telangana, and Bengaluru in Karnataka are prominent examples. The population of these cities is several times larger than those of the second largest cities in those states—Kolkata's is nearly 12 times than that of the second largest city in West Bengal, Asansol; Hyderabad's population is almost 16 times that of Warangal and Bengaluru's population is nearly 9 times than Hubli-Dharwad.

The concept of primate cities was first propounded by the geographer, Mark Johnson in 1939. He described it as being "at least twice as large as the next largest city and more than twice as significant" (Johnson, 1939). The significance could extend to the economic, financial, social and political aspects.

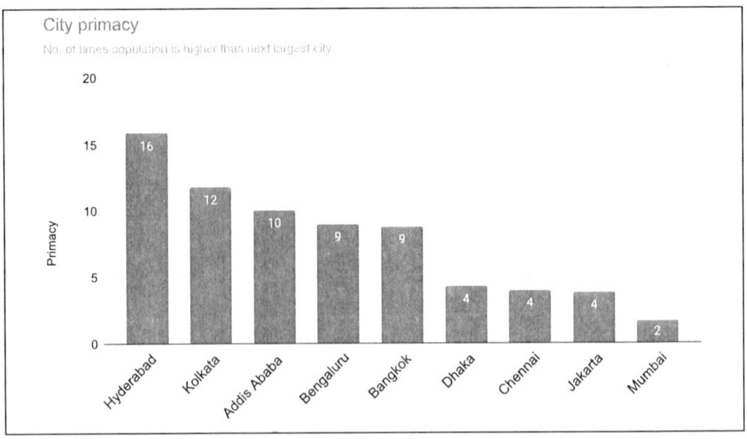

Fig. 9.2: City primacy of select cities in India and other developing nations.
Source: Swastik Harish, compiled from various sources on population data.

This phenomenon is true of several other Asian countries like Thailand where Bangkok with a population of 10.5 million dominates the urban scene, the next city, Chiang Mai housing 1.2 million people. In Indonesia, Jakarta (10.6 million) is nearly 4 times larger than Surabaya (2.8 million), and Dhaka in Bangladesh (22.5 million) is 4.25 times bigger than Chittagong (5.3 million). Such primacy of cities is partly the result of colonial legacy and partly the way urban policies of the country have operated. Some countries have smaller capitals compared to the economically and social thriving larger cities like in US-Washington the capital being much smaller than New York or Los Angeles, in Turkey, the capital Ankara and huge Istanbul, and in Australia, the tiny capital of Canberra and the metros of Melbourne and Sydney.

Primate city is an indicator of imbalance in the urban development of a country or a state in large countries such as Brazil, China and India. They enjoy unrivalled supremacy in the economic, social and cultural spheres and the politics of the country too wherever they happen to be the capitals, but they depend on the peripheral agglomerations and other regions for their labour force and other resources. They are usually marked by a large migrant population and cosmopolitan character.

Megacities and Regions

The urban phenomenon in India has for long been dominated by the large cities of Delhi, Mumbai, Kolkata, Chennai, Bengaluru, and Hyderabad which have now graduated from the metropolitan to the status of megacities with a population exceeding ten million. The continuous expansion of large metropolitan cities and adjoining agglomerations beyond their boundaries has led to the concept of Metropolitan or City Regions. Many urban agglomerations in Asia are evolving into mega urban regions and urban corridors. They are large urban areas the size of fully-fledged regions and are often referred to as Extended Metropolitan Regions (EMR) (UN-Habitat, 2010). The unbridled growth of Delhi gave rise to the formation of the National Capital Region (NCR) bringing under its umbrella the adjoining areas of the three states of Haryana, Rajasthan, Uttar Pradesh and the Union Territory of Delhi. The NCR is spread over a vast area of

55,083 square kilometres with a population of over 46 million (2011). Set up in 1985, its mandate includes planning the development of the region and "to evolve harmonized policies for the control of land-uses and development of infrastructure in the region" (Ministry of Housing & Urban Affairs, 2019). The other megacities of Bengaluru, Chennai, Hyderabad, Kolkata, and Mumbai have set up Metropolitan Region Development Authorities to serve the capital cities and the surrounding agglomerations with somewhat similar objectives.

Metros and Non-Metropolitan Cities and Towns

The economic growth and rapid strides taken by the service sector in the twenty-first century have spurred the growth of the second order metro cities with a population of one million to less than ten million. The metro cities can again be classified into two categories: one to five million and five to ten million. Cities like Ahmedabad with a population of 5.5 million in 2011 (estimated at 8.1 m in 2020), and Pune with an estimated population of 6.6 million in 2020 which have developed as important centres of industry, business and education can be included in the latter (United Nations: World Urbanisation Prospects, 2018 revision).

It is heartening to note that some of the smaller cities and towns in India are also exhibiting rapid growth. A survey conducted by the Economist Intelligence Unit (EIU) in January 2022 revealed that six small cities in India have found a place in the list of the world's fastest growing urban areas, of which four are in Kerala—Malappuram, Kozhikode (Calicut), Kollam and Thrissur, one in Gujarat—Surat and the other, Tiruppur in Tamil Nadu (India Today, November 21, 2022). According to Hurun India Report which compiles an annual India Rich List, more than a thousand people in India had a net worth of Rs 1,000 crores plus in 2022, of which one hundred and seventy eight or 17 per cent are small town tycoons. Tier-2 cities (1-5 million population) like Bhubaneswar, Chandigarh and Jaipur have exhibited significant economic progress, as reflected in the salary trend report of Randstad (2021). Randstad's MD & CO, P.S. Viswanath (as cited in Singh, 2022) comments on secondary cities sound optimistic:

> We firmly believe that they (tier-2) are the future talent hubs and job-creation centres. Our conviction has been borne out by the fact that tier-2 cities have made great strides in salary levels due to a lot of investments in building excellent physical and social infrastructure. This is also an indication of an exciting trend that emerging organisations have discovered the advantages of having a borderless, multifaceted workforce that can deliver 'anytime, anywhere' work. So, we could say that work is seeking out talent in this new model, right up to tier-2 cities.

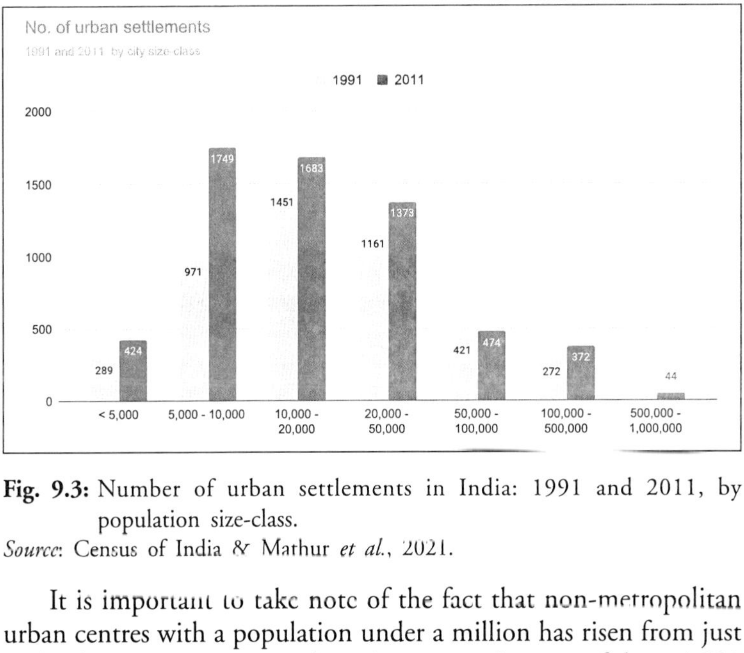

Fig. 9.3: Number of urban settlements in India: 1991 and 2011, by population size-class.
Source: Census of India & Mathur *et al.*, 2021.

It is important to take note of the fact that non-metropolitan urban centres with a population under a million has risen from just under 4,600 in 1991 to over 6,100 in 2011, an increase of about 1,500 cities and towns. About a third of the urban population of the country lives in towns with a population of less than a lakh (Census, 2011). These smaller urban centres play an important role in serving as links between the rural and the urban economies including the global.

> Small and medium-sized cities often serve as 'stepping-stones' for rural migrants on their way to further destinations. In many countries, these subsequent urban-

> to-urban migration streams are as significant as rural to urban flows. The bulk of urban-to-urban migration is from small and medium-sized cities to larger ones. In mega urban regions, this may also involve migration from large to small or medium-sized cities in the periphery.
>
> (UN-Habitat, 2010, p. 59)

Small Towns and Local Economic Development

Local Economic Development (LED) is "a process by which public, business and non-governmental sector work collectively to create better conditions for economic growth and employment generation" (World Bank, 2006). The strategy of LED can be deployed in promoting the local economy of small towns and village clusters in the manufacturing sector. The share of manufacturing in the economy has been stagnant for many years, touching a low of 14.9 per cent in 2018-19. According to a report by the Centre for Economic Data and Analysis, Ashoka University, India lost ten million jobs in four years between 2016-17 and 2019-20 and if the pandemic is considered, the loss could be 40 million. Expansion of the manufacturing sector can go a long way in generating more employment.

The Government of India has launched several programs like Make in India, Skill India, and Digital India to give fillip to employment generation. Small scale units for manufacture of some items listed under Make in India scheme like textiles and apparels, leather and footwear, food processing and jewellery can be set up in rural areas/towns where local skills are available. Simultaneously, training centres can be set up for skill development. What is important, however, is to ensure quality of the products which can propel the export market. The economic miracle of China is attributed mainly to its exports in a variety of products, riding on the back of Foreign Direct Investment (FDI). It is often argued that to compete with China is a tough task. If we build state-of-the-art infrastructure and produce world class goods, there is no reason why we should lag. It also calls for policy reforms towards ease of doing business. Tiruppur town in Tamil Nadu is a shining example of what was once a village, developing into a thriving manufacturing centre of 100 per cent export of garments, and emerging as the knitwear capital of India. We need many more Tiruppurs in India.

Bhagyanagar is a small town in Koppal district of Karnataka, and the hub of the human hair-processing industry. It accounts for 40 per cent of the hair processed in India, an approximately Rs. 3,000 crore business annually. While raw human hair is generated by the offerings of devotees across many temples (the largest being the Tirupati Venkateshwara temple at Tirupati, which records an annual revenue of Rs. 150 crore from selling hair), the processing of human hair is a skilled job. Processing involves many steps such as cleaning, washing and drying by lengths and thicknesses of hair. Processed hair has a huge demand from the export market. According to Mattanna Vaddar, a hair-processing unit owner and aggregator at Bhagyanagar, as Indian hair quality is considered good, there is a huge demand from countries like China, Myanmar and parts of Africa, where they turn it into different types of wigs and hair extensions, to be shipped in turn to USA and Europe. As exporters from cities like Bengaluru, Chennai and Hyderabad command the market for such exports, it hinders the growth of the local wig industry. In such cases, the state government would do well to take the initiative in imparting the necessary skills to workers in the hair-processing industry, so that we gain the capacity to export finished hair products, thus generating more value from a valuable resource and skilled employment (*Times of India*, August 1, 2023).

Another case of small town entrepreneurship comes from Udupi in coastal Karnataka. Rohit Bhat had the audacity to set up a technology company in a small town with a population of about a lakh in the early 2000s. He went to Japan in 1992 to work for a company in Osaka. He was so impressed by the progress made by that country and their work culture that after a few years, he decided to return to India. About the Japanese, he says: "They were so hi-tech, so humble. Their work ethic was amazing. Japanese companies were buying Hollywood studios. Their car companies were upstaging Detroit ones. A country destroyed by World War II had picked themselves up to become the world's second largest economy. I decided then that I'm going back to India and build something world class". He came back, not to the IT city of Bangalore, but to his native town of Udupi, 400 km away from the metropolis and built a company, Robosoft Technologies, which has emerged as one of India's best app developers. Bhat's words should instil hope about the potential of small towns in India:

> One of the misconceptions people have is that they need to be in a larger city to start something big. When I moved to Udupi, people said nobody will give you work...you can't innovate out of Udupi...you can't raise funds in Udupi. But as soon as I moved, we got one of our biggest customers then—Hewlett Packard, we started getting into newer areas like apps, game porting, we raised three rounds of funds. Then they said you can't get an exit sitting in Udupi. We got that too. Take care of your customers and people, and everything takes care of themselves. (From *TOI*, September 1, 2021).

Technology and e-commerce in particular have revolutionized the way businesses operate in places far beyond big cities, in lower-tier cities. According to a report published in *Business Today* (14 November, 2021), small cities and towns are driving online sales during the festive season as top e-commerce players steadily make inroads into tier-3 towns and beyond—in Alwar (Rajasthan), Anantapur and Visakhapatnam (Andhra Pradesh), Silchar and Tinsukia (Assam) and Patna (Bihar). Online shopper base expanded by 20 per cent in 2021 and tier-2 and beyond cities accounted for more than 60 per cent of online orders. Data by the CMIE shows that the increase in employment ahead of the festive season was disproportionately higher in rural India, with 6.5 million out of 8.5 million jobs added in September 2021 coming from rural regions. In its monthly bulletin for October 2021, the RBI stated "...The digital payment ecosystem is poised for stronger growth on the back of the growing footprint of e-commerce in lower-tier cities and rising awareness about digital modes" (RBI, 2021).

An analysis of industrial development in Kerala, West Bengal and Tamil Nadu reveals that decentralised industrial strategy of manufacturing dispersed over many districts is fairly successful (Kumar, 2022). A strategy of economic and urban development that relies only on a few metros need not be the only paradigm of development in a large and developing country like India. Pointing out that intermediate/middle order towns play a critical role in the development of regional economy in developing countries, Amitabh Kundu observes that a large part of contemporary growth in India occurs outside the hegemonic power structure of globalisation and metropolitanisation and hence the need to build a narrative from below and bring dispersed urbanisation into the centre of research and policy agenda (Kundu *et al.*, 2016).

Hill Towns

India has a number of towns located in hilly regions—hill stations as they were called during the British period, which have turned into summer resorts. Over the years, the inflow of visitors/tourists from cities has increased necessitating more construction to accommodate tourists and develop the required infrastructure. One can see several constructions along the road leading to hill town—like Mussoorie, for instance. The residents of Mussoorie have highlighted that a section of Landour, a popular tourist thoroughfare was 'sinking'. The National Green Tribunal had pointed out that "the carrying capacity (of the town) was studied by the Lal Bahadur Shastri Academy of Administration in 2001 which suggested that no further constructions are viable. The Mussoorie Dehradun Development Authority has failed to go by the said study and take preventive and remedial measures. Excessive traffic congestion adds to the traffic burden on the mountain roads". The government has also taken up large projects in some of these towns. All this has resulted in serious damage to the environment, leading to disasters such as the one in the Himalayan town of Joshimath which witnessed unprecedented devastation in January 2023. Buildings developed cracks and people suffered loss of life and property. People have attributed the occurrence of the disaster to the construction of a thermal power project and a hydro-electric project by the government.

What is Happening to Shimla, the Queen of Hill Stations?

Manoj Kumar was getting ready for work when his doorbell rang. It changed his life forever. On the other side of the door were the police. Within minutes, the forty-eight year old the shopkeeper lost his house and found himself standing under an umbrella on the roadside with his wife and children. Dumbstruck, they watched the building adjacent to their house crumbling down. His family was among the many residents who were vacated overnight in September 2001 as the Darshan Cottage, an adjacent nine-storey building was going to collapse.

"It was the worst time of my life. I don't even want to recollect it" Kumar said. One of the victims of Shimla's poor development and callous neglect by the authorities, he couldn't return to his home for a year. It was a precarious structure that could meet the same fate as Darshan Cottage.

Situated at a height of 2,276 metres, with a population of nearly 3 lakhs, the capital city of Himachal Pradesh is struggling to accommodate people. The city is expanding horizontally but in an unplanned manner. With an additional floating population of about 70,000, Shimla experiences massive traffic jams "as notorious as Bengaluru and is running out of parking space…it is running out of water too".

For over four decades, Shimla's infrastructure was based on an interim development plan formulated in 1979. The recent 2041 plan draft development plan introduced in February 2022 was struck down by the National Green Tribunal. The Hazard Vulnerability and Risk Assessment (HVRA) report notes that 65 per cent of the city's buildings are categorised under 'high vulnerability' and warns that anywhere between 5,000 and 20,000 people are likely to die in the event of an earthquake.

"Even the town hall building built in 1888 is earthquake-proof, but not the newer ones" according to Chantranta Singh, convenor of the Shimla Upnagar Jankalyan Samiti. "The northern slope of the ridge is sinking. The Grand Hotel West is going down". In July, another four-storey building had collapsed, and instances of landslides are becoming a regular feature (Misra, 2022).

Hailed as the queen of hill stations and one of the finest Himalayan towns, this beautiful city has become a victim of outdated planning and poor governance.

Urban-Industrial Corridors

The National Industrial Corridor Development Programme, a joint venture between the centre and the states is aimed at developing industrial townships located in different states running along a highspeed corridor with a view to expanding industrial output, increasing employment opportunities and provide better living and social facilities for the growing workforce. GOI has approved the development of eleven Industrial Corridors:

Delhi-Mumbai Industrial Corridor (DMIC), Chennai-Bengaluru Industrial Corridor (CBIC), Extension of CBIC to Kochi via Coimbatore, Amritsar-Kolkota, Hyderabad-Nagpur, Hyderabad-Warangal, Hyderabad-Bengaluru, Bengaluru-Mumbai, Vizag-Chennai, Odisha Economic Corridor and the Delhi-Nagpur Corridor.

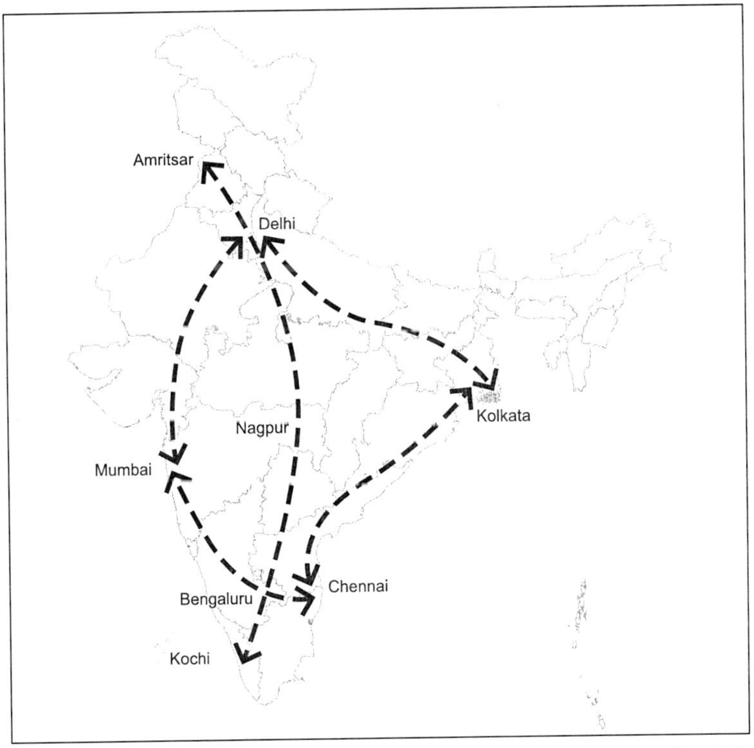

Fig. 9.4: Some of the proposed and under-progress economic-industrial-logistics corridors.

Source: Swastik Harish, based on various reports, map not to scale.

Knowledge Explosion and Its Impact on Cities

> "Never before in history have so many people, from so many places, had so much power at their fingertips."
>
> (Schmidt & Cohen, 2013)

This observation by Eric Schmidt and Jared Cohen in their brilliant book, *The New Digital Age* (2013) brings home the impact of digital revolution and shows how it is "reshaping the future of people, nations and businesses". The growth of IT in the third quarter of the 20th century acted as a driving force in two areas: first, it accelerated the pace of globalisation, and secondly, it played a key role in the globalisation of cities. The human impacts of telematics-driven globalisation moved towards a theorisation of space, and in particular new understandings of the city (Beyers, 1989). The structure and growth of cities came to be determined by the patterns of capital accumulation and urban sites became bases of production and markets in a hierarchical network of inter-linked spaces (Heitzman, 2004). Cities like London, New York and Tokyo became centres of corporate headquarters, finance and consulting, and performed a key function of coordinating the flow of capital across the world. The idea of 'world cities' and 'global cities' came into being, creating a global hierarchy of cities performing similar functions at regional and national levels, 'an urban architecture of global networks' as described by Sassen (2002). Thus, Singapore emerged as key technology hub in Asia, Mumbai became the financial capital of India and Bangalore its IT capital. The new millennium saw other major cities in India such as Hyderabad, Chennai, Pune, and the Delhi region (Gurgaon, Noida) making rapid progress in the IT sector.

Communication technologies have advanced at such a rapid pace that the number of internet users in India increased from 0.5 per cent of the population in 2000 to 7.5 per cent in 2010 and 43 per cent (of 1.37 billion) in 2020 (World Bank, 2022). Much of the adoption of the internet has so far been in urban areas, and a significant majority of internet users are residents of the largest nine metropolitan cities (Govt. of India, n.d.). The new and emerging technologies such as Internet of Things (IOT), Artificial Intelligence (AI), Machine Learning (ML) and Robotics have radically altered the nature of work and human activity. This has impacted the city in many ways. More that 40 million people from feature phones to smart phones in 2021.

The central government disbursed Rs. 37,601 crores in 2021-22, Rs. 4,000 crores more than the previous year under the PMMY (Prime Minister's Mudra Yojana) for petty businesses in cities and countryside. 110 per cent increase in UPI based digital transactions in volume between June 2020 and June 2021. Thirty per cent Indians ordered food through home deliveries during the pandemic, signalling a shift to online consumption.

The rapid shift to digital payments over the past year indicates significant formalisation of the Indian economy. Banks achieved digital coverage of 95.9 per cent of individuals and 89.8 per cent of businesses. It is worth mentioning that most jobs were generated in the lower income category—deliveries, ride-sharing, care and wellness and other microtasks (Boston Consulting Group & Michael & Susan Dell Foundation, 2021).

Technologies such as Artificial Intelligence (AI), Robotics and 5G are expected to play a big role in driving innovation and economic growth. In 2022, an Artificial Intelligence Park (ARTPARK) was set up in the Indian Institute of Science, Bengaluru. It aims to bring together industry, academia and the government to help creating the next model of job growth outside of metros by leveraging cutting edge digital technologies. According to PricewaterhouseCoopers (2020) research, the AI-driven experience economy would result in $15.7 trillion of new economic value by 2030.

It has often been argued that increasing use of technology results in unemployment. Technology may disrupt jobs but reduces costs dramatically, making services accessible to all. Two significant trends can be noticed: first, a shift in the composition of the economy—from agriculture to manufacturing to services, reducing marginal cost to zero and shift from non-renewable to renewable energy, leading to near zero marginal costs in energy (Rifkin, 2014), and second, a technology mediated 'dematerialisation'—use of less material in almost every product (for instance, use of less fuel and less number of parts in a car) to produce the same product (McAfee, 2019). Lower marginal costs and 'dematerialisation' will improve affordability. It is likely that future growth will be determined more by technology and enterprise than use of labour force. Countries like India where unemployment is high, and creation of jobs is an imperative will have to contend with this problem.

Let us look at some examples of the use of technology by states and cities in India and how they have benefited the people. Electronic or e-governance has been introduced in almost all states for a variety of purposes. Karnataka, a leading state in technology adoption, has introduced the following measures:

- **E-Janma** data base that captures timely and regular data on births and deaths.
- **Bhoomi:** Right to Land—a digitised land record system; the latest version, Bhoomi 7.0 is an extensive and holistic web-based platform that aggregates data from Taluks to a secure and safe centralised data base.
- **Dishank:** a mobile app that provides any citizen located anywhere in the world with a virtual, wireless and complete land map. Very useful to landowners as proof of land title, and to those who purchase land, especially to investors.
- **E-Office:** paperless project aimed at improving productivity and accountability.

Urban scholars have time and again expressed concern about the availability, credibility, and quality of data on urbanisation and urban development. Although the situation has improved in recent years, there are gaps which act as serious constraints to planning and management of cities. In particular, the non-availability of timely 2021 census data, work on which is yet to start must be considered as a serious gap in planning for the future. During the pandemic, the use of technology played a significant role in generating reliable data for tracking and tracing infected persons, identifying hotspots and container zones, and monitoring hospital admissions and discharges. It is to the credit of the urban local governments that they played a leading role in this effort. Bangalore Municipal Corporation was a pioneer in setting up a War Room to exclusively attend to this work; this was a major factor in planning and providing relief measures. Other cities also undertook emergency measures. Such city level experiences in dealing with crisis situations can offer useful insights in using technology and mobilising technical manpower in speedy data collection of ongoing activities.

Modern India is characterised by urban explosion and the ICT revolution, both occurring somewhat simultaneously. This has led to generation of an unprecedented amount of data about different aspects of cities and urban spaces. Much of these data are hidden in the records of urban institutions running a city. These data relate to land use patterns and changes, property transactions, mobility patterns, water and energy use and other dimensions of city life which carry great value in decision making. Yet, several decisions made the government are not necessarily supported by data, more specifically, accurate data. While progress is being made in digitalisation of activities generally, there is an absence of a structure for data collection and release in the municipalities and urban development agencies.

Karnataka, a leader in IT, had as far back as 2008 set up a Karnataka Municipal Data Society (KMDS) with the objective of strengthening Urban Local Bodies through e-governance (mrc.gov.in, accessed 25 Jan., 2023). Recently, KUIDFC has, in collaboration with the Vidhi Centre for Legal Policy, has developed the Karnataka Municipal Data Policy to facilitate proactive access to municipal data in digitally accessible formats. This is expected to improve data collection on the hand and help in actively sharing data with the public. This will be a major step in promoting transparency and accountability in the functioning of urban local bodies.

Shifting Nature of City Jobs—Digital Era

Cities have emerged as major platforms for technological innovation and wealth creation; secondly, urban settings serve as a breeding ground for entrepreneurs, in fact, they have let loose the animal spirits of entrepreneurship. India is witnessing a surge in digital startu-ps and with rising e-commerce, it is attracting venture capital like never before. The year 2021 alone was expected to bring in about $30 billion acting as boost to the unicorns.

The covid pandemic, for all the suffering it has caused, has actually triggered the dawn of a new digital era in India. More and more people not only in urban but rural areas are adapting themselves to the smartphone screen. What was primarily a communication and entertainment device, has turned into a minicomputer in the hands of the general populace, serving multiple purposes. The citizen, urban and rural, with a smart phone and a digital identity (Aadhar) that has now covered practically the entire population can learn a skill and find a job, and with a bank account transact online or invest money. Digital transactions are no more confined to the English-speaking elite but has penetrated to all strata of society encompassing local language populations. This is a stupendous achievement in terms of democratising access to the digital world.

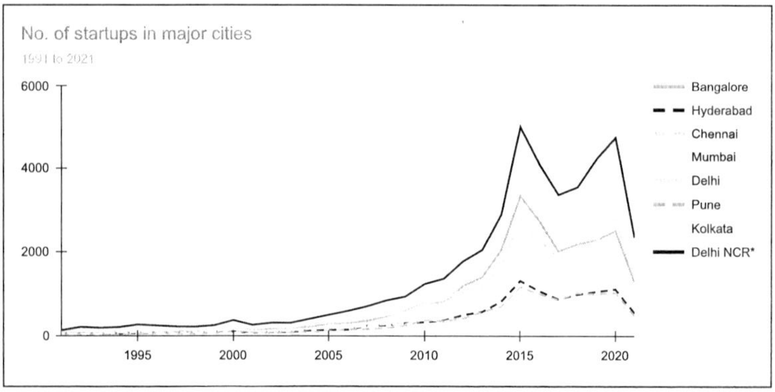

Fig. 9.5: Number of start-ups in major cities.

Source: IIM, Bengaluru.

The most widely talked about change ever since the onset of the pandemic is what has come to be known as 'work-from-home' (WFH), which in a way, has transformed the world of work. Companies and employees embraced this change as it proved beneficial to both; companies saved money and employees were more comfortable to work from their homes and free from the hassles of commuting in big cities. The question being asked now is whether such remote work will continue or will the companies go back to physical presence. Prithviraj Choudhury, Lumry Family Associate Professor of Business School, at Harvard Business University has been studying remote work even before the pandemic. He is firmly of the view that there is no going back. He calls remote forms of work WFA (work from anywhere) and says it allows the individual to choose where to live and then decide to work from home or a co-working space or a cafeteria. Employers can hire from anywhere and the world becomes your labour market.

WFA also has the potential to revitalise tier-two and three cities (TOI Interview, March 27, 2022). According to a study by the US National Bureau of Economic Research, working from home is saving commuters working the world 72 minutes a day.

There is another viewpoint. According to a NASSCOM survey, 70 per cent of organisations are looking at hybrid work models. Different companies will define roles depending on the organisation structure, culture and goals. Moreover, during the COVID-19 pandemic, people missed out on the social capital, which is also important in building the culture of the organisation (TOI, Feb 16, 2022). Ultimately, what is likely to prevail is a hybrid model, the ratio of Work from Home (WFH) and Work at Office (WAO), varying from one organisation to another, depending on their requirements. This has resulted in recognition of talent in smaller cities, particularly in tier-2 cities. According to the Randstad report (2022) on salary trends, cities like Bhubaneswar, Chandigarh and Kochi have seen a sharp rise in salaries. The accompanying figure shows the salary trends in Tier I and Tier II cities at three levels. In salaries paid, Chandigarh tops the chart at junior and mid level categories; at the senior level, Bhubaneswar leads followed by Kochi and Chandigarh.

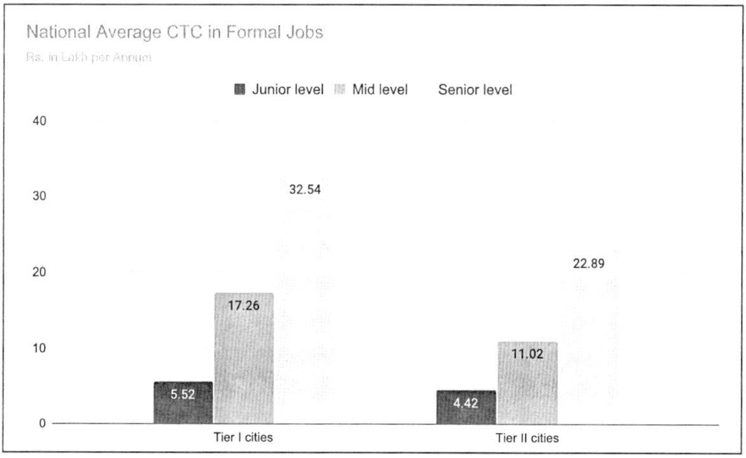

Fig. 9.6: Average salaries at the junior and mid level in Tier II and Tier I cities beginning to compete with the same in Tier I cities. At the same time, between 2011 and 2021, more than 25,000 tech startups were recorded in India. Just in the year 2021, India added 42 'unicorns' in the tech sector, while total investment in startups in the same year was to the order of 24 billion USD.

While WFH will result in loss of some jobs, the widespread use of technology has the potential to create jobs in several other areas. The ramifications of technology are so widespread that the demand for technologically oriented jobs in diverse fields will only increase with time. The new jobs of the 21st century will include the following:

- With increasing urbanisation, the demand for city planners, engineers qualified in transportation, water supply and sanitation, experts in waste management, finance, e-governance and a host of other jobs has been rising.
- Architects and building engineers need to adapt themselves to new designs in construction technology such as green buildings and space optimisation.
- In the background of the pandemic, the need for more epidemiologists and scientists who can analyse and communicate how diseases spread, more chemists to deal with processes to clean offices and public spaces, and more public health specialists in general are needed.
- The rising number of patients in cities suffering from non-communicable diseases like diabetes, hypertension, heart ailments, mental health problems such as stress and depression requires more health professionals in general and in specialised disciplines.
- With increasing life span, the need to pay greater attention to ageing and elderly health care.
- Online delivery of public services by various government agencies.
- As meetings, conferences and webinars are taking to the online mode, greater the need for more communication and virtual meeting specialists. Learning and education have also gone online with business opportunities (Byjus, Coursera, Udacity, etc.).
- Technology literate journalists with skills to articulate and communicate news and events to a non-technical audience.
- With arts gaining popularity in cities, the need for more broadcasting and theatre technicians.

- Issues related to urban data—lack of urban data on aspects of urbanisation and urban development, as well as the accuracy and reliability opens up a new profession in urban research, theory and practice.

More can be added to the list. Whatever the type of job, technological skills are becoming essential and hence the need for employing technology specialists in almost every activity, be it data management, communication, sport, entertainment, or office management. Apart from science and technology, a new theme has entered the job market, viz. art. To the long propagated combination of STEM (Science, Technology, Engineering and Mathematics) is now added Arts, thus transforming STEM into STEAM. The world of art and culture has now started thriving in India and has opened new opportunities for jobs in music, dance, visual arts, designing and broadcasting. As some of the old jobs disappear, new jobs are emerging. The existing skillsets are becoming obsolete in a few years and hence the increasing importance of skilling, reskilling, and upskilling.

The revolutionary changes in the job market brought about by technology, as significant as it is, is only one part of the story. At the end of 2022, the employment scenario in the country presents a bleak picture. The unemployment rate had touched 7.14 per cent, i.e., 37.1 million labour force out of 443 million (CMIE: media reports, *India Today*, 13 February 2023). Sector-wise break-up of jobs shows that 46 per cent are employed in agriculture, 21 per cent in industry and 32 per cent in services. Even the big tech companies like Amazon, Google, Meta, Microsoft, and IBM are laying off employees. And with agriculture showing a declining trend, it is essential to expand the scope for employment in the infrastructure and industrial sectors, particularly in manufacturing. The central budget for 2023-24 has provided a huge outlay of Rs. 10 lakh crores (3.3% of GDP) for capital investment, an increase of 33 per cent compared to the previous year which is expected to drive infrastructure development and boost employment. Transport infrastructure has been accorded priority with a massive outlay of Rs. 2.4 lakh crores for Railways and Rs. 75,000 crores for 100 critical transport infrastructure projects for last- and first-mile connectivity for ports, coal, steel, fertiliser and foodgrains sectors. An encouraging feature of the budget for the urban sector is the proposal to set up an Urban Infrastructure Development Fund (UIDF) for public agencies to create infrastructure in Tier-2 and 3 cities which can generate considerable employment.

The projects and financial provisions may look impressive, but success depends on effective execution and delivery. This also calls for creation of new jobs and upgrading skills of existing personnel. The importance of skilling has been recognised with the Technology proposal to launch Pradhan Mantri Vikas Yojana 4.0 to train lakhs of youth during the next three years, which would include new-age courses like coding, and launching a Unified Skill India platform to enable demand based formal skilling with employers, including MSMEs and facilitating access to entrepreneurship schemes. Translating the budget promises into reality will be a huge challenge.

On the whole, there is lot of optimism in the tech industry about the capability of India in playing a leading role in shaping technology innovations for the entire world.

Chapter
10

The Discontents

The Informal Economy of Indian Cities

> *"India's economy is the informal economy—the rest simply can't work without it".*
>
> (Harris-White, 2021)

India's informal economy was deliberately created by the late colonial and newly independent state which needed to minimize regulative obligations to labour and small firms (*Times Evoke*, 2021). Now, India's informal economy is the biggest in the world, supporting possibly 400 million households, or 80 per cent of all workers (WIEGO, 2020) with no sector or region exempt. It is important to recognize that the informal workers possess a variety of skills, ranging from basic construction and street vending which may be considered as low-skilled to carpentry and welding learnt through a little training and experience, to high-skilled work like weaving and jewellery making. Many female workers are engaged in manual labour, mainly in domestic chores, rolling *beedis* (local cigarettes rolled in dried leaves) or incense sticks and construction labour, carrying loads of bricks.

In recent years, another class of informal workers known as 'gig' workers has emerged, i.e., those who represent short-term work, 'outside of the traditional employer-employee relationship'. They include platform workers who work as delivery boys or cab drivers and are employed or rather 'engaged' by aggregators who treat these workers as 'independent contractors', meaning they are free from labour laws. Rough estimates put their number around 7 million currently and expected to grow to 23.5 million by 2019-30 (Niti Aayog, 2022). This could include workers with higher skills in technology and management sectors like IT and design or wellness services and teaching. At present, the big four platform companies—Swiggy, Zomato, Ola and Uber employ a substantial number.

What about their working conditions? Being 'independent contractors' or 'delivery partners', they are outside the ambit of labour laws and are not guaranteed minimum wages. They mostly work on a target and incentive model and how much they earn depends on how many hours they work and how many orders they comply with. The government brought in a new Code on Social Security which describes the status of gig and platform workers as "persons in a work arrangement outside of traditional employer-employee relationship". It provides for social security funds for the welfare of workers, but the source of funding is left vague, although it includes sources such as government contribution, Corporate Social Responsibility (CSR) funding or a 1-2 per cent cess on revenues of these companies.

Story of One of the World's Biggest Slums with a Big Informal Market

This is the story of not only the biggest slum in India and one of the world's largest, but perhaps the most talked about and written about human settlement, popularized through internationally acclaimed movies—*Slumdog Millionaire* and *Gully Boy*. Its origin goes back to over 150 years. It rose on a marshy land and a dumping ground for waste in the heart of what is now one of the largest metropolises and the financial capital of India, Mumbai. It is called a 'city within a city', home to nearly a million people in an area extending over 500 acres. It is also an industrial township, housing about 15,000 small-scale units, manufacturing a variety of products—leather ware, jewellery, textiles, etc., but without the infrastructure and civic amenities of a planned township like Durgapur or Jamshedpur, one created in the public sector and the other in the private sector. So, the people live in closely huddled houses, lacking proper sanitation and other civic amenities.

Attempts to redevelop the slum and rehabilitate the dwellers into a better and healthy environment has been going on for decades. The process is interesting. After several half-hearted efforts, a Dharavi Action Plan was drawn up and a Special Planning Authority for the purpose was created in 2003. In 2007, Dharavi redevelopment was declared a Vital Public Purpose Project but was embroiled in hurdles like population density, mixed land use, proximity to airport, eligibility criteria and so on. In 2018, another Integrated Redevelopment project came up and bids were invited for execution. SecLink Technologies Corporation, a Gulf based firm won the bid, but the entire deal was cancelled in 2020. Again, this year on October 1, 2022, fresh tenders have been invited with a proposal to set up a Special Purpose Vehicle (SPV) with equity being shared by the government and a private player. The project is estimated to cost Rs. 23,000 crores and will include preparation of a master plan, and construction of houses and civic infrastructure.

Commentators have pointed to several complexities involved in the implementation of the project: ownership of the land, part of it being owned by the municipal corporation; building plan, vertical development replacing low-rise structures; survival of multiple businesses; population from different ethnic and religious backgrounds; terms and conditions of allotment of housing units; the existing units being of different sizes and high densities—these and more could pose serious problems. Nevertheless, the Dharavi Redevelopment Authority is confident of overcoming the hurdles.

In the meanwhile, one of the residents, Devanna Bhandari, who has lived most part of his life in Dharavi, decided recently to move out of the slum, for the simple but a very weighty reason—the walk to the community toilet for a family of eight members, had become too much.

As of 2022, the Maharashtra government has announced that it has awarded the Dharavi Redevelopment Project to an Adani Group company. Residents of Dharavi are keeping their fingers crossed about their future.

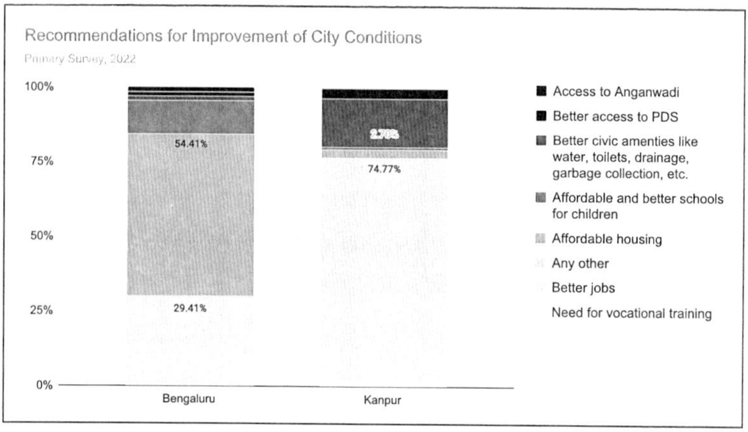

Fig. 10.1: Migrant workers' recommendations for improvement in city conditions.

Source: Author, primary survey, 2022.

In recent primary research with migrant workers in Bengaluru and Kanpur an overwhelming number of respondents made a case for better jobs in their cities. In Kanpur, a massive three quarters of migrants felt that better jobs would be key to making their city better.

Street Vendors

Street vendors in Indian cities constitute a large workforce. In 2006, the Government of India estimated that there may be between 17 and 25 lakh street vendors in urban India (Government of India, 2006). More recently, it has been estimated that street vendors may constitute about 2.5 per cent of the urban population (SPRF, 2020). By many accounts, they lead an uncertain life, subject to severe occupational hazards. The street vendors face harassment from officials of municipal and police departments who collect their *mamools* (a kind of 'protection money') resident welfare associations who want footpaths to be free from encroachments and pedestrians who find them as obstructions almost daily. Their income keeps fluctuating from day-to-day and can particularly suffer when there are weather conditions and of course, during crises periods like COVID-19.

The Street Vendors (Protection of Livelihood and Regulation of Street Vending) Act, 2014, is considered a progressive legislation. The Act provides a framework for street vending, with four basic provisions. There will be a survey of all existing hawkers. Instead of licenses, certificates of vending will be issued to all existing hawkers identified in the survey. There will be provisions to demarcate vending and non-vending zones and all hawkers will be accommodated in the vending zones, and no hawker will be evicted from his or her spot until the survey is completed and certificates of vending issued.

The highlight of the Act is the setting up of a Town Vending Committee (TVC) with representatives from street vendors, traffic police, Resident Welfare Associations (RWAs), market associations and the planning authority and headed by the municipal commissioner. Its functions include organizing the survey, deciding on vending/non-vending zones, deciding on vending fees hawkers should pay the municipality and publishing the street vendor's charter. A truly democratic structure and a participatory process that virtually takes away the powers concentrated in the municipality and the police and sharing it with various stakeholders. However, the implementation lags. TVCs are yet to be set up in many cities, let alone taking action on others. Although the Act has tried to balance the livelihood rights of hawkers and the right to free movement of pedestrians, there are several practical problems, that I myself have experienced as the Municipal Commissioner. In many places, the pavements are so narrow that it becomes extremely difficult to accommodate the interests of both. Secondly, finding adequate public spaces at the right spots is not easy. And the hardest task is arriving at a consensus among all stakeholders; cooperation by stakeholders and a patient approach can, however, yield results. So, by and large, things continue as before.

Informal work is heterogeneous in nature and identifying specific target groups within the larger informal workforce is difficult but essential for policy making (Sethuraman, 1976). Indian Institute for Human Settlements undertook a study of 'Neighbourhoods and their Impact on the informal food economy of Bangalore' (IIHS, 2018) with the aim of capturing a city-scale understanding of food business and a structural understanding of how neighbourhood types affect business outcomes. It carried out a survey of one thousand informal food business across the city of Bangalore in September 2018. The findings showed that different neighbourhood types create particular kinds of opportunities through the pattern of previous occupation and how these relate to particular places. The study shows how business outcomes vary across neighbourhoods, and how socio-economic networks are embedded in place.

The study concluded that majority of the sample constitutes well established businesses who have been in operation for many years and have never moved their location. Another significant finding is that vendor outcomes remain static over time even for business, implying that stability of time and place do not necessarily lead to better financial gains. The findings of this study stand in contrast to the literature on precarity of street vendors in relation to eviction and displacement, as the authors of the study themselves have pointed out. The spatial location and other circumstances relevant to understanding such an outcome requires further investigation.

A National Social Security Board has been proposed to be set up recommend to the central government formulation of schemes for different sections of the unorganised sector workers, but the new Board is yet to see the light of day. Sometimes, delivery workers are treated badly by customers. But they are also mistreated by restaurants. Many times, the food delivery boys can't use the rest room there. They have to pick up the order from outside. There is no space for them to stop and rest for even 10 minutes.

Many delivery workers are logged in for more than 12 hours, but they have no canteen facility. Even a basic meal on the street costs Rs. 45 in Bengaluru today. The least these companies could do is at least tie up with restaurants to provide a basic meal to their workers for a reduced price in a few locations.

> Forget this, most of these workers are prone to accidents. Assume that these people work for three or four years. They definitely get severe back pain, haemorrhoids, spondylitis and other issues. But there is no law that applies to these workers.
>
> (Vinay Sarathy, V., President, United Food Delivery Partners Union)

The informal economy has positive and negative implications for city economy and society. On the positive side, it provides employment to a large number of people—the poor, disadvantaged, migrant and to the lower middle class deprived of jobs and to the small entrepreneurial class willing to experiment new types of businesses. Secondly and very importantly, it makes available cheap food to the working class near their work spot, though the space food vendors occupy may be considered illegally occupied. On the negative side, informal workers lack security, especially in times of calamities, as it happened during the COVID-19 pandemic. The uncertainties of earning a livelihood and the far from satisfactory living conditions including security of tenure are matters of serious concern and government's intervention is sorely needed. The two cases of Dharavi slum dwellers and of the street vendors discussed above bring out both sides of the story.

It is not that the government has not bestowed attention on the plight of informal workers. It has implemented a number of initiatives through legislation and welfare programmes such as the National Social Security Act, 2008, Atal Pension Yojana, Pradhan Mantri Bhim Suraksha Yojana, and the Skill India Mission aimed at imparting and upgrading skills. The problem really lies in their implementation, which is a governance issue.

State of Infrastructure and Services

Performance of Cities

Where do the cities stand in terms of infrastructure development and delivery of services? How do we measure their performance? For the first time, The Ministry of Housing and Urban Affairs (MoHUA) undertook this task in 2020 and assessed the performance of cities under two categories: Municipal Performance, and Ease of Living.

The Municipal Performance Index 2020 (Ministry of Housing and Urban Affairs, 2021) is aimed at assessing the critical input-level parameters enabling better provisioning of municipal services to citizens (p. 26) using the following five parameters: (1) Services, (2) Governance, (3) Finance, (4) Planning, and (5) Technology. The municipalities have been classified under two categories—million+ (with population of over a million), and those with a population of under a million. The ranking of the top and bottom cities is shown in the Table 10.1.

Table 10.1: Ranking of Million+ and Less than Million Municipalities in the Municipal Performance Index 2021

Rank	Million+ Municipality	Less than Million Municipalities
1	Indore	New Delhi MC
2	Surat	Tirupati
3	Bhopal	Gandhinagar
4	Pimpri-Chinchwad	Karnal
5	Pune	Salem
47	Aurangabad	Dehradun
48	North Delhi MC	Rourkela
49	Srinagar	Port Blair
50	Kota	Diu
51	Guwahati	Agartala

Source: MoHUA, 2021.

Of the 51 million+ cities, Indore, Surat, and Bhopal occupy the first three positions and Srinagar, Kota and Guwahati are the last three. Among the larger cities, while Greater Mumbai figures in the top ten, Hyderabad and Chennai are in the middle and surprisingly, Bengaluru, the IT capital, is pushed down to the bottom half along with the three municipal corporations of the national capital—South, East and West Delhi. Under the less than a million category, New Delhi MC, Tirupati and Gandhinagar have emerged at the top and Kohima, Imphal and Shillong figure at the bottom. In terms of performance on the basis of the four parameters, in the million+ category, Ghaziabad, Indore and Rajkot are ranked the first three under 'Services'; Indore, Surat and Chennai under 'Finance' and Indore, Raipur and Bareilly under 'Technology (Ministry of Housing and Urban Affairs, 2021b).

The framework for the Ease of Living Index (EOLI) was prepared by MoHUA with the Institute for Competitiveness. EOLI measures well being of citizens across the three pillars of Quality of Life, Economic-ability, and Sustainability; carrying a weight of 35 per cent, 15 per cent and 20 per cent, respectively. A new dimension added in this survey included Citizen Perception Survey with a weight of 30 per cent. In the million-plus category of cities, the top three ranks were awarded to Bengaluru, Pune, and Ahmedabad and within cities with less than a million population, the awards went to Shimla, Bhubaneswar, and Silvassa (Dadra and Nagar Haveli) (Ministry of Housing and Urban Affairs, 2021).

An overall assessment of the performance of cities reveals that some cities do well under some categories but not so well under certain others, as exemplified by Bengaluru, topping under Ease of Living Index but faring rather poorly under municipal functions. The ranking of cities based on their performance gives a comparative picture of where they stand at the national level and should help spur competition towards better performance. There are certain issues which are fraught with serious problems, going beyond municipal capabilities and require the intervention of state and central authorities.

Four Critical Issues in Urban Governance

Taking a medium and long-term view, there are four critical key issues to be addressed: (1) water supply, (2) land and housing, (3) mobility/transportation and; (4) climate change and environment.

There are other issues like road infrastructure, electricity/energy, waste disposal etc. but the above four are not only crucial but also fraught with serious problems. Hence, these are dealt with at some length.

Water Supply: Will there be a Water Famine?

The supply of water to urban areas cannot be considered in isolation, purely in terms of the needs of cities but in the overall context of requirements for other purposes like irrigation, industries and rural population, as the sources of supply could be common and may be located anywhere. Surface water comes mainly from rivers which may run through some cities but originate from afar and groundwater can be tapped from both rural and urban areas. With growing urbanisation, water requirements for large cities are now partially met from groundwater in the periphery beyond the metropolitan boundaries.

Let us first look at the question of water availability across the country. The annual per capita availability of water has declined by 75 per cent in the 75 years since independence—from 6,042 cubic meters to 1,486 cubic meters. While surface water is getting polluted,

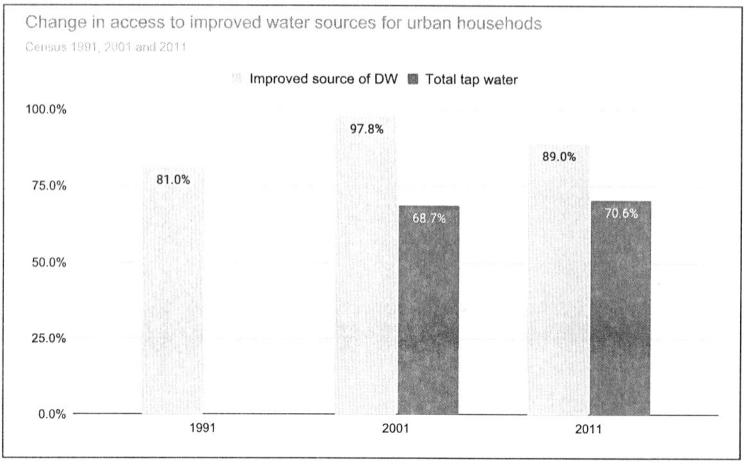

Fig. 10.2: Change in access to improved/tap water sources in urban India. *Source:* Wateraid report on state of urban water supply in India, 2018.

groundwater is getting depleted. The first census of water bodies in the country (2017-2018) reveals that out of 9.45 lakh water bodies, 18,691 or 2 per cent have been encroached. The maximum encroachment of water bodies is seen in the state of Tamil Nadu (8,366 encroached water bodies out of a total of 1,06,975, or nearly 8%), followed by Telangana (3,032 encroached water bodies out of a total of 64,056, or nearly 5%), Andhra Pradesh (3,920 encroached water bodies out of a total of 1,91,777, or 2%) and Punjab (1,578 encroached water bodies out of a total of 16,012, or nearly 10%) (Ministry of Jal Shakti, 2022). A number of lakes, ponds and wetlands in cities have vanished. Bangalore, for instance, which used to be called a 'city of thousand lakes', was left with only 280 lakes by 1960, only 80 by 1993 and is now left with merely 17 healthy lakes, the rest becoming victims of encroachments or neglect (Firstpost, 19 September 2016).

Groundwater depletion continues to happen on a large scale. The share of groundwater in net irrigated area has increased to 60 per cent, and about 85 per cent of drinking water needs are fulfilled by groundwater (Narayanmoorthy, 2022; World Bank, 2012). The story of Punjab, once the land of five rivers (now reduced to 2.5), is particularly alarming. Groundwater extraction has exceeded availability by 164 per cent, as 97 per cent of the water extracted being used for agriculture. Water tankers, never seen before in the state, have now become a common sight. Ironically, the Green Revolution which ushered in prosperity in the Punjab is also said to be the cause for the water crisis in the state. Farmers switched over to the water intensive crop of paddy and is now grown in 75 per cent of the cultivable area; worse still, 73 per cent of irrigation is now dependent on groundwater. Incentivising such inefficient practices is the policy of providing free electricity for the farm sector.

In urban India, several cities suffer from water shortage. The MoHUA has fixed 135 lpcd (litres per capita per day) as the norm for water supply. A number of projects have been executed for augmenting water supply to towns and cities. However, the per capita supply in most urban areas continues to be uneven, ranging from 37 lpcd to 298 lpcd in various cities (Wateraid, 2018). It may appear the average supply is nearer or more than the norm, but the data hide more than what they receive. The actual supply of water is between 1 and 6 hours per day; in some cities, the supply is restricted to once in two, three or four days a week. One positive achievement is the improvement in coverage. Today, piped water supply has been extended to many more households, a marked improvement from 1991. However, there is still a high dependency on bottled and tanker water within urban India.

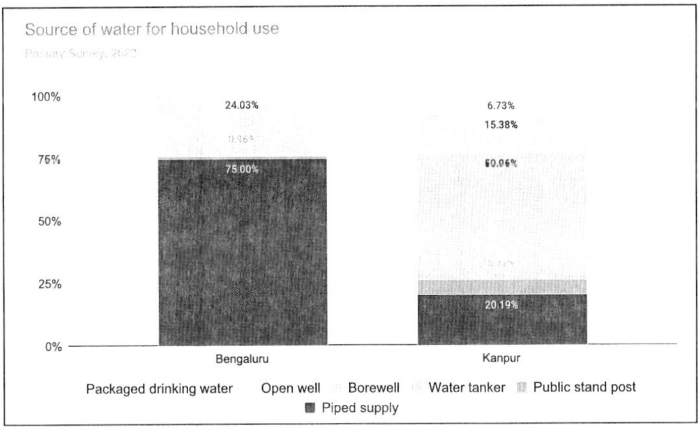

Fig. 10.3: Source of domestic water supply, migrant workers in Bengaluru and Kanpur in 2021. Bengaluru seems to have much higher penetration of piped water supply, that is however supplied every alternate day. Nearly a quarter of the migrants surveyed still depend on groundwater drawn from a bore well. In Kanpur, only about a fifth of the migrants surveyed have access to piped water supply. Nearly half of the migrants depend on water tankers, that in turn, most likely draw water from bore wells.

Source: Author, primary survey, 2022.

From a primary survey of migrants in Bengaluru and Kanpur, a mixed picture of water supply to vulnerable segments of the urban population emerges. Bengaluru seems to have much higher penetration of piped water supply, that is however supplied every alternate day. Nearly a quarter of the migrants surveyed still depend on groundwater drawn from a bore well. In Kanpur, only about a fifth of the migrants surveyed have access to piped water supply. Nearly half of the migrants depend on water tankers, that in turn, most likely draw water from bore wells.

Major issues in urban water supply

The major issues in supply of adequate and safe water to cities are the following:

1. **Lack of water sources in or close to cities** necessitate sourcing from distant places, making water supply projects capital-intensive. In Bengaluru, water is pumped from nearly 100 kilometres, sourced from the river Cauvery at massive capital and operating expenses. Chennai sources its water from a similar distance, from the river Krishna.
2. **The cost of water** supply schemes is borne by the state and central governments and through external assistance. Between 2016-2019, it is reported that over $75 billion was spent on water supply by states and the central government, and this would increase to $270 billion in the next 15 years (Aniruddh, 2019). Though water supply forms a major component of central urban development projects such as JNNURM, AMRUT and Jal Shakti Abhiyan (JSA), the future requirements are huge. For example, against the total plan size of Rs.77,640 crore of all the State Annual Action Plans (SAAP) under AMRUT, Rs. 39,011 crore (50%) has been allocated to water supply.
3. **Water losses** on account of leakage, or non-revenue water, ranges from 40 per cent to 70 per cent of supply (World Bank, 2011).
4. **Inequitable distribution** within a city. Water supply and distribution are marked by spatial variability. In Bengaluru, for instance, at least 20 per cent of the city population does

not have access to piped surface water supply simply based on their location. The peripheral areas which have grown faster that the central areas rely entirely on groundwater and bear disproportionate financial burden (Malghan *et al.*, 2013).

5. **Depletion of groundwater** and the inadequacy of piped water supply inevitably leads to reliance on groundwater, estimated to cater to 85 per cent of all drinking water needs (World Bank, 2012). Many of the apartment complexes in peripheral areas and some within the city depend on groundwater, whose supply has turned into a huge market in large cities. The 'tanker mafia' exploits consumers by overcharging, particularly during acute scarcity of water during summer months. Groundwater rejuvenation projects in some cities like Bangalore have shown positive results with rise in the levels.
6. **Water Quality** of water bodies and groundwater in several cities are found to be highly polluted. According to an analysis of critically polluted water bodies done by Central Pollution Control Board (CPCB), for the years 2013-2017, Bengaluru tops in water bodies with chemical pollution (17), followed by Telengana (12) and Kerala (6) ("Bengaluru Tops in Water Bodies with Chemical Pollution", 2018).

The Niti Ayog sounded the alarm bell in 2018 by pointing out that India is undergoing its worst water crisis in its history. There are already more than 600 million people facing acute water shortages and the critical groundwater resources which account for 40 per cent of our water supply are being depleted at unsustainable rates (NITI Aayog, 2018, p. 27). A Composite Water Management Index, said to be the country's first comprehensive and integrated national data-set for water was generated. Their predictions for India are truly frightening:

- 40 per cent of the population will have no access to drinking water by 2030.
- 21 cities including Delhi, Bengaluru, Chennai and Hyderabad will run out of groundwater by 2020, affecting 100 million people.
- 6 per cent of GDP will be lost by 2050, due to water crisis (under business-as-usual conditions).

The answers to these issues have been articulated from time to time by experts and policy makers are aware of them. What has been lacking is the will to implement. Action must be taken before we run out of both time and water. In the following section, the issues of implementation are discussed.

Approaches to solving the urban water crisis

In the first place, we must get the policy right. Although the National Water Policy of 2012 makes grandiose statements, implementation leaves much to be desired. Water being a state subject, inter-state conflicts between states over water sharing turn into political battles, which is borne out by my own experience in the case of Cauvery water dispute between Karnataka and Tamil Nadu. Eshwer Kale, lead researcher at the Watershed Organisation Trust puts it aptly: "The present policy environment in the water sector is very fragmented and facing 'hydro-schizophrenia'. There is no integration of surface and groundwater, drinking water and irrigation, and departmental coordination. The national water policy is very irrigation-centric" (Mohan, 2022).

It is therefore essential to adopt a holistic approach in addressing the multiple problems of water supply: rural-urban, drinking water-irrigation, sourcing supply-distribution, wastewater treatment-reuse, costs-pricing-subsidies, inter-state conflicts, and governance. The following issues need to be addressed on priority:

1. **Efficient use of water:** In agriculture which consumes over 80 per cent of fresh water, the issue must be addressed on two fronts: (a) excessive water used for the cultivation of paddy and sugarcane—the imperative need for changes in the cropping pattern emphasising switching over to crops that are less water intensive, and (b) scrapping the policy of free power supply for irrigation, which encourages wastage of water and cultivation of water intensive crops, apart from causing heavy financial losses to the state.
2. **Reuse of wastewater:** Managing waste or sewage flowing out of the city is as important as managing water flowing into the city for ecological sustainability. The infrastructure for treating wastewater is woefully short in Indian cities. Underground sewerage connections have touched only a small proportion

of the urban population. An interesting study by Centre for Science & Environment (Narain *et al.*, 2012) presents a particularly alarming picture of how we are 'soaking up water, polluting rivers and drowning in our own excreta'. The solution lies in treating and recycling all the wastewater generated and using it for primarily for non-potable purposes. At present, the quantity of wastewater recycled is far below the potential. We can also explore using recycled water for drinking purposes after treating it up to the required standards, as is done in Singapore (NeWater). But then, it must be made acceptable to the people by creating awareness.

3. **Regulating groundwater extraction:** Despite laws and regulations, this problem has eluded a solution. Given the increasing demand for water in urban areas and shortage of surface water supply by the municipal authorities and water supply boards, this is a challenging task. Some states have regulatory laws but implementation is lax. A participatory process is likely to yield better results.
4. **Water conservation:** It is common knowledge that considerable quantity of water-supplied by nature or in our daily use is wasted and if conserved, can serve as a solution to the water problem. For instance, according to some experts, the quantity of rainfall received in Bengaluru (800 mm per year), should suffice to meet the water needs of the city. Though late, the central government has woken up to the crisis and launched the JSA in 2019 to promote water conservation, recharge and rainwater harvesting, initially in 256 water stressed districts in the country and later covering all the 740 districts. States are also preparing an inventory of water bodies which is expected to help in preventing or dealing with encroachments.
5. **Water pricing:** A highly politicised and sensitive issue, pricing continues to be a ticklish problem. Drinking water is considered by some as a basic right and a public good and by some others as an economic good. There is a wide gap between the cost of production and supply of water and the revenue derived from levy of water charges. What should be the right or appropriate

price to be charged by consumers has been the subject of much discussion. Water being a state subject, different states follow different methods, broadly based on metered and non-metered systems, with variations in actual determination of the price. The National Water Policy of 2002 laid down the principle according to which water charges should be fixed in such a way that they cover at least the operation and maintenance charges of providing the service initially and part of the capital cost subsequently and the subsidy to the disadvantaged and poorer sections of the society should be well targeted and transparent.

6. **Water governance:** Reforms in the water sector are long overdue. A number of studies have been conducted and recommendations made on the structure of water pricing, private sector participation, reducing water losses, and overall, improving the efficiency as well as lowering costs and ensuring equity. Sooner the states wake up to the urgency of implementing necessary reforms, the better. The political, economic and technical issues involved in the water sector demand a strong coordination mechanism and an effective implementation strategy. A high-level decision making body headed by the Prime Minister, with Ministers of Water Resources, Urban Development and Rural Development as members at the national level, and one headed by the Chief Minister, with Ministers of concerned departments as members at the state level must be set up with agenda to resolve issues from time to time.

As the latest World Water Development Report, 2023 warns: the global urban population facing water scarcity will touch 2.4 billion and India will be the most severely affected country (WWDR, 2023).

Land and Housing

The ramifications of urban land problems have been traversed in Part II. Urban land may be considered one of the most complex issues in the overall context of urban development. Within this paradigm, the issue of affordable housing needs to be addressed on priority. Yet, at the heart of the question of affordable housing is the question of land.

With unregulated prices, the provision of affordable housing depends on the vagaries of the land market. The competition for land is so intense that encroachments have extended to private lands. The land mafia in large cities have become a serious threat to individual life and property. In the city of Bengaluru, for instance, the author is privy to several cases ranging from minor encroachments of a neighbour's property to large scale encroachments of public and private land. The following instance is cited for illustration.

Chikka Kallasandra Lake

The lake that was originally spread over an area of 12.5 acres has now shrunk to five acres of a stinking water body. Connected to two valleys in the city, it helped in irrigation of hundreds of acres in the surrounding area and in balancing excess water upstream and reducing flooding. The lake now looks like a wasteland with piles of garbage, sewage, and illegal structures.

The issue of lake encroachments was first raised by the residents when heavy rains during 1993-1994 had brought construction debris into the lake but it was only in 2006 that case were filed against 48 encroachers. But no action was taken till 2014 when the Tahsildar demolished and cleared encroachments from seven acres of land. But the encroachers returned in a matter of weeks, after either obtaining stay orders from the courts or through political influence. According to a resident, the corporator had played a major role in the encroachment and other illegalities. During 2012-2013, those who went to survey the land were threatened and one official was locked up. A mahzar report filed by the villagers of Chikkalasandra had named several individuals of constructing buildings and renting them out which went to prove that the encroachers were not poor individuals without a roof on their head (Kulkarni, 2022). The case highlights encroachments on land and lakes in cities take place in defiance of the law, corruption amongst the authorities concerned, politicians and officials connive and even encourage such illegal activities. The people who raise these issues are threatened and silenced.

Housing Shortage

The urban housing shortage in India was estimated at 18.78 million dwelling units in 2012 by the Technical Group constituted by the Ministry of Housing and Urban Poverty Alleviation (MoHUPA) (at the commencement of the 12th Five Year Plan), of which 95.6 per cent came under the Economically Weaker Sections (EWS) and Low Income Group (LIG) categories. Though committed to providing housing for all, Government of India's housing policy has been shifting over the years, from being provider to facilitator to communities and markets, to self-help housing, to once again direct provision since 2005 (Batra, L., 2009). The Housing Policy of 2015 outlining its vision "to create a vibrant, sustainable and inclusive housing market in India", adopted a muti-pronged approach that included, inter alia, participation of the private sector, cooperatives, industrial sector (labour housing) and NGOs, reiterating goal of 'Housing for All' by 2022—the 75th year of our independence. This dream remains unfulfilled.

The irony of the urban housing situation in India is that on the one hand, there is a huge shortage and on the other, there are excessive stocks of vacant properties. As per the 2011 Census, 11 million housing units were vacant across cities in the country. The empty stocks pertain mostly to the higher and upper mid-housing segments built in the private sector while the demand is in the lower end categories to house the economically weaker and low-income sections. It can be argued that both the public sector (land and housing agencies) and the private sector (developers) have failed to deliver what is really required at the right time and the right price. The parastatal agencies are constrained by limited resources and capacity resulting in delays in land acquisition, construction and supply of sites or houses and services. Private housing where builders expect a higher premium has become unaffordable not only to the poor but to the middle classes who resort to home loans with Equated Monthly Instalments (EMIs) taking away a fair chunk of their income.

Taking into account the economic, social, spatial and political dimensions of the problem of this peculiar demand and supply situation, what are the options to find a viable solution to the housing problem in India?

Affordable Housing

The term 'affordable housing' can be understood in different ways by different sections of people based on their incomes and willingness to pay a certain amount of money to meet their housing needs. As per government definition, in general terms, it can refer to any house, rented or owned, in which the costs comprise less than 30 per cent of the household monthly income. In specific terms, the MoHUA provides a definition based on factors like the size of the house, its price and income of the household, as shown in the table below:

Category	Size (sq ft)	Price (Rs. lakh)	EMI (Rs./month)
EWS	300-500	< 5	4,000-5,000
LIG	500-600	7-12	5,000-10,000
MIG	600-1,200	12-50	10,000-30,000

The Reserve Bank of India, based on loans given by banks for building houses or buying flats, defines affordable housing as one where the cost of a residential property is less than Rs. 65 lakhs in metro cities and less than Rs. 50 lakhs in non-metros.

Several affordable housing programmes have been implemented by the government with varying degrees of success in different states. The models include Basic Services for Urban Poor (BSUP) under JNNURM, Rajiv Awas Yojana (RAY), Pradhan Mantri Awas Yojana—Urban (PMAY-U) and Slum Rehabilitation Schemes by state governments, primarily aimed at the weaker sections. The success rate has, however, not been encouraging. Under BSUP, the largest housing programme in India, out of 1517 projects approved, only 22 were completed, and many houses allotted to beneficiaries were unoccupied. "Only 52 per cent out of the total one million approved housing units were constructed and out of the approved, only 36 per cent are actually occupied" (Patel, Sluizas *et al.*, 2015). In Bengaluru, about 57 per cent of BSUP stock was left unoccupied, and in Hyderabad, a staggering 90 per cent (Mahadeviah, Datey *et al.*, 2013). The story of affordable housing in the private sector is more disappointing. It catered to only one per cent of the shortage recorded by MoHUPA, with only 78,000 units launched all over India (Monitor, 2013).

Analysing the poor performance of affordable housing, be it rehabilitation or subsidized housing or private sector, Dubagunta and Patel (2015) conclude that from the perspective of end user, "spatial location of site, access to employment opportunities, tenure, affordability, presence of infrastructure, access to amenities, community relations and design of unit have proved to be the significant factors influencing the success rate of any model. Negligence of a single factor may lead to underperformance of the overall model". Scaling up of affordable housing provision by the private sector faces the dual challenge of high input costs and a much more lucrative premium housing market (Mint, May 5, 2023). These challenges, in sum, lead to the risk of impoverishment leading to lower occupancy ratio in rehabilitation housing, presence of high rental component against policy guidelines in subsidized housing.

Impact of Displacement and Resettlement of Slum Dwellers in Bengaluru

The Bengaluru Metro Rail Corporation Ltd. (BMRCL) was set up in 2005 with the objective of facilitating the development and construction of metro rail to meet the commuter needs of the rapidly growing metro city of Bengaluru, with a population of over 10 million. The project entailed acquisition of properties, public as well as private. Most of the people affected by the acquisition of land and property happened to be slum dwellers and informal settlers in the city and were subject to displacement, eviction, or relocation under the rehabilitation package. Rehabilitation can be of two kinds—in situ, i.e., rehabilitation in the same place or relocation to another place. In this case, the latter policy was adopted.

Smitha & Pal's (2008) study pertains to relocation of slum dwellers from two slums, one in located in Basaveshwara Nagar, and the other in Jai Bheema Nagar. The former was centrally located, just about a kilometre from the city railway station and the central bus station. Out of the 120 affected families, 65 families accepted the rehabilitation package while the remaining 55 opted for cash compensation. In 2010, the 65 families were relocated in Srigandada Kavalu, about 16 km from the earlier location. Those residing at Jai Bheema Nagar, located on Sampige Road, a busy locality in the city, were shifted to Peenya, near Yeshwantpur. The new areas were thus away from the city centre, about 7-10 kilometres from the original location. The study of the two resettlement projects yielded interesting results.

The relocated areas affected the occupational pattern in both cases. Overall, the proportion of male members engaged in the informal sector declined. The process of spatial relocation has had both positive and negative effects on the occupational status of both men and women. Some families did benefit from rehabilitation, particularly those shifted to Peenya which happens to be large industrial belt. There was upward mobility among a few men and women who were better educated. A clearly beneficial impact on women was in their being relatively freed from daily burdens like fetching water, fuel wood etc., which also resulted in increase in the supply of young female labour. The adverse impact of rehabilitation to a new place was clearly seen in the occupational profile of women. On the whole, post-rehabilitation, both men and women had to commute longer distances after relocation to access workplace, market, health care and educational facilities, thus incurring higher expenditure, resulting in erosion of real income and purchasing power of households, and women in particular.

In all, the study reveals that the new residential complexes to which the slum dwellers were relocated had all basic amenities and a better living environment but access to multiple employment opportunities were lost and access to services mentioned above became more difficult. A valuable finding is the fact that education and acquisition of skills provide better and higher income job opportunities.

Rental Housing

A strategy highlighted in the 2015 policy relates to the importance of promoting Social Rental Housing with a focus on urban poor and vulnerable sections with government support. Arguing for a market driven approach, it called for removal of legal, financial and administrative barriers and converting slums on municipal land for rental housing. The target groups were identified as migrant labour, working women and men, students, widows, transgender persons or any other vulnerable groups. The GoI also prepared a Model Tenancy Act to overcome the complex tenurial problems. It urged the states to reflect these reform measures in the state housing policies and the ULBs to play a proactive role in implementing them.

In India, there is a predominant preference for home ownership. In metros, the first thing youngsters look for soon after getting a white-collar job or getting married is buying a house. Banks with their mantra of EMIs, are only too eager to welcome them and offer the required loan. The distribution of households as per 2011 census shows that 87 per cent (rural and urban) are owned and only 11per cent are rented. In urban areas, 68 per cent of the houses are owner occupied and 28 per cent rented. Several other developing countries such as Brazil (25%), South Africa (22%), Thailand (13%) and Mexico (11%), and developed economies such as USA (34%) and UK (31%) seem to prefer owned houses. Exceptions are a country like Germany which shows a high preference for rentals (60%). However, many among the low income sections of the population, particularly in large cities, cannot afford home ownership and are forced to go in for rental accommodation.

Rental housing has several advantages—affordability as there is no investment cost and no need to borrow, lower transaction costs, hardly any maintenance cost, and immediate shelter for migrants. For students pursuing education (increasing numbers moving to big cities), employees shifting to another city on transfer and those seeking temporary accommodation, it is particularly beneficial. The major constraints are: high rents in big metros, huge deposits demanded by landlords and reluctance on the part of some landlords to let out to persons belonging to certain communities, which is a social problem.

2011 census says that there were 21 million households living on rent. But the housing market is unregulated and the old rent control legislations in states having lapsed or not in operation. They were considered as overwhelmingly being in favour of the tenant, giving rise to bitter disputes between the landlord and the tenant, and hampering construction of new houses. The Model Tenancy Act seeks to put in place a uniform set of regulations which would be fair both to the tenant and the landlord. It aims to eliminate ambiguities in rental agreements and introduce consistency in matters relating to security deposit, termination of the agreement, rent escalation, maintenance of the property etc. It has also proposed setting up a Rent Court to resolve disputes and protecting the tenant from unjustified evictions while protecting the landlords from illegal possession by notorious tenants.

The onus of implementing the Model Act lies with the states who must pass separate legislations and bring them into force. As of now, only a few states seem to have modified their rent control laws. Going by the past experience of the operation of earlier laws, enforcement is not going to be easy. It is important to ensure that the new law is free from ambiguities and cases before the Rent Court are disposed of within a specific time frame.

Affordable Rental Housing Complex (ARHC) Scheme under the Pradhan Mantri Awas Yojana—Urban (PMAY-U)

During the COVID-19 pandemic and ensuing lockdown, a very large number of migrant workers were unable to earn money and therefore pay rents in the destination locations. This resulted in a mass reverse exodus of migrants back to their origin locations, which was widely publicized in Indian and international media. In the wake of this crisis, the Government of India announced the Affordable Rental Housing Complex (ARHC) scheme, as a component or vertical of the PMAY-U. The aim of the scheme was to enable access to decent, affordable rental housing for migrants and the urban poor. It consisted of two models of rental housing provision—one wherein existing vacant government-built housing (under previous schemes) could be converted to rental housing through a concession agreement with a private entity, while the other encouraged private and public landowners to contribute their land towards developing rental housing for their own workers and others (Harish, 2021).

As of writing, the scheme is yet to mature but there seem to be some takers for such partnerships. One such case is in Ahmedabad, wherein a private developer has repaired and retrofitted about 1,300 houses near the Ring Road of the city and is now letting these houses out for a rent of Rs. 5,000 per month. While such a rent is unaffordable to a vast majority of poor migrant workers, the developer has accommodated lower-middle to middle-income households in their project. At the end of year 2022, the project seems well maintained and the developer claims that there is a huge waiting list of households who want to live here on rent. While this can serve as an example of how rental housing markets may be instituted in the country's cities, it is to be seen how the projects and scheme will develop over the 25 year time period, the concession agreements are supposed to run.

Fig. 10.4: An Affordable Rental Housing Complex (ARHC) project at Thaltej, Ahmedabad.

Source: Swastik Harish.

Future trends and challenges in urban housing

It must be recognized that both the public sector and the private sector have contributed in a big way to the housing demands of the people, yet there are shortcomings in delivering adequate, satisfactory and timely final products to the consumers. Successful interventions by the public or private sector or in a Public Private Partnership model

(PPP), have shown that it is possible to achieve the desired results where people, be they slum dwellers or other income categories of people are taken into confidence during the planning and execution process. In the Slum Rehabilitation Scheme of 2010 in Ahmedabad, land was handed over to the private developers with additional FSI to rehabilitate the slum dwellers at the same plot. "In this scheme, the developer gains TDR (Transfer of Development Rights), slum dwellers gain Improved housing units with leasehold unit for free, and finally well being of the poor without any financial commitment" (Dubagunta and Patel, *op cit.*). The role played by an NGO, the Mahila Housing Trust strengthened the process by bridging the gap between suppliers and beneficiaries. There are similar success stories of rehabilitating slum dwellers in other states like the Lakshmipuram case in Bengaluru (see Part II).

Private developers have of late, turned their attention to what they consider affordable housing. The problem with the real estate sector is lack of transparency and non-adherence to their promises made in advertisements with respect to completion of works and handing over possession of flats as per the time schedule. The bad quality of work, demanding high security deposits which gets locked up if there are delays in execution, etc. lead to hardship to the consumers. The central government enacted the Real Estate Regulatory Authority Act (RERA) in 2016 to reform and regulate the real estate sector by ensuring greater transparency, financial discipline, and accountability. But the functioning of the RERAs during the last few years leaves much to be desired. A recent case reported in the media in Bengaluru (2022) serves as a sharp illustration. About 100 people from Maple Park West Allottees Association in Binnypet area went on a protest demanding the builder to honour his commitment. Their list of woes include—non-completion of the work even 27 months after the delivery date (December 2019), extraction of 80-90 per cent of the cost from the home buyers, diversion of funds, getting three extensions from RERA and to cap it all, the developer asking the allottees to sign a compromise document with January 2024 as an exit clause and 15 months no delay compensation. The Karnataka Home Buyers Forum has said that most of the housing projects in Bengaluru have been delayed for more than three years and expressed its disappointment at the failure of RERA to provide relief the buyers, suspecting corruption in the organisation.

The solution lies in formulating an appropriate policy framework that provides for a participatory approach involving the government (concerned local housing/local authority), the private sector/developer, the consumers/people for whom the projects are undertaken and a non-governmental organisation to act as a bridge to coordinate with all stakeholders in the planning and execution of housing projects, with transparency and accountability as the guiding principles. There is also need for an effective monitoring mechanism involving the key stakeholders to ensure smooth implementation.

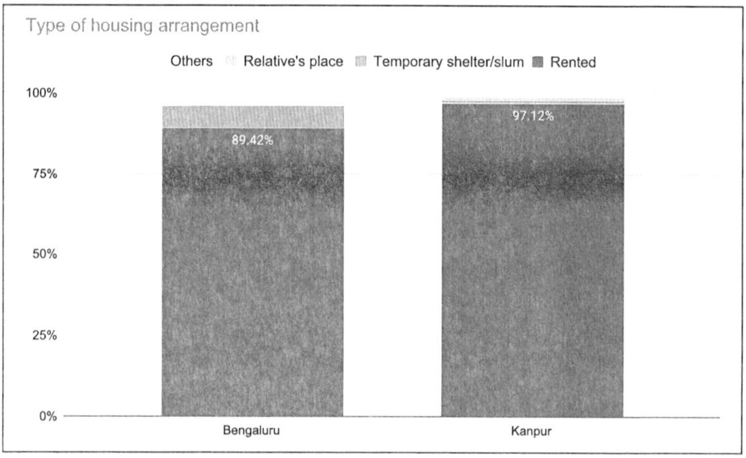

Fig. 10.5: Type of housing arrangement, migrant workers in Bengaluru and Kanpur.

Source: Author, Primary Survey, 2022.

From this primary survey of migrants in Bengaluru and Kanpur, a picture of housing arrangements of vulnerable segments of the urban population emerges. The vast majority of migrants surveyed in Bengaluru and Kanpur live in rented accommodation. This is a common feature for a lot of migrants as they might not want to own a house in the destination city and/or may not have the means to afford one. The Government of India has recently launched the first national level rental housing scheme—the Affordable Rental Housing Complex (ARHC) scheme as part of the Pradhan Mantri Awas Yojana-Urban (PMAY-U). The housing/slum upgradation programme which served a useful purpose seems to have been, unfortunately given up. Serious thought must be given to revive this scheme in an appropriate manner.

Mobility: Evading a Solution

The MoHUA brought out a National Urban Transport Policy in 2006 whose stated objective was "to ensure safe, affordable, quick, comfortable, reliable and sustainable access for the growing number of city residents to jobs, education, recreation and such other needs within our cities" (Ministry of Housing and Urban Affairs, 2006, p. 3). The objective was sought to be achieved through a multi-pronged approach that would revolve around the following measures:

1. Integrating land use and transport planning.
2. Equitable allocation of land space.
3. Priority to the use of public transport, its quality and pricing.
4. Technologies for Public Transport.
5. Integrated public transport system.
6. Financing-encouraging high capacity public transport systems through the mechanisms of Special Purpose Vehicles (SPVs) and providing viability gap funding.
7. Priority to non-motorised transport.

Even after seventeen years since the announcement of this policy, we cannot claim to have made substantial progress in any of the seven areas. Urban transport in India is a shining example of the French proverb, "*plus ça change, plus c'est la même chose*" (the more things change, the more they remain the same). Let us look at the key issues.

Exploding number of vehicles

The number of auto-mobile vehicles has shown a continuously rising trend resulting in increasing congestions and pollution.

There is hardly any city in India where integration of land use and transport planning has been achieved. Although it may form part of the master plan, on ground, there is little evidence of it. Large portions of land space including road space is occupied by private vehicles. Efforts to provide separate lanes for buses have met with little success.

Parking of vehicles has emerged as a serious problem with private vehicles encroaching on every available vacant public space including those used by pedestrians.

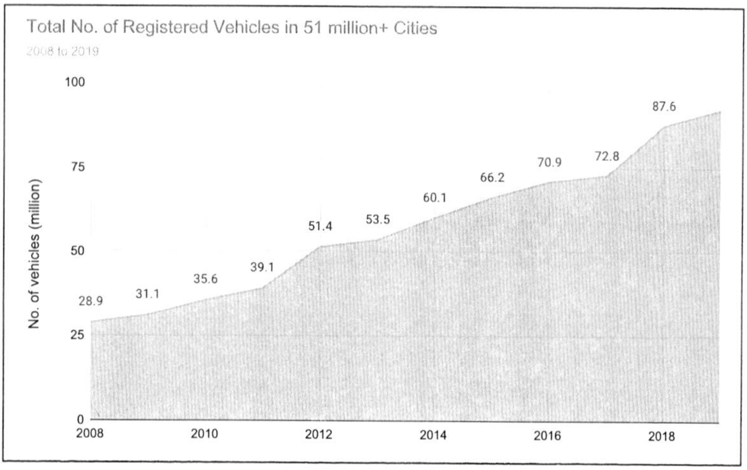

Fig. 10.6: Number of vehicles registered in 51 million plus cities of India, 2008 to 2019.

Source: MoRTH, (2019).

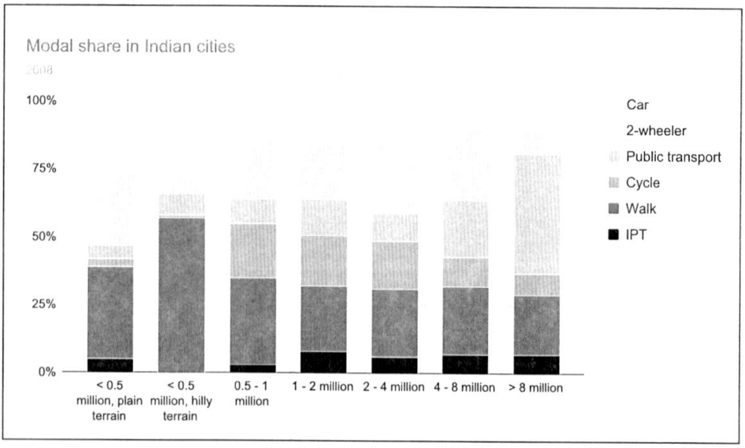

Fig. 10.7: Modal share in Indian cities, 2008.

Source: Wilbur Smith Associates, 2008, p. 32.

Government's aim of increasing the share of public transport to 70 per cent is yet to be realised. In fact, the World Bank (2014) reported that the share of public transport in Indian cities declined from 70 per cent in 1994 to 40 per cent in 2007 (The World Bank, 2014). City category wise data on modal share (from 2008) can be seen in Fig. 10.7.

Public vs. Private Transport

Failure to promote public transport is the primary cause for increase in the use of private transport and the consequent problems of traffic congestion, use of land space and parking and more pollution. Fig. 10.7 shows that except cities with a population exceeding 8 million, the share of public transport is very poor. Intermediate private transport such as autorickshaws and cabs, especially Olas and Ubers are serving a very useful purpose in providing long distance as well as last mile connectivity. However, regulation of private transport needs closer attention to enable ease of commuting by this mode.

Metro vs. Bus Transport

Metro Rail was first introduced in the megacities of cities of Delhi, Bengaluru, Chennai, Mumbai, Hyderabad and Kolkata and has now been extended to 15 other cities. While it is a very good form of public transport (less travel time and pollution-free), it is highly capital-intensive. It is therefore essential to examine the cost-effectiveness of metro rail projects before launching them, especially in smaller cities. Do we really need metros in cities where the population is less than 25 lakhs such as in places like Agra, Meerut, Patna and Varanasi? Would it not be more prudent to improve the bus transport and the road infrastructure which would cost far less and serve the purpose? It is essential to fix a norm for the size class of cities where metro rail can be introduced; 50 lakh population appears to be a viable proposition in a country like India.

Cost of Commute and Financial Viability of public transport undertakings

Provision of Affordable Transport is a key element of urban transportation policy. How affordable is public transport in India? Estimates may vary from city to city but the generally accepted norm it should not be more than 10 per cent of the household income. Unless made affordable, public transport is likely to lose passengers, as seen in the case of Bengaluru where two-wheeler is considered the cheapest mode of transport, which also accounts for the largest number of two-wheelers in the country (about 7 million). If the total cost of commute is taken into account, i.e., where a person has to use different modes of transport to reach her destination—bus+metro or bus+auto or bus+metro+auto (last mile connectivity), then even a car can work out cheaper. If the proportion of household expenditure towards transport among the poorer sections is high, it seriously affects their livelihoods. In a city like Bengaluru, the cost of travelling by public transport is considered high compared to other major cities in India.

As the investments needed for the transport industry are huge, service providers end up making losses and fixation of tariffs to suit the purse of the common man becomes problematic, given the price sensitivity of the Indian commuting public. Government subsidy therefore becomes inevitable. The question is how much subsidy? It has also been argued that subsidies can lead to inefficiencies. What is the scope for non-fare revenues apart from advertisements? These issues need to be examined in depth and a viable pricing for public transport must be worked out. The underlying policy must be to promote public transport and discourage use of private transport, failing which traffic in our cities will become more chaotic.

Integrated Urban Transport System

Despite the emphasis on an integrated transport system, in reality, the approach continues to be conventional. The critical issue relates to lack of effective coordination amongst the multiple agencies engaged in managing mobility—road transport corporations, metro rail companies, private transport, traffic regulators etc. The proposal of the Central Government to set up Urban Land Transport Authorities in metro cities has not been effectively implemented. Only very recently, Bengaluru has established a Bengaluru Metropolitan Land Transport Authority that is tasked with integrating all modes of transport within the city (*News Trail*, Dec. 27, 2022).

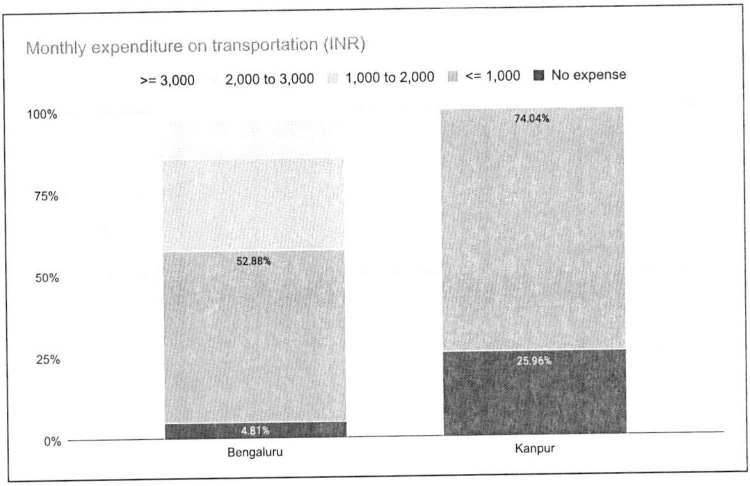

Fig. 10.8: Monthly expenditure on transportation, migrant workers in Bengaluru and Kanpur.

Source: Author, Primary Survey, 2022.

From a primary survey of migrants in Bengaluru and Kanpur, a picture of transportation expenses of vulnerable segments of the urban population emerges. It is obvious from the primary survey that most migrants spend quite less on intra-city commuting. A quarter of the surveyed migrants in Kanpur spend no money at all, and the rest spend less that INR 1,000 per month. The sum of these categories in Bengaluru is just over 50 per cent. There are very few migrants that seem to be spending a significant amount on transportation. This implies that their work is likely close to their accommodation.

Apart from integration within the sector, it must be recognised that urban transport is closely related to issues like housing, land prices and environment (congestion, air pollution, waste production). The way to move forward is, as Satterthwaite (2021) has suggested, restructuring urban transport policies in a way to not only restrict their benefits towards better urban mobility but also solve other urban agendas such as improving housing, reducing poverty (by increasing income earning opportunities, and lowering transport cost), reducing disaster risk, and adaptation and mitigation of climate change. A focus on 5 Ds may be able to generate better results: Density, Diversity of Land Uses (jobs and homes, provision for walking, bicycles and cars),

Design (of street layout that encourages pedestrians and bicycles), Destination Accessibility (what can be reached within 30 minutes—the idea of a 15-minute city), and Distance to Transit.

There is also the problem of human behaviour-reluctance to use public transport in view of lack of last-mile connectivity, and most importantly, the greater convenience offered by private vehicles. Essentially, it reflects human behaviour, with personal interest overriding public interest. Public education needs to be taken up to induce change towards better law compliance.

Ensuring safe, affordable and reliable urban transport in general and prioritising public sector in particular will perhaps be the biggest challenge in managing our cities.

Environment and Climate Change

"It took just 120 years for humans to alter the planet's climate."
(Inter-governmental Panel on *Climate Change*, 2021)

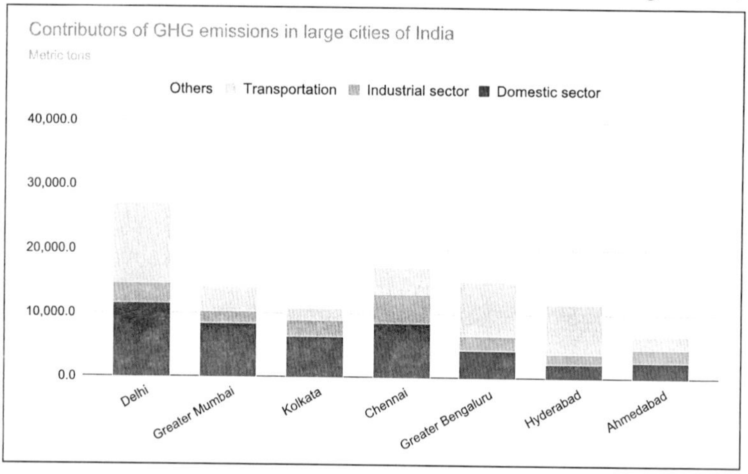

Fig. 10.9: Contributors of GHG emissions in large cities of India.

Source: Ramachandra, 2015.

The data produced by the above report says it all: in the first two decades of the twenty first century, the average total global surface temperature was 0.99 degrees higher than the 1850-1900 level. This is an indicator of the unprecedented levels of warming caused by human beings. "Since 2001, concentrations (of GHGs) have continued to increase in the atmosphere, reaching averages of 410 ppm (parts per million) for carbon dioxide (CO_2), 1,866 ppb (parts per billion) for methane (CH_4), and 332 ppbs for nitrous oxide in 2019". These greenhouse gases emitted on account of human activities have been the primary driver of tropospheric (the first and lowest layer of the earth's atmosphere) warming since 1979.

Cities and greenhouse gas emissions

Cities are responsible for producing over three quarters of the world's carbon emissions that cause climate change.

Unprecedented rains and floods in Bengaluru in August 2022 lead to demolition of several structures that had cropped up encroaching storm water drains and causing serious hardship and loss of property to a large number of people residing in vulnerable areas (slums) and low lying areas. The coastal cities of Chennai and Mumbai are subjected to flooding almost every year. During a water scarcity in Maharashtra in 2010 water had to be shipped on trains to affected areas. In November 2021—Janpath area in Delhi recorded a PM2.5 reading of 655—43 times above WHO's safe level.

Air pollution causes over 7 million premature deaths across the world. India accounts for nearly 25 per cent of these deaths (World Health Organisation, 2021). The impact of air pollution costs the economy over 3 per cent of GDP or approximately Rs. 3.9 lakh crores (Dalberg *et al.*, 2021).

According to World Economic Forum (2022), 33 coastal cities are sinking at the rate of one cm every year; they include Tianjin (China), Jakarta (Indonesia) and Houston (US). The sinking is caused because of three reasons: (a) people pumping water from ground, (b) oil and gas drilling, and (c) rapid construction. Thirty years ago, Jakarta was sinking at 30 cm a year. The government of Indonesia banned extraction of groundwater for a year in North Jakarta and found tremendous improvement. Indonesia is now shifting its capital 100 miles away to Java Island with a view to protect ten million residents from more flooding.

The GoI has formulated a National Action Plan for Climate Change (NAPCC) and set up eight Missions to implement the Plan.

They relate to solar, enhanced energy efficiency, sustainable habitat, water, sustaining the Himalayan ecosystems, forest, sustainable agriculture, and strategic knowledge for climate change. Subsequently, three more were added: (1) National Coastal Mission, (2) Human Health and Climate Change, and (3) Sustainable Transport. All the eleven missions are, directly or indirectly are relevant to the urban environment and city activities. The success of the missions depends a great deal on the state and local governments. GoI has asked the states to align their action plans to be in sync with the NAPCC. Some states like Tamil Nadu have made considerable progress while a majority are yet to wake up to the realities of climate change. The missions are expected to help us "achieving the goal to reduce overall emission intensity".

The climate crisis and the role of cities

One of the toughest challenges cities have to face will be to protect the environment and tackle the climate change. There is no dearth of literature depicting the dangers of ignoring action to reduce the risks posed by rise in temperatures, pollution of air and water, loss of tree cover, disasters like heavy and untimely rains, floods, cyclones, droughts, fires, and heat waves.

The Inter-Governmental Panel on Climate Change (IPCC) Report (2022)—presents a detailed assessment of climate change impacts, risks and adaptation in cities. Briefly, the following picture emerges:

> By 2050, almost 70 per cent of world's growing population will live in urban areas, many in unplanned or informal settlements. As a result, today's children and future generations are more likely to be exposed and vulnerable to climate change and related risks such as flooding, heat stress, water scarcity, poverty and hunger…

Stressing the imperative need to keep the global temperature increase within 1.5° to 2°C limits, the Report warns that failure to do so will lead to more challenging climate extremes which will be irreversible. The urban scenario is alarming:

- Cities will be subject to the worst impacts of climate change-larger carbon footprints, intense air pollution, heat waves, variability of rainfall, water drought, incessant precipitation leading to flooding and rising sea levels posing grave risks to coastal cities (we have a coastline of 7,500 kms) such as Chennai, Mumbai, Kolkota and Vishakapatnam.

- India has 43 of the world's most environmentally risky cities.
- Climate change will make farming less viable and migration to cities will grow.
- If not managed in time, the city could transform itself into its dark twin, embodying vulnerability, inequity, and instability.

The IPCC had observed that our cities and hills are witnessing unplanned and unabated development, turning environment into a state that cannot absorb flood water or heat anywhere, there is a need to redesign them; climate change may be global, but the challenges are local (2022). Holding out a dire warning about the consequences of inaction, Chairman of IPCC, Hoesung Lee quotes the example of Bengaluru:

> Bengaluru where local communities traditionally managed a network of water tanks of immense ecological importance, provides one such example of inaction. In the last half-century, urban development has threatened the blue network to such an extent that Bengaluru now depends on long distance water transfers that create political conflict and a dense network of private bore wells depleting the city's water resources.

The report also flags some of the best practices in India, referring in particular to the adaptation measures in cities such as Bhubaneswar, Indore and Surat (p. 964) which have enabled people to make cities resilient to climate change.

Here are some remedial measures:

1. Develop climate resilience in city life by adopting the required climate adaptation measures and planning for climate mitigations.
2. Augment water conservation through rainwater harvesting and increasing green spaces, lakes and wetlands; remove

encroachments on water bodies and storm water drains, minimise large project oriented expensive long distance water transfers.

3. Use principles of passive architecture for buildings in cities-building with nature, not against it (traditional Indian practice), instead of unsustainable glass facades. Research by Centre for Science and Environment (CSE) has shown that when temperature exceeds 28 °C, the energy demand for cooling soars in cities.
4. Increase public transport connectivity, reduce use of private auto vehicles, provide more walking and cycling spaces.
5. Increase tree cover, especially in places where poorer people live; the shade that trees provide is an important form of climate adaptation measure (Delhi has much more tree cover in richer areas than in poorer places).

The Food and Agriculture Organisation (FAO) of the UN has recommended urban agriculture including animal rearing within cities as a useful means to promote sustainable city practices and to tackle poverty. Encouraging horticulture, fish farms, domestic animal farms and wetland development would contribute to poverty alleviation and food security. The World Food Summit in 1996 (Food and Agriculture Organisation, 1996) highlighted the need to increase access to food in the wake of increasing urbanisation. Some cities have introduced innovative practices towards this end. Kolkata, for instance, has established a 3,900 acre wetland in the peri-urban area for the purpose of fisheries that has yielded immense benefits—several ponds benefiting from 1,300 MLD treated waste water discharged from the city, 13,000 tons of fish providing livelihoods for 60,000 people, 150 tons of vegetables.

Governing the Urban Commons

The importance of 'Commons' or common properties was first highlighted by Ostrom (1990), a political scientist who won the Nobel Prize for Economics in 2009, in her book 'Governing the Commons and the Rational Choice Controversy'. As commonly understood, the 'commons' include all public land, forests, tanks and other water bodies, wetlands, grazing land, pathways, beaches in coastal towns and other spaces not owned by any private individuals. In a modern economic context, 'commons' is taken to mean any open and unregulated resource such as the atmosphere, oceans, rivers, ocean fish stocks, or even an office refrigerator (Rowe, 2007). As economic development gathered pace and the demand for natural resources increased, protection of the commons has proved extremely difficult.

The 'urban commons' include, apart from those mentioned above, streets, footpaths, parks, playgrounds, and other public spaces. The increasing demand of land for urban uses has resulted in an intense competition between public and private spaces, and encroachment of public spaces. Government and the public agencies have lost vast extents of valuable urban land to land grabbers in cities and recovering the lost land is a Herculean task, many of them involving litigation. The metropolitan regions of large cities include vast extents of public land earmarked for public uses. While protecting them by itself is a huge task, the real threat comes from private developers and political interests. As cities expand in space and grow in population, what we are witnessing is nothing less than a 'tragedy of the commons', the concept popularized by Hardin (1968), an American ecologist, that drew attention to "the damage that innocent actions by individuals can inflict on the environment".

The world has changed a lot since 1968, particularly so India where damage to the environment is inflicted not by innocent actions but by deliberate design. A recent instance of an attempt to converting grasslands near Bengaluru (part of the BMR) throws light on how vested interests circumvent honest attempts by committed officials to protect sensitive environmental areas).

The Case of Hesaraghatta Lake in Bengaluru

Hesaraghatta is a large village with a population of a little over 8,000, located in Bengaluru North Taluka, about 20 kms from the main city. The lake served as the first source of water supply to Bengaluru right from 1896, and the National Institute of Horticulture is situated here. In 2020, the Chief Conservator of Karnataka (CCF) submitted a proposal to the government to declare the lakebed and grasslands as a conservation reserve as they constituted important reservoirs of biodiversity and a refuge for endangered species of birds, butterflies and mammals. The proposal was considered by the Karnataka State Wildlife Board (SWB) which surprisingly rejected the proposal, though it was chaired by the chief minister and consisted mostly of professionals. A PIL was filed in the High Court of Karnataka alleging that the Board's decision taken under duress, be set aside. The Court allowed the plea and went on to observe that the CCF's proposal had been rejected in a cryptic and cavalier manner, ignoring the provisions of the Wildlife Protection Act, 1972, and suffered from the vice of non-application of mind.

It later came to light that when the deliberations of the SWB were going on, the MLA of the area in whose constituency the grasslands fall, had barged into the Board's meeting hall in January 2021 and exerted pressure on the Board members to reject the proposal to declare the grasslands as a reserve area, obviously with an eye on using the place for some non-public purpose. There were attempts in the past to set up a film city or a holiday theme park which somehow did not fructify. The matter is expected to come up again before the SWB shortly to reconsider its earlier decision.

Clearly, this is a case of misgovernance. It is mostly the zeal and persistent efforts of certain individuals and groups committed to environmental protection that has to a limited extent controlled the damage at least in certain areas. Ostrom (1990) rightly observed: "Neither the state nor the market is uniformly successful in enabling individuals to sustain long-term, productive use of natural resources systems with reasonable degrees of success over long periods of time" (p. 1). While protecting the natural environment of the urban habitat is important in the interests of the health of the people and a certain spatial order of the city, in developing societies, the state has a responsibility in promoting economic development. Striking a balance between the two will be a continuous struggle.

Matters of Daily Concern to Citizens, Still Unaddressed

While water, land and housing, mobility and climate change constitute the major problems, certain other issues which matter in city management are briefly discussed below.

Land Titles: Problem-ridden

The right to property is recognized by the constitution but not the title to property. Property has two characteristics, (1) 'possession', implying control of possessor over the property, and (2) 'title', that is, the right against others who shall recognize the right of the person to control the property even when it is not in the possession of the person who owns it.

At present, the rights of the people with respect to their properties are governed by a set of complex statutes and state authorities. The existing legal system in India does not provide for registration of title over property, it is only registration of deeds of sale; in other words, there is no guarantee of title over property. The ownership of property and title is only presumptive in nature, not conclusive. The risk of authenticity of title is thus borne by the buyer or possessor of the property. This raises the question of the role of the State in assuring a right of clear title over the property of its citizens.

In several democratic and developed countries, there exists a guaranteed title certification system by which the state provides for clear title over property. The most well known is the Torrens System in Australia where property records mirror the ground reality or the actual facts, the operating principle being 'title by registration' than 'registration of title'. In US, the Title Insurance system operates where the title holder insures through an insurance policy and the Insurance Company indemnifies the title holder of any loss.

The advantages of guaranteed title cannot be overemphasized. It provides reliable data on property, helps reduce litigation, can prevent encroachments, provide improved access to credit, facilitate accurate assessment of land market valuation and improve urban planning and management. In 1989, the Planning Commission appointed D.C. Wadhwa, as a one-man Commission on Land Records to suggest measures to generate reliable data on land and property. Wadhwa submitted his report in 1989, recommending guaranteeing title to land. In 1990, the Ministry of Urban Development in its draft Housing Policy, suggested to state governments introduction of registration of title as opposed to registration of documents. In 2019, the Niti Aayog circulated a model Land Titling Act. However, states are yet to take action to pass their own legislation in this matter.

It must be stated that this is a complex task in view of the multiplicity of land laws and in the absence of a single authority to maintain all land records. Moreover, state governments are reluctant to take on the burden of guaranteeing title to land as it would have to bear the risk of making good any loss to the landowner. Nevertheless, this is an extremely important issue, not to be ignored. McKinsey consultants had estimated that land problems in India cost the nation one per cent of its GDP (McKinsey Global Institute, 2010). Moreover, the benefits of a guaranteed land title are enormous, as pointed above. The state will gain in revenue which now gets diverted to professional middlemen, while individual land/property owners will be sure of their titles. It is high time this matter receives priority attention of the state governments to enact suitable legislation to find an answer to one of the most complex, yet critical land problems in India.

Roads

The focus is on building main roads, flyovers, subways, particularly in metropolitan cities. Here again, except for New Delhi that enjoys a special status as the national capital, in many other metros, it is the central/CBD area that receive attention, neglecting the interior roads including footpaths, drains, street lighting and cleanliness where people reside. Even in a city like Bengaluru, the 'tech' city, the quality of several roads is poor and potholes are a common occurrence, causing accidents and at times, deaths. The planning, designing and execution of road infrastructure which includes footpaths, roadside drains, parking space, intersection design, flyovers and subways in most Indian cities leaves much to be desired. This can be primarily attributed to lack of well trained professional personnel in municipalities, inadequate investment (cost per kilometre) that ensures quality and delays in execution. An unstated but well known reason is the wide scope for corruption which dilutes the quality of roads. The result is potholed roads, more accidents and urban flooding.

Urban Flooding and Drainage

The recent torrential rains, rising of the Yamuna and intense flooding of the national capital, Delhi (July, 2023), that resulted in serious damage to life and property, is proof enough that no city is free from the ravages of nature. Drainage management has not received the attention it deserves. Some measures have been taken like preparation of plans for restoring storm water drains, mapping of surface water bodies under AMRUT scheme, rejuvenation of water bodies and rainwater harvesting, desilting and deepening drains but government action is falling short. In particular, attention must be paid to the removal of encroachments on storm water drains and water bodies, desilting and deepening storm water drains, water conservation, especially rainwater harvesting and establishing real-time flood warning systems.

Urban flooding is caused by natural as well as human factors. The natural includes meteorological resulting in very heavy rainfall and hydrological—when there is a change in the course of a river and the presence of high tides. The human is accounted for by increasing urbanisation, loss of lakes and other water bodies, encroachment of drains and low-lying areas and the damage to roads and buildings designed without regard to flood risk. The drainage systems in our cities hardly meets the present exigencies. The storm water drains constructed years ago, meant to carry rainwater, are not only encroached but filled with garbage, obstructing the flow of water. The problem is compounded by the lack of adequate water conservation infrastructure.

Flooding has become a common risk to urban ecosystems and we need to enhance our preparedness to meet such situations when risks become hazards.

Waste Management

According to World Bank estimates (Kaza *et al.*, 2018), India generates the highest quantity of waste in the world, more than the most populous China, and in another 30 years, double the quantity—from

Fig. 10.10: A crowd-sourced map of inundated roads and areas during the floods in Chennai in 2017.

Source: https://osm-in.github.io/flood-map/chennai.html#13.65/13.0436/80.2219

277 million tons in 2016 to 548 million tons by 2050. But India is among the lowest per capita generators—0.57 kg, compared to developed countries (US-2.24, Russia-1.13, world average-0.740). Our cities face many problems in the area of waste management with respect to collection and disposal of different kinds of waste-municipal solid (wet and dry), hazardous, bio-medical and electronic waste. While a lot of the waste does gets collected, disposal is beset with numerous problems. The traditional dumping on vacant sites in and away from the city that causes pollution and has an adverse effect on health is sought to be replaced to scientific landfill sites, and adopting the 3 Rs—reduce, recycle and reuse and move towards zero waste. This is easier said than done. The progress is very slow and old practices continue in most urban areas. Civic bodies are insisting on segregation at source which is catching up in some cities. Disposal of bio-medical waste that requires careful handling has received little attention. The quantity of electronic or e-waste is increasing by the day but only about a third is being processed in a scientific manner or recycled (*The Tribune*, 2023), and the balance being processed in the informal sector with exposure to health hazards.

There is also a human problem. Manual collection of waste and cleaning of streets by *poura karmikas* or *safai karmacharis* poses health risks to the workers. The ragpickers use their hands to pick the usable material from the garbage thrown in waste bins and streets to earn their livelihoods. Adoption of safe collection practices and mechanical devices is a tardy work-in-progress. One of the most obnoxious practices still prevalent in many urban areas is the manual scavenging system. The law mandating its discontinuance, Employment of Manual Scavengers and Construction of Dry Latrines (Prohibition) Act, 1993 was passed three decades ago. The Act clearly prohibits any person from engaging in or employ for any other person for manually carrying human excreta or construct or maintain a dry latrine.

The system of managing waste by ULBs lends itself to malpractices. Corruption has become part of the contracting system of collection and transportation of waste, resulting in severe financial losses and low productivity. Municipal services mostly continue to be inefficient, with people's grievances not receiving the attention they deserve in a democracy. E-governance has no doubt helped enhance efficiency and speedy delivery where online services have been introduced but its reach is limited to the educated class mostly in larger cities. This state of affairs must be viewed against the background of the investments made in the sector. Greater priority has been accorded to physical infrastructure than social infrastructure that improves the quality of life, such as clean air and water, solid waste and wastewater management and decent housing to the poor and vulnerable. This has resulted in lopsided development, underscoring the oft-repeated observation that conventional city planning must make way for holistic planning that integrates the economic, social, spatial, and environmental dimensions.

Secondly, implementation bottlenecks have led to time and cost overrun. They rarely get executed as per schedule, resulting not only in delays but in cost escalation. The Smart Cities Mission was announced in 2015, but it took years for the guidelines to be published and the process of selecting 100 cities took another couple of years. Thereafter, the formulation of schemes and the selection of project management consultants took some more years. Finally, out of 6,130 planned projects, 5,486 are in work order stage and about 2,898 have been completed (Observes Research Foundation, n.d.).

A glaring example of mismanagement of municipal solid waste came to light recently. The Brahmapuram dumpyard in Kochi in Kerala is a 110 acre plot that receives 390 tonnes of waste everyday. 65 per cent of it biodegradable but much of the plastic remains in the dumpyard as only recyclable plastic is retrieved by the company running the plant. One day in March 2023, intense heat experienced in Kerala triggered a fire in the dumpyard and toxic fumes engulfed the city for over a fortnight causing severe respiratory problems for the residents in the vicinity, forcing many of them to shift from the area. Many offices and most schools in a 50-100 sq km area had to be closed. The intensity of the fire was such that it required 200 fire force personnel, 68 civil defense personnel, 55 Kochi Corporation staff, 48 home guards and many more to deal with tragedy. It is alleged that the company that was awarded the contract for treatment of the waste was not qualified to do the job well. The history of award of contracts, cancellations and funding is said to have called for the intervention of the National Green Tribunal. The incident also highlights the problem of dealing with plastic waste which is assuming serious proportions.

Manual Scavenging: A Glaring Governance Failure

> *"In no country people are sent to gas chambers to die. Every month 4-5 people lose their lives due to manual scavenging."*
>
> (Supreme Court of India, 1991)

It is nothing but appalling that deaths on account of manual scavenging should have become a recurring phenomenon in a country nine years after its Parliament enacted a law (Prevention of Employment as Manual Scavengers and their Rehabilitation Act, 2013) and eight years after it launched a Mission on Cleanliness (Swachh Bharat). The Act abolishing the dehumanizing practice was a landmark legislation aimed at correcting the historical wrongs done to the SC and ST community for centuries.

In 2021, the government informed the Rajya Sabha that 66,692 manual scavengers had been identified so far but denied occurrence of any death due to manual scavenging; however, it admitted that more than 900 people had died while cleaning sewers and septic tanks. In April 2022, the number of deaths was reported as 161 during the three years, 2016-2018, and 129 between for the two years 2019-2020. Apart from the inconsistency in providing information, the artificial distinction between scavenging and manual sewers betrays a flawed approach because it is the manual scavengers who clean sewers. According to Bezwada Wilson, Founder of the *Safai Karmachari Andolan*, the practice of cleaning dry latrines is very much prevalent in UP, MP, Bihar, and Jammu & Kashmir.

> We have evidence for this and each time we try to share the same, the *safai karamcharis* are harassed by the government and the police…in such circumstances, people may not come and openly give a statement.
>
> (Bezwada Wilson, n.d.)

The stark reality is that the local authorities have failed to implement the 2013 Act that laid the responsibility on them to use modern technology for cleaning sewers. As far back as 1956, the Kaka

Kalelkar Commission had called for mechanisation of sewer cleaning, yet the manual practice continues till today even in some large cities. In 2011, Justice Singhvi of the Supreme Court observed: "The human beings who are employed for doing work in the sewers cannot be treated as mechanical robots, who may not be affected by poisonous gases in the manholes". The perpetuation of this social evil is a clear case of governance failure where the law is not enforced and the policy statements are allowed to remain on paper.

Litigation in ULBs—costing dear

There is a mountain of cases piling up against ULBs in almost every state of India. Unfortunately, data is lacking on this important aspect of urban administration. In my own work experience, these cases pertain to municipal properties, personnel matters, unresolved grievances of individual citizens, and matters of public interest such as the state of urban roads. In 2022, about 7,588 cases were pending in cases pertaining only to BBMP. Such cases lead to enormous financial losses to local bodies, apart from litigation charges (lawyer fees). In this way, lessees of municipal properties occupy on valuable properties leased long ago for a pittance. Land acquisition cases pending for years mostly result in enhancement of compensation. Most cases are not represented properly as municipal and government advocates do not have enough interest in fighting them, and the legal staff in corporations is usually meagre. Such a state of affairs reflects a failure in governance and needs serious and urgent attention of the concerned authorities.

How safe are our cities

Safety is an area of major concern in Indian cities, especially in bigger cities. Urban safety has several dimensions. Public spaces, private spaces, buildings, traffic—all of these carry a safety dimension. Let us look at the state of safety in some cities.

In 2015, a Street Quality Index released by *Janaagraha* showed that 51 per cent of the city's' streets have 'lux'(one lumen per square metre) levels below the safety benchmark of 10 lux making them unsafe for pedestrians. In the 3,075 km of streets surveyed, the average was only 8 lux, lower than the minimum safety requirement (*Janaagraha*, 2015). Recently, the Bangalore Political Action Committee (B-PAC) carried out an audit of city's public infrastructure in terms of safety, walkability, accessibility, and quality and found that in one of the city's oldest areas, 23 per cent of the 73 audited streets scores poorly in lighting and general safety and in one of fast developing areas, 50 per cent of the 35 major streets were poorly lit. The two surveys reveal not only the poor state of lighting in a major metropolis like Bangalore but worse, there was hardly any improvement in street lighting even after several years.

The poor quality of roads (potholes, roads dug up for laying water/ sewage pipes) has resulted in accidents causing injuries to commuters and deaths. Several pedestrian subways are dark, dingy and unsafe. A Performance Audit of the Karnataka State Road Safety Authority (2022), responsible for planning and monitoring road safety, conducted by the Comptroller & Auditor General has highlighted the lack of initiative in coordinating safety measures for motorists, pedestrians and citizens. It pointed out that the authority conducted 36 meetings between April 2014 and March 2021, but no meeting was conducted between January 2018 and January 2019. More importantly, some crucial issues were not even considered in any of the meetings.

Construction sites and buildings put up ignoring safety norms carry serious risks. Building collapses and fire hazards have cost several lives. Delhi witnessed a devastating fire in May 2022 claiming 27 lives. In Bengaluru, in April 2021, two elderly women were charred to death trapped inside a 5-storeyed building that caught fire. The firemen who rushed to the spot found the grill of the balcony blocked fire access and it was not possible to rescue them (*DH*, May 22, 2022).

Women's safety has been a very major concern in urban areas, particularly in metros. The Nirbhaya episode in Delhi in 2012 when a female student was gang raped in a moving bus, resulting in her death sparked a nationwide debate and led to the passing of the Criminal Law (Amendment) Act, 2013, which broadened the definition of rape and made existing offences more stringent. Nevertheless, the problem continues, and women still walk in the city streets in fear.

According to R. Swaminathan, Senior Fellow at Observer Research Foundation and is a specialist in social construction of urban spaces, real safety is a combination of four factors: the first is intelligent designing of architecting of urban spaces; the second is technology in the form of a networked blanket of high-resolution and hi-quality CCTVs; the third is enforcement of rules, regulations and norms, which we broadly call law and order, and the fourth is a sense of community support. "At a basic level, a city is nothing more than a collection of people. Individually, each one is unsafe. But network them, and suddenly the concept of safety starts acquiring collective overtones" (*Governance Now*, March 16-31, 2013, pp. 60-61).

Public Order

The City Police constitute an important part of a city's governance, yet they hardly find a place in deliberations or writings on urban issues. The police are involved primarily in three crucial areas of governance: law and order, crime control and investigation, and traffic regulation. How effectively these functions are performed varies from city to city and is dependent on a number of factors. In researching for this book, I held discussions with Bengaluru Police Commissioner and his team to gain insights into the problems faced by them in managing their statutory duties and the possible solutions.

The major problem pertains to shortage of manpower. As against the UNDP norm of 222 police personnel per 1,00,000 population, Bengaluru has only 131, leaving a huge gap, particularly in comparison with the multifarious functions they need to perform. They are forced to work long hours, with little rest and denied leave during big events or emergency work. It is therefore essential to recruit more personnel on priority to improve the overall efficiency of the police force. Public agitations and protests for various reasons are increasing and the police are required to take preventive action. In spite of their best efforts, things, at times, go out of control. Whatever the reason, the responsibility falls on police' shoulders. One suggestion made was to earmark 4-5 sites (open grounds) in bigger cities to hold rallies in a city to deal with simultaneous events, which will help in minimising public inconvenience and law and order problems. The want of adequate staff hampers the prompt dealing with increasing number of complaints. Registration of online complaints has improved matters, but many citizens are not able to access the online system.

Traffic problems in large cities pose serious problems in view of the increasing number of motor vehicles on the one hand and the inadequate infrastructure on the other. People don't often realise that the job of the police is restricted to regulation while traffic management involves several other factors like land use planning, road design, traffic engineering, construction infrastructure and behaviour of the commuters. Coordination with other agencies like the municipal corporation, city planning authority and public utilities is poor.

There is also a jurisdictional problem. The territorial jurisdiction of the City Police does not coincide with that of the Municipal Corporation or other city agencies, and this causes confusion not only between the different agencies but also in the minds of the public. There is, however, no quick answer to this question as it is not easy to alter municipal boundaries. An effective information and coordination system is essential to deal with matters in the peripheral areas of a city.

The Pandemic and the Migrant Crisis

In the introduction to the book, a brief narrative was given about the COVID-19 pandemic, its origin and impact, causing enormous suffering and loss of lives and the measures taken by the government to contain the effect of the deadly virus. Here, we look at the issue from the perspective of governance—the role played by government and other stakeholders, the health professionals, the hospitals, the civil society in dealing with the crisis, and its impact on the migrant population. A migrants' survey was conducted in two cities, Bengaluru in the south and Kanpur in the north to gain first hand knowledge of the problems faced by them during COVID -19.

First, the government at all levels, the central, state and local, were fully seized of the crisis at hand and devoted their full attention to it. With cases piling up every day, it had to deal with several problems at the same time—keeping track of the number of people getting infected by the virus, testing them, arranging for their treatment, the travelling public, quarantine arrangements, admissions to hospitals, adequacy of beds, drugs, health staff etc. The long lockdown announced by the government without any prior notice created unprecedented hardship to all classes of people, especially the poor, the vulnerable and the migrant class—loss of jobs and income, closure of offices, workplaces and educational institutions, confinement to the house, difficulty in procuring essential items—all these meant dealing with an emergency of gigantic proportions.

How did the government deal with the situation? Initially, it looked like the government acted in panic. Declaring a lockdown throughout the country with hardly any time for the people to prepare themselves created lot of confusion and a panic reaction among the people. As government hospitals proved inadequate to cope with the increasing number of patients, private hospitals had to be roped in and they were asked to earmark a certain number of beds for COVID cases. In view of the restrictions on movement, those travelling to hospital or other emergency work, had to obtain a permit from the police. Enforcing the ban on movements and wearing of masks was another tough task. Rations had to be arranged for the poor to meet their daily needs of food consumption. The migrant workers who wanted to go back to their villages, at times in large numbers, had to be provided temporary shelter and transport facilities. And above all, vaccines had to be procured and administered to the entire adult population to prevent spread of the disease, which was no easy task.

There were several shortcomings and numerous complaints. Patients had to wait at the hospital gates for admission, at times, for an unduly long time, for want of beds inside and some even lost their lives, just waiting for health care. Disposal of dead bodies posed another kind of problem. The bodies ended up in queues at the crematorium/ burial ground. Perhaps the most distressing situation one confronted was the inability of the family members of the deceased to perform the last rites of their loved ones (they were asked to keep off for fear of infection). And there were other kinds of woes like getting confined to the house, remaining in quarantine for 14 days, cases of depression and so on. Despite the myriad problems and deficiencies, it must be said that overall, the entire covid situation spread over a period of two years in two phases was well managed in India, compared to even some of the advanced countries of the west.

The pandemic, extremely painful as it was, has some valuable lessons to offer in governance. First and foremost, public policy must give due importance to public health issues. In the present rigid hierarchical system, over a third of the positions of doctors and nurses is vacant or absent, especially in Primary Health Centres (PHCs), with most of the staff concentrated in larger cities. Supply of drugs and medicines suffers from pilferage. It is time to reform the public health system in India, making it more flexible to meet routine as well as emergency situations efficiently. Our neighbouring country, Thailand's 30-Baht Health Reform, 2002 holds out a model worth considering. It seeks to achieve the goal of universal health care by linking the public and private health care systems. The Health Ministry comprises two parts—one an agency that buys health care for all citizens based on outcomes, from competing public and private hospitals, and the other that runs government hospitals. Rural areas are served by primary care community-based networks manned by trained doctors.

The need for a robust data system came out strongly during the pandemic. A number of cities did set up War Rooms to collect and transmit data on tracing, testing, hospital admissions, vaccination and some like the ones in Bengaluru and Mumbai did an excellent job. But there were questions on the accuracy of data including the number of infections and deaths and suspicion about under reporting. India is now quite advanced in the use of technology and all state health departments should ensure that the quality of data is not comprised. This is also essential for data-based policy making and taking timely decisions. Coronasafe network, a war room capability network developed by IT professional volunteers enabled Kerala government to monitor its hospitals' parameters in real time, from oxygen supply to capacity utilisation of hospital beds, ventilators and status of recovery of patients. Kerala's pandemic management won lot of praise from different quarters.

Administering timely vaccines is extremely important to prevent spread of infections and instilling confidence in the public. Though initially there was a delay in procuring vaccines on the part of India, subsequent action ensured that the vast majority of the population received the two prescribed doses. Indigenous production of vaccine was a major factor in achieving success in such a large-scale operation.

The lesson here is ensuring perfect coordination in the supply chain activity, which can be replicated in other activities of health care.

People's participation played a crucial role in supplementing government's efforts at the local level. A number of voluntary organisations and individuals helped out in providing food and shelter to the needy, transporting them to hospitals, supply of oxygen cylinders etc. This reinforces the argument for greater decentralisation and empowering ward committees and resident welfare associations in solving local problems. Citizens do rise to the occasion when the situation demands.

However, the management of the migrant crisis left a lot to be desired. Starting from the sudden announcement of the lockdown to their losing jobs overnight to handling their movement back to their own places of residence, leaving many stranded, government's approach came under severe criticism.

Even under normal circumstances, migrants face problems of exclusion. The Congress party which came to power in Karnataka in May, 2023 had promised five guarantees in its election manifesto: 10 kg free rice to Below Poverty Line (BPL) families, free bus travel for women within the state, free electricity up to 200 units of electricity, Rs. 2,000 per month to BPL women and an unemployment allowance of Rs. 3,000 per month to unemployed graduates, Rs. 2,000 to diploma holders for a period of one year. However, these benefits will be provided only to those who are domiciled in the state and those utilizing them must provide their identity cards. These schemes, however, exclude a large number of migrant women, who commute from their residence to their workplace. Even if they possess identity cards, if they lack domicile certificates, they are ineligible. On the other hand, the scheme of free bus ride is offered to all women, irrespective of their economic status (indeed, it has been a big hit and they are using it liberally). It has been argued that Bengaluru being one of the biggest destinations for migrant workers from all over the country, denial of such benefits to one of the most marginal groups who contribute substantially to the city's production and services, while subsidizing mobility of the better-off sections who can afford to pay, would be iniquitous and an unnecessary financial burden of the state government.

Report on the Impact of the Pandemic and Lockdown on Migrant Workers in Bengaluru and Kanpur

The COVID-19 Pandemic has had a major impact on migrants and informal sector workers in several cities across India. The World Bank observed that the "crisis induced by COVID-19 could be long, deep, and pervasive when viewed through a migration lens" (The World Bank, 2020). Migrants have faced impacts on several fronts such as loss of employment, wages, and lack of health insurance coverages. To better understand the dimensions of this phenomenon, the author, with the support of the Public Affairs Center (PAC), Bengaluru undertook a primary survey of migrants and informal sector workers in two cities in India: Bengaluru and Kanpur; the results of which provide useful insights. While some of these insights have been provided in various sections of this book thematically, this section briefly summarizes the report for a broader understanding.

About a hundred migrant workers were surveyed in each city. A majority of them were single male short-term migrants of OBC category. The major reasons for migrating to the city were access to better jobs and therefore incomes, while some migrants in Kanpur also claimed that better health facilities in the city were also a pull-factor. Yet, there were considerable challenges in accessing basic services in both cities, with Bengaluru doing better in some respects (toilets and sewage) and Kanpur doing better in some others (water supply). A vast majority of the migrants in both the cities live in rented accommodation. Bengaluru turned out to be generally a more expensive city to live than Kanpur, both in terms of rent and cost of subsistence. Overall, migrant workers in Kanpur had a higher probability of saving their income as compared to those in Bengaluru. As reported elsewhere in this book, migrant workers in Bengaluru were looking for better housing options while those in

Kanpur were looking for better quality jobs. Across both cities, awareness of government schemes and identity documents was limited to ration cards.

A big negative impact on children's education was perceived in migrant households. Many migrants claimed to have lost more than a year of education for their children, as online education was unaffordable. More distressingly, several migrants reported job loss of between a year and two years due to the pandemic and lockdown. They had to compensate for this income loss through their own savings and substantial loans. Government support during those times was largely restricted to supply of food packets.

Chapter
11

Rich Cities, Poor City Government

Governance Issues in Financing City Services and Development

Municipal Finance

It is an irony that while Indian cities are getting richer and contributing in a greater measure to the national GDP, the institutions that are expected to provide civic services and develop infrastructure are financially weak. The huge resources generated by cities in the form of taxes (Income Tax, GST, Excise duties etc.) are appropriated by the central and state governments and only a very small share trickles down to the local bodies. The ratio of municipal revenues to GDP in India is pitifully small—less than one per cent, compared to other developing countries like South Africa (6%) and Brazil (7.4%) (Ahluwalia *et al.*, 2019). According to a study by the Reserve Bank of India, the total revenues of ULBs have been growing at a rate lower than that of combined central and state revenues, leading to a decline in their share in total government revenues. The Reserve Bank of India (2022) reports that the share of municipal revenues/expenditures in the country's Gross Domestic Product (GDP) has stagnated at around 1 per cent for the last decade (between 2009-19), as compared to 7.4 per cent in Brazil and 6 per cent in South Africa (Reserve Bank of India, 2022). The same report goes on to say that the revenue receipts of all municipal corporations would amount to 0.61 per cent (2017-2018) to 0.72 per cent (2019-2020) of GDP.

The requirement of funds for city development and services have been studied by a number of government committees and private researchers. The High Powered Expert Committee (HPEC) chaired by Isher Ahluwalia estimated the investment requirement as Rs. 3.2 million crores over a period of 20 years between 2012-31 (HPEC, 2011). The McKinsey Report arrived at an estimate of Rs. 9.74 million crores (McKinsey Global Institute, 2010). Both the reports indicated huge resource gaps. On ground, we find that the own revenues of the municipalities are woefully inadequate, making them heavily dependent on the higher levels of government and eroding their fiscal autonomy. In short, the local fiscal governance suffers from inter-governmental imbalances on account of policies of fiscal federalism, resulting in an urban fiscal crisis. This raises serious issues about the entire fiscal governance system.

The functional domain of the municipalities is enumerated in the 74th constitutional amendment—12th schedule to the constitution which has listed 18 functions ranging from urban planning to infrastructure and services to environment to welfare and regulatory activities. All these functions are not strictly 'municipal', some of them being performed by other parastatal agencies as in the case of water supply (Water Supply Boards in large cities) and departments of the government in case of forestry (Forest Department), planning for economic and social development (Planning Department) and safeguarding the interests of weaker sections (Social Welfare Department). Then again, the constitution provides for a District Planning Committee and a Metropolitan Committee to prepare District Development Plan for districts and Metropolitan Development Plan for metropolitan cities (million plus cities). This overlapping of responsibilities has created confusion and raises questions in expenditure assignment: which are the functions that are purely 'municipal', which are to be divided or shared between different government agencies, and between urban and rural local bodies?

In the matter of revenue assignment, the powers vest with the state government in respect of assignment of taxation and grant-in-aid, and with municipalities in case of levies like fees, charges, tolls etc. The only tax power vested in local bodies is levy of property tax on immovable property, which is also the most important source of own revenue. Unfortunately, the valuation of properties bristles with difficulties and the valuation methods followed have remained irrational and opaque, and breed corruption. Although efforts have been made to rationalise the system by prescribing certain criteria for valuation and a self-assessment system has been introduced in a number of states, its full potential has not been realised (see Box—Rationalising the Property Tax in Part II). In any case, the revenue from property tax alone cannot meet the financial requirements of running the city administration. This is true even if revenue from other levies like charges and fees are included.

A city is not run only with the revenues of municipal governments. The parastatal authorities provide essential services like water, electricity and public transport, but they are also controlled by the state authorities and lack autonomy in in matters of fixing tariffs. The user charges levied by them fall far short of the costs of managing their services and often of meeting even the operation and maintenance costs and they look forward to subsidies and grants from the government. For the purpose of infrastructure development and execution of major capital works, both the municipalities and the parastatals resort to borrowings from banks and financial institutions; here again, the state government's support is required for standing guarantees. As such, the parastatals are also dependent on the state government to run their organisations.

Comparison with other countries is instructive. In Brazil, municipalities have access not only to property tax but to other sources such as federal income tax, motor vehicle tax, real estate transfer tax, service tax on base other than that assigned to states and a few others. In China, local taxes include real estate tax, business tax, urban land use and appreciation tax, fixed assets capital gains tax, vehicle tax, share in income tax, domestic value added tax and so on. In the United States, the tax assignment rules are transparent and flexible enabling the local finance system to run smoothly. The municipalities have the option to access to local income tax, excise tax, gasoline tax, general sales tax, tax free municipal bonds etc. In England, there exists a system of exchequer grants like the Revenue Support Grant (RSG) intended to compensate local authorities for differences in the cost of providing municipal services; the central grants actually constitute more than 50 per cent of the local body expenditure. Thus, the urban local governments in many of not only the developed but developing economies have a broader revenue base unlike in India where it is very narrow.

The mismatch between functions and finances leaves the ULBs inadequately and unpredictably financed. The situation was well summed up in a study conducted by the Asian Development Bank (2013) on municipal finances in India:

> The municipal finance system in India has limited autonomy in fixing tax rates, determining the tax exemption policy, accessing capital markets or restructuring personnel policy. Their taxing and spending powers have existed under the provisions of state laws which often deny municipalities the power either to impose a particular tax or to impose a tax on a particular class of taxpayers. The state laws do not provide for the protection of municipal fiscal domain nor do these lay down a policy governing transfers. There exist no performance standards or measures for municipalities, with the result that the finance system at this level is extremely 'soft'. (p. 30)

This brings us to the fundamental governance question in fiscal federalism: 'Who should tax, where and what?'

The Local Resources Conundrum

The Indian Economic Survey of 2017-2018 (Ministry of Finance, 2018) highlighted four aspects about urbanisation:

1. Broadly, urbanisation has increased per capita GDP, but the pattern of urbanisation is rather unusual. Smaller cities are too small, and seemingly the largest cities are also too small. This could be due to factors like overburdened infrastructure in cities, distorted land markets leading to unaffordable market rents, that, in turn, discourage migration and strong place-based preferences embedded in the deep social networks in the country,
2. Service delivery is strongly correlated with urban capacities, financial and personnel, and better service delivery is positively correlated to capital expenditure and services, adequacy of staff and services. Resource mobilisation, therefore, remains one of the key challenges,

3. ULBs' financial capacity is not necessarily constrained by taxation powers; there seems to be no clear relationship between taxation powers and actual mobilisation of resources. ULBs like Mumbai and Pune with low taxation powers show better performance in revenue mobilisation than those like Kanpur and Dehradun with higher taxation powers,
4. Property tax potential remains unexploited across ULBs and tax collection is far below potential. An analysis based on satellite imagery for the 2017-2018 Economic Survey has shown that Bangalore and Jaipur collect only 5-20 per cent of their tax potential.

The Economic Survey has captured in a nutshell what are known facts. The hard reality is urban local bodies are woefully short of resources. The share of municipal revenues to GDP remained as low as 0.70 per cent in nineties (Finance Commission India, 2000) moved up marginally to 0.94 per cent in 2007-2008 (Finance Commission India, 2009).

Fiscal federalism is generally discussed in the context of sharing of resources between the central and state governments and the extent of fiscal autonomy states enjoy and does not extend to the local government. The 74th Amendment to the constitution provides for the creation of a State Finance Commission (Art 243Y) to make recommendations on the grants to be provided to the urban local bodies and suggest methods to improve their resources. The Central Finance Commission also recommends certain grants to be released to the local bodies.

The resources of ULBs are derived from three sources: (a) own revenues consisting of taxes and charges, (b) grants from the government, and (c) borrowings. It is a well known fact that they are unable to mobilise adequate resources to provide for all the urban services and infrastructure. According to the latest 'Report on Municipal Finances' published by the RBI in November, 2022, the revenue receipts of ULBs from their own tax and non-tax revenue were budgeted to be a meagre 0.45 per cent of GDP in 2019-2020. Of the total revenue receipts, 31-34 per cent is accounted for by own tax revenue, 30 per cent by non-tax revenue, and 35-40 per cent by transfers from the CFC and state governments. The Report further observes: "The share of own revenue (both tax and non-tax) in the total revenue of ULBs in India has declined over time while that of government transfers (both Union and States) has increased. Empirical evidence has shown that greater dependency of local governments on upper tiers for meeting their expenditure needs makes them more vulnerable and less efficient" (Reserve Bank of India, 2022).

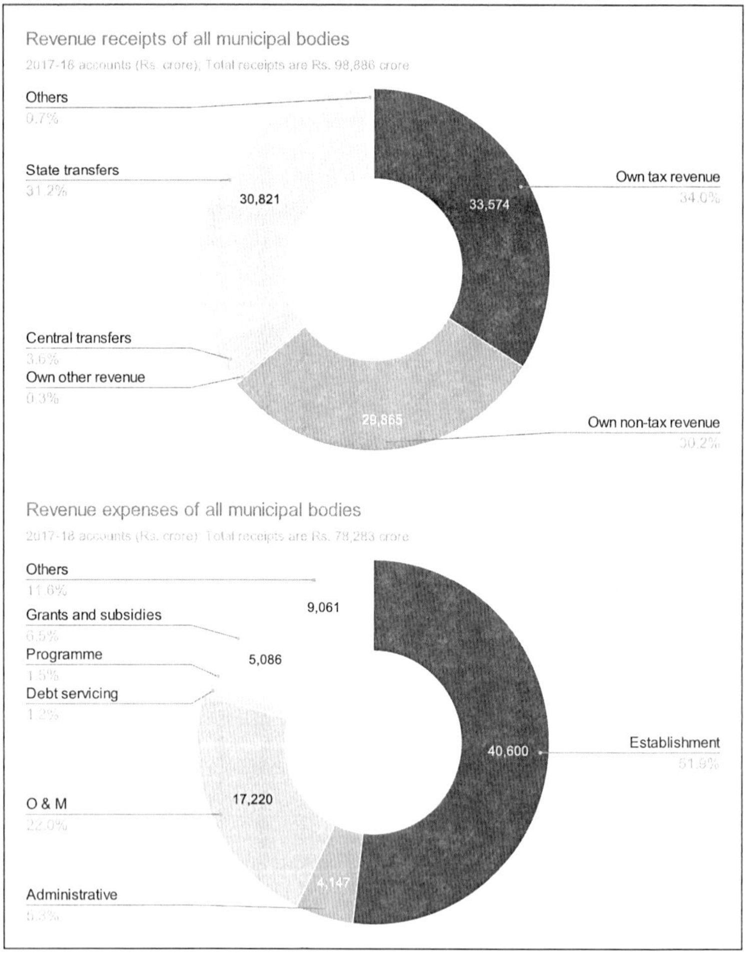

Fig. 11.1: Revenue receipts and expenditure of ULBs, 2017-18 accounts.

Source: RBI report on municipal finances, 2022.

This increasing 'dependency syndrome' of the municipal bodies is the crux of the problem, calling for a thorough examination of the question of fiscal federalism. Analysing the issue, Bibek Debroy and Aditya Sinha (Chairman and researcher respectively, PM's Economic Advisory Council, *The Economic Times*, 18 Nov. 2022) identify three inherent reasons for the prominence of government transfers over municipal revenue.

The Union Finance Commissions have increased their transfers to ULBs/PRIs over the years. The Union FCs are not really supposed to give grants to ULBs, they are only to recommend measures to augment the consolidated fund of a state to supplement the resources of municipalities, while the State Finance Commissions are to recommend the distribution of the net proceeds of taxes leviable by the state between the state and local bodies. Unfortunately, many states have failed to constitute the SFCs and where constituted, their recommendations are not accepted.

States are not ready to devolve fiscal powers to local governments; as a result, the dependency of ULBs on transfers by union and state governments increases, and while it is ideal that ULBs have financial autonomy, the question generally asked is—are ULB officials and elected representatives equipped enough to take sound financial decisions? There may be some truth in this, but the argument cannot be used to deny them adequate powers to spend on matters that are local. Some limits can be considered in expenditure relting to big projects where state and central funds are provided. It is however, imperative that the municipal personnel undergo training in financial management.

The authors also refer to what is called the 'Wicksellian Connection'—the connection between the revenue and expenditure decision and until that happens, it will be difficult for ULBs to provide basic infrastructure and services and for citizens to make ULBs accountable for providing services commensurate to tax payments. I fully endorse this observation on the basis of my own experience. I found the municipal budgets were inflated on account of the pressure of elected representatives to provide for expenditure items far in excess of what the revenues could accommodate. However, in respect of (c) above, the argument linking financial autonomy to the (in-)

competence of the ULB personnel, while factually correct, cannot be held against the need for fiscal decentralisation. The problem does not lie so much in training the personnel, which can be done, as with elected representatives who need to orient towards a sense of fiscal responsibility.

A World Bank Report (2022) has highlighted that "low tariffs are weakening the financial viability of civic bodies. Pointing out that the current trend of low revenue of ULBs and less than required spending on urban infrastructure would hurt India's growth story, it emphasizes that the country needs to increase investment by more than 300 per cent for the next 15 years to meet future needs. This translates into an annual investment of $55 bn (Rs. 4.46 lakh crores) in urban infrastructure compared to the current rate of $16 bn (Rs. 1.3 lakh crores). Policy decisions to keep tariffs and services charges below levels required for cost recovery and financial sustainability are contributing to low revenue, ULBs and utilities are generally unable to recover O&M costs, let alone capital costs, of providing services such as water supply and sewerage". The average O&M cost recovery of water supply charges is around 45 per cent and barring a few cities like Surat (93%), Bengaluru (72%) and Delhi (69%), most cities show less than 50 per cent recovery.

It is time the state governments and the ULBs address the issue of augmenting the revenues seriously failing which our growing cities will face a financial crisis. The Fiscal Responsibility Acts of states must include provisions for fiscal responsibility of local bodies with penal provisions if they fail to adhere to certain norms.

One good source of revenue could be to share a part of the Goods and Service Tax (GST) revenue that looks very buoyant. Another source could be to provide a substantial share of the wealth tax and the recently proposed 28 per cent GST on gaming and betting. After all, a lot of this wealth is produced in cities and it is only fair that city governments, which provide the necessary infrastructure and the facilities to such economic activities should benefit from it.

Public Utilities: The Challenge of Financial Viability

Three essential services in a city—water, power and public transport are the responsibility of public utilities under the state governments.

Although water supply is a municipal function, in many large cities, it is entrusted to water supply boards. The power sector has been corporatised but the power supply and distribution companies are mostly government-owned, except in a few cities like Delhi and Mumbai where private distribution companies operate. City bus transport is again mostly in the public sector and so is the metro rail transport. All these utilities perform extremely important functions but are financially losing enterprises raising serious concerns about their operational and financial viability.

The Niti Aayog has estimated that the cumulative losses suffered by the ESCOMs in the country in 2021 amounted to Rs. 90,000 crores (Niti Aayog & RMI, 2021). A recent study of Karnataka's energy sector (2022) reveals that five ESCOMs in the state carry a debt burden of Rs. 29,764 crores at the end of the financial year 2021-2022 and incurred cumulative losses to the tune of Rs. 9,821 crores. This is attributed mainly to the inadequate billed and metered energy sold and expensive long-term power purchase agreements.

In the transport sector, according to Annual Report 2018-2019 (Ministry of Road Transport & Highways, 2019) 55 state road transport undertakings had shown a loss of Rs. 14,231 crores. A study pertaining to Karnataka (Losses of four RTCs in Karnataka touch Rs. 4,540 crore, *The Indian Express*, February 2017, Bengaluru) shows the outstanding liabilities of the four state-level Road Transport Corporations' (RTC) as Rs. 4,426 crores at the end of 2022 and the accumulated losses till 2020-2021 as Rs. 4,989 crores.

At the root of the several problems—technical, commercial, financial and administrative—lies the governance issue, which needs to be addressed on priority. Although termed 'autonomous', public utilities function under the control of the state governments and are therefore subject to constraints in fixing their tariff and taking policy decisions. The main concerns are under pricing of services, physical losses in respect of water and energy managerial inefficiencies.

Governance reforms are imperative to make public utilities in the states financially viable and improve their services in an era where economic goods and services are subject to the market forces of demand, supply and pricing. First, they must be insulated from external interference and allowed to function on commercial lines. The state governments must separately provide subsidies to make good the shortfall in revenues where services to certain sections of the population are to be under priced. Secondly, where incentives are essential to promote a particular cause in public interest as in the case of public transport, governments must provide assistance for capital investments. Third, upgradation of the capacities of the staff must be addressed in all seriousness. This would mean formulating a sound personnel policy that includes manpower planning, training, and human resource management.

The entry of private sector is held out as one option to meet the deficiencies in the public utilities. The operation of private power entities Delhi and Mumbai are cited as examples. Their performance is considered more efficient as they have the capacity to make the investments required for infrastructure and the freedom to fix the tariff on commercial lines. They can also quickly adapt to the use of modern technologies, as in the case of Tata Power, the power distribution company in Delhi, Mumbai, and Odisha. According to its CEO, Praveen Rao, over the past few years, their engineers have built world class solutions, involving the use of technologies like IOT (for smart meters), AI and ML.

There are examples of private sector participation in the water sector such as the 24/7 water project in Hubli-Dharwad and a few other cities in Karnataka and permitting private transport operators in some states which have shown mixed results. The option of private entry in water, power and transport must be kept open and decisions taken on the merits of the case in each city/state.

Reforming the Property Tax System

The most important source of revenue for the urban local bodies (ULBs) has also been the most complex. Property Tax which accounts for 50-60 per cent of the total revenue of any municipality had its origins during the British rule. It was primarily based on the concept of 'Annual Rateable Value'(ARV), derived from the Valuation (Metropolis)Act of 1869 in England—the rent received or receivable from a property became the basis for valuation of a property of towns and cities in India.

As Commissioner of the Bangalore Municipal Corporation, I found that the valuation of properties was done arbitrarily and did not reflect the true value of a property. It was based more on the discretion of the tax officials than on objective criteria. Most often, a property was either undervalued or overvalued, resulting in loss to the municipality or harassment of the taxpayer. The collection efficiency was also poor, rarely exceeding 55 per cent. Reducing arbitrariness in valuation and maximizing collection of property tax, therefore, presented a serious challenge.

As I was brooding over the possible solutions to the knotty problem, one fine morning, it occurred to me, why not consider something similar to the Income Tax model? What appealed to me in this system of central tax was the trust placed in the taxpayer to declare the income earned by him from different sources and determine the amount of tax to be paid as per the formula prescribed by the Income Tax department. So, why not the local body, much closer to the people, trust the property taxpayer to calculate the tax of his property based on the criteria to be provided by the Corporation? I decided that we would evolve a new system of property tax that would yield revenue to the local government and free the taxpayer of tyranny of the tax inspector. It was a sort of Eureka moment—devising, if not inventing a new method of tax determination and payment.

I called a meeting of the concerned officials and revealed my idea to mop up tax revenue. At first, it was received with shock—giving the discretion to the property owner to fix his own tax? It would result in decline in revenue etc. I then set up a committee to deliberate the issue thoroughly and come up, in the first place, with rational criteria for valuation of a property. Finally, the following parameters were prescribed to calculate tax:

1. Location of the property
2. Total built area
3. Quality of the building-type of flooring, roof etc.

The next step was to devise a proper form containing all the particulars to be filled by a taxpayer that was simple and clear. The new scheme was named as Self Assessment Scheme (SAS). The more important task was to convince the stakeholders. First, the elected body of councillors to whom an elaborate presentation was made and after several rounds of discussions, they finally gave their approval. Then the people, the taxpayers had to be educated. Meetings were held with Resident Welfare Associations to explain the new scheme. Finally, the SAS was brought into force in Bangalore city during the year 1997-1998, but the coverage was only partial. It was not an easy transition. After passing through an experimental phase and some modifications, the new rationalized property tax system stabilized and was hailed as 'people-friendly'. Happily, it has stood the test of time and survived till now.

Finding adequate resources for city services and development has been a perennial problem, linked as it is to the broader issue of fiscal autonomy and taxation powers of the urban local bodies and concentration of fiscal powers in the state governments. This also raises the larger governance question: who should run the city—the state or the city government?

SUMMING UP

With growing urbanisation, the requirements of our cities are so many, the available resources are so short, and the local capacities are so low, that we must set our priorities right so that money is spent on first things first. For the poor and common citizens, regular water supply, and safe and affordable public transport is more important than a flyover which only makes way for more cars. In many ways, the urban revolution of the previous century, has created its own discontents.

There have been various attempts over the period of 1950-2000 to regulate and direct urbanisation. These included new industrial policies, town planning regulations and master planning, developing new cities, urban development seems to have followed a logic of its own in the country. What we see therefore today, are primate cities, megacities and regions, a growing segment of non-metropolitan cities and small towns in some states, and even cities such as 'hill towns' and 'temple towns', that have a unique character of their own. Of late, there has been a stronger emphasis on encouraging urbanisation in 'urban-industrial infrastructure corridors', of which nearly a dozen are in the pipeline.

In this context, the rapid expansion of information technology capabilities has led to the very nature of jobs in our cities change from industrial production to knowledge production. Incomes have increased across the board, in large and small cities. This is a highly leveragable development for structuring urban growth. Yet at the same time, the discontents are highly visible, whether they are the tribulations of the burgeoning informal economy, growth of slums and informal settlements of the urban poor, or the general state of infrastructure in most of our cities.

What is most strikingly visible about Indian cities is the state of its basic physical infrastructure and the housing settlements, particularly of the poor and vulnerable sections. It must be clarified that what was earlier limited to public works such as roads, drains, sewers and other physical installations, the term 'Infrastructure' has now been extended to include water, electricity, transportation and communication systems, and social overheads or 'soft infrastructure' like health, education, and other support systems considered essential for economic growth. Infrastructure is considered a prerequisite to rapid urban development. Infrastructure is now considered a 'crucial enabler of growth' and central to raising India's competitiveness and achieving the planned target of $5 trillion economy by 2025.

Keeping in view the gaps in infrastructure and the availability of funds, and the real needs of the people, it is essential to prioritize projects that can be taken up in the short, medium, and long-term. This is bound to vary from city to city and it is inevitable to carry out a city-level exercise, giving up the one-size fits-all approach. Four critical and immediate issues may be identified—water supply, land and housing especially for the urban poor, urban mobility, and the changing climate and its relationship to urbanisation. Each of these need separate and combined attention. Many matters of daily concern are also yet to be addressed but may be seen as a corollary to the four identified critical areas of work.

Budget allocations for expenditure in municipalities and other city-level service organisations do not always match the actual requirements of the city. A large proportion of allocation generally goes towards construction works, roads, subways, and flyovers, while the amounts marked for Operations and Maintenance (O&M) are pitifully low. In the transport sector, for example, while there is a lot of noise about promoting public transport, the alternatives within the sector in terms of cost-benefit are not properly evaluated. Priorities seem to be lopsided, as can be seen in the case of launching high cost metro rail projects in smaller cities where improvement of bus services would suffice. In the water sector, water conservation is ignored, and huge water supply projects are taken up, drawing water from long distances. Sanitation, which should receive the highest priority is ignored, while our cities continue to look dirty. With the background of the COVID pandemic, focus on public health should figure high on priority lists, both in terms of manpower and infrastructure. The entire subject of priorities for cities and appropriate allocations of funds needs a thorough review.

Part IV
Rethinking Governance and Planning for Tomorrow's Cities

Chapter

12

What is Governance?

Governance is distinct from 'government', which refers to the institutions and authorities exercising statutory power. The concept of 'governance' encompasses not only the traditional arms of the government but also other stakeholders who are part of civil society. Urban governance involves a range of actors and institutions and the relationships among them determine the outcomes in a city. To effectively manage urban transformations, governments at all levels must play a strategic role in forging partnerships with and among key stakeholders (UN-Habitat & UNESCAP, 2010, 2015). The quality of urban governance hinges on two fundamental questions: **'Who' Governs, and 'How'**.

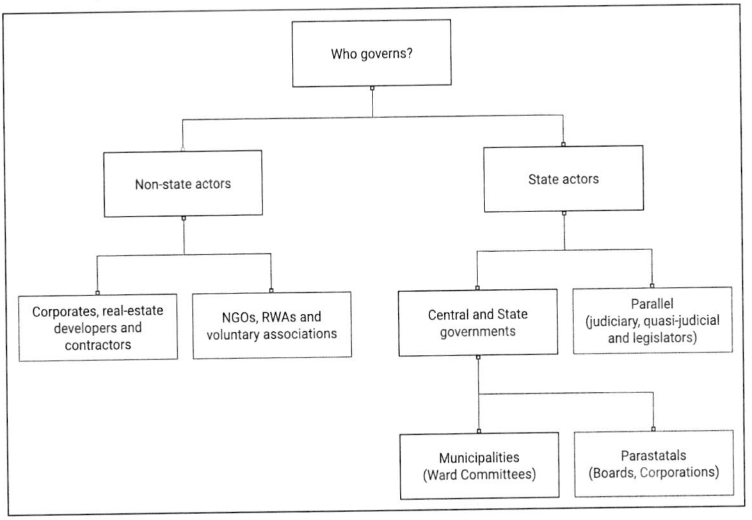

Fig. 12.1: Key stakeholders in urban governance.

Source: Author.

Governance processes deal with the laws, rules and procedures established by those who govern, as well as the manner in which they are implemented. These processes include various aspects such as how plans are formulated and financed, how laws are enforced, how services are delivered, and how resources (including political power) are allocated. As highlighted by (Devas *et al.*, 2004), "It is therefore profoundly political, influenced by the creation and operation of political institutions, government capacity to make and implement decisions and the extent to which these decisions recognise and respond to the interests of the poor; it encompasses a host of economic and social forces, institutions and relationships. These include labour markets, goods and services, household, kin and social relationships, and basic infrastructure, land, services and public safety."

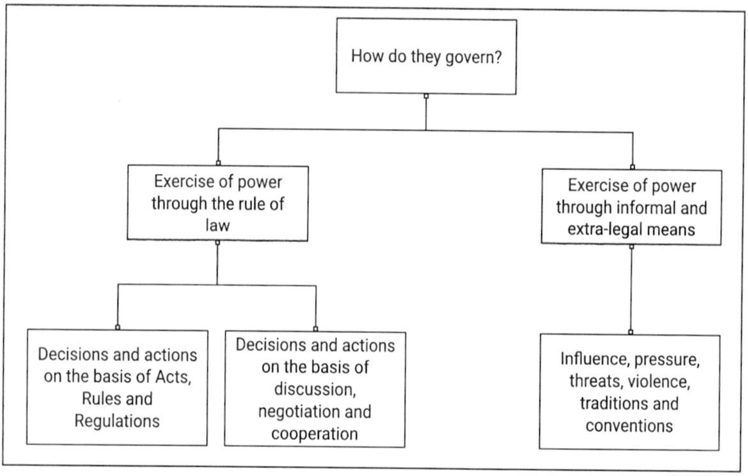

Fig. 12.2: Exercise of power in urban governance.

Source: Author.

The way in which these processes have unfolded in India reveals a complex picture of interacting factors and actors that make it difficult to achieve the intended goals. A multitude of laws and regulations, a fragmented authority structure at the city level, inadequate institutional frameworks, and a lack of capacity within urban local bodies have contributed to poor outcomes. A number of initiatives have been undertaken in the past two or three decades with the objective of improving city infrastructure and services. Nevertheless, the challenges persistently overshadow the achievements and presents a new set of issues.

Urban Visions and Contradictions

> *Cities are perhaps one of humanity's most complex creations, never finished, never definitive. They are like a journey that never ends. Their evolution is determined by their ascent into greatness or descent into decline. They are the past, present and the future.*
>
> (UN-HABITAT, 2008)

In his Independence Day speech on August 15, 2021, Prime Minister Narendra Modi set a new vision for India for the next quarter century: "Next 25 years will be India's *Amrit Kaal* (the Golden Age) whose purpose will be to better the lives of citizens, lessen the development divide between villages and cities, reduce government interference in people's lives, and have the latest technology so that we are not behind any country in the world". Finance Minister Nirmala Sitharaman echoed this vision in her Budget Speech on February 1, 2022, stating, "We are marking Azadi ka Mahotsav (celebration of Independence) and have entered into Amrit Kaal, the 25-year long lead up to India". The budget is aligned with the seven key areas of PM's Gati Shakti Plan—National Master Plan for Multi-modal Connectivity—roads, railways, airports, ports, mass transit, waterways, and logistics—that aims to bring together 16 ministries for integrated planning and coordinated implementation of infrastructure connectivity projects. This will significantly improve connectivity between cities and major metros. The finance minister also emphasised the importance of a 'circular economy' and recycling in generating new businesses and generating jobs. An Action Plan will be developed for 10 sectors, including electronic waste, end-of-life vehicles, used oil waste, and recovery of toxic and hazardous industrial waste, with a focus on infrastructure, reverse logistics, technology upgrades, and integration with the informal sector.

These measures are expected to positively impact the country's economic growth and foster urban-rural integration. However, translating this vision into reality will require effective governance strategies.

In his book, 'Order without Design: How Markets Shape Cities', Bertaud (2018), argues that the order in cities is primarily shaped by market forces, while urban planners attempt to modify it through regulations, infrastructure development, and public spaces. The allocation of land in cities is determined by norms established by planners, architects, and engineers while land use transformations are driven by land prices. The reason why some cities grow while others do not is because the rate of population growth is determined by the comparative advantage of a city's location and capacity for innovation, in addition to the efficiency of its labour market. The effective size of a labour market depends on travel time and the spatial distribution of jobs. While the land market, labour market, and transport system drive a city's growth, urban planners' designs can impose limitations on growth.

Bertaud (2014) refers to the 'Anti-Big City Bias' of planners, highlighting attempts to balance growth through the Industrial Policy Resolution, 1956 that encouraged location of new industries in backward areas. It later prescribed that new industries should be located 50 km away from a city with a population of more than 2.5 million and 30 km from cities with a population range of 1.5-2.5 million (1988). Despite these efforts, industries continued to thrive in Mumbai and Bangalore, both with a population exceeding 2.5 million. As firms and households 'vote with their feet' by choosing to move to cities with greater potential, planners' attempts to redistribute city sizes are unlikely to succeed.

The common concerns that dominate conversations around the future of Indian cities include traffic congestion, air pollution, the state of infrastructure, water scarcity, waste management, power supply issues, urban flooding, and illegal constructions. Informed individuals may delve into topics such as population density and concentration, inequalities, urban poverty, slums, architecture, and social and cultural life. Others may praise the advantages offered by cities, including leading educational institutions, the modern healthcare facilities, entertainment options, and vibrant nightlife, depending on the city's size and the social and economic class of its residents.

These three visions represent the aspirations of a political leader, the analysis of an expert urban scholar and the concerns of common citizens, which the National Urban Policy Framework embodies.

The National Urban Policy Framework

Nearly three decades after the constitutional mandate and two decades into the twenty-first century, the Ministry of Housing and Urban Affairs (MoHUA) introduced the National Urban Policy Framework in 2020. This framework recognises the significance of rapid urbanisation in India, with a projected urban population of 558.8 million by 2031, which "places cities at the centre of India's development trajectory" and highlights that urban development "plays a critical role in the structural transformation of the Indian economy and sustaining a high economic growth".

The policy framework identifies 10 essential functional areas, including urban planning, urban economy, physical infrastructure, social infrastructure, housing and affordability, transportation and mobility, urban finance, urban governance, urban information systems, and environmental sustainability.

An 'outcome matrix' has been developed for each of these areas to empower ULBs and make them self-reliant. The central government's budget for 2022-23 has proposed the establishment of Centres of Excellence for Urban Planning in five higher educational institutions. While the details of the scheme are yet to be announced, these centres are expected to play a crucial role in modernising and strengthening the urban planning systems in the country. Important as all these ten functional areas are, there is a tendency to treat them as separate entities, overlooking the city's overall phenomenon as a unified entity. This is evident in the multitude of agencies managing a city, leading to fragmented governance systems and complicated service delivery.

Fragmentation within the urban sector is only one dimension of the problem. Fragmentation between the 'urban' and the 'rural' is another one. The growth of a city is not confined to municipal limits; as towns and cities expand, agglomerations emerge to include adjoining rural areas into the urban fold. This process of urbanisation of villages and spatial expansion of cities will continue in the coming decades, necessitating a broader policy framework that encompasses both urban and rural development. Reclaiming our cities requires a paradigm shift in the overall development strategy at the national, state, city, district, and local levels.

Chapter 13

Planning for the Future

Urban planning involves taking into consideration the prevailing economic, social, and environmental conditions of a territory—the city—and the surrounding urban areas or agglomerations, which may include villages. Pani (2022) distinguishes between the static notion of a 'city', defined by boundaries, and the dynamic concept of the 'urban', which escapes the 'territorial trap' and involves a 'multitude of relationships' found in a set of processes. He refers to the World Cities literature, which initially examined cities in terms of generating hierarchies (Taylor, 1997) and later focused on processes in Global Cities (Sassen, 2009), both emphasising Command and Control centres of globalisation. Hence, "today urbanisation is a process that affects the whole territory of the world and not only isolated parts of it" (Brenner & Schmid, 2014, p. 21). Scott & Storper (2015) explain the urban "around the processes of agglomeration and polarisation and associated interactions within the urban land nexus" (p. 9).

Here, the emphasis is on the 'process', where the process of agglomeration is accompanied by polarisation, which also explains the difference between the urban and the city. The nature of processes may differ with reference to a situation and a point in time. In medieval India, cities had fortresses where people from neighbouring villages would move during times of war, whereas in the present day, they move in search of work or for what they consider to be a better life. The rapid urbanisation of China has transformed villages into cities, and cities have expanded into metropolises. The case of Shenzhen in southern China is often cited as an example of a small town being transformed into a globally recognised metropolis. In such transformations from a rural/semi-urban to urban, a large number of economic, political, and social processes are at work. The local manifestations of the state—from the local governments to parastatals to national governments—may be seen within the territorial boundaries of the urban, which may include the rural, and each of them would be accountable to make laws by which the city is to be governed.

Pani (2022) quotes the example of the local manufacture of global garment brands in Bengaluru that follow different labour and environmental standards, where the sovereignty of the state is overtaken by demands of global brands. Similarly, within a city, the supply of water is governed by the regulations of the parastatal water supply board, and traffic moves according to the rules framed by the state government. Another manifestation of the diversity in the urban is the presence of IT parks representing the local end of high-technology globalisation alongside poorer colonies of low-end industries. What we witness is fragmented territories of a large city; the continuous changes taking place in the urban further limit the relevance of territorial classification of town, city, or metropolitan.

In light of these factors, the approach may vary from place to place and from time to time. Hence, in a country like India with wide regional variations, a 'one-size fits-all' or a single and uniform approach cannot hold good for the entire country. The national policy can provide a broad framework, enabling states and cities to develop planning models relevant to their areas and conditions. The central government should focus on matters of national importance, such as infrastructure relating to connectivity, physical as well as digital macroeconomic issues that affect states and large agglomerations; inter-state issues pertaining to migration, and movement of people and goods across state borders without hurdles; and sharing of common resources.

The approach to state policies will depend on the level and pattern of urbanisation, the state of the economy, infrastructure requirements, the educational facilities, and so on. At the city level, the major policy issue will be the degree of autonomy to be provided to local governments to raise resources and manage their own affairs, keeping in view the functions they are required to perform, primarily pertaining to planning and delivery of services to the citizens. Thus, the five southern states of Andhra Pradesh, Karnataka, Kerala, Tamil Nadu, and Telangana, and the two western states of Maharashtra and Gujarat, with higher levels of urbanisation and economic growth, would have to adopt policies quite different than those relevant to northern states of Bihar, Uttar Pradesh, and Rajasthan with lower urbanisation rates and economically and socially backward conditions. The approach of the eastern states like Odisha, West Bengal, and Assam, and the hilly north-eastern states will have to be different from both.

An overall review of the policies and plans adopted hitherto and the resultant action on the ground reveal that we have failed in five fundamental tasks:

1. Providing legislative, institutional, and regulatory systems that suit the changing requirements of dynamic city growth and facilitate ease of living for its citizens.
2. Developing the necessary infrastructure and ensuring all citizens have adequate and equitable access to basic services such as safe drinking water, sanitation, housing, public transportation and public health facilities, and effective service delivery.
3. Protecting the environment from increasing pollution, and the ravages of the construction industry and the reduction of natural spaces essential for healthy and comfortable living.
4. Empowering local urban institutions politically, administratively, and financially to effectively discharge their functions.
5. Facilitating adequate public participation in the governance of the country, from grassroots to higher levels, particularly in urban areas.

Addressing these questions and exploring the answers call for a rethinking of the entire systems and processes of urban and rural governance, as well as our capacity to reflect on the lived realities, including the political economy that has shaped urban growth. Let us explore an integrated model of development that shifts the focus from mega and metro cities to smaller cities, towns, semi-urban centres and large villages with potential for economic growth, which can help contain migration from villages and small towns to manufacturing clusters. The larger cities are more likely to grow in the service sector, especially in technology-related areas. Along with economic development, education and skill development must receive priority in rural and small-town areas. We are already witnessing a trend of people from these places sending their children to nearby cities for education, including higher education. It is not uncommon to see students hailing from villages and towns exhibiting their talent by obtaining top ranks in degree and postgraduate courses.

Going forward, the reconfiguration of developmental and regulatory governance in India involves reconciling what may appear as contradictory processes: economic growth and environmental sustainability; rapid urbanisation and rural transformation; rising inequalities and uplifting the poor and low-income groups. The challenges to resolving these contradictions, as viewed from the prisms of some scholars, are:

1. The imperatives of national growth and transactional finance inducing large-scale land dispossession (Harvey, 2003; Sassen, 2014).
2. States promoting 'world-class' real estate and infrastructure projects that threaten lives and livelihoods in city regions (Goldman, 2011; Watson, 2014).
3. The dual role of local states in advancing urban entrepreneurial strategies and global market-oriented reforms while also responding to the uneven social fall-outs of these interventions (Brenner, 2004).
4. The centralising tendencies of national and state governments along with the demands of local democracy.

Need for a Paradigm Shift

Moving the Centre of Power: Voice and Accountability

Through much of the twentieth century, even as the State was gaining more power, the plight of the average citizen was worsening. Despite numerous urban development projects, cities were deteriorating. Roads and walkways were in a bad state, urban waste was scattered, sanitation was poor, traffic was chaotic, and there were inadequate water supply, housing, and transportation facilities. Civic services, such as obtaining birth and death certificates and building licences, were plagued by significant delays. Tax matters were subject to arbitrary actions, corruption was rampant, and the authorities paid little attention to addressing public grievances. In short, the voice of the ordinary citizen was ignored, and they had no significant role in the affairs of the state.

Given these circumstances, the major challenge in a democratic society was how to shift the centre of power from the State to the Citizen. People had to raise their voices to hold the state accountable and demand their right to participate in the planning and governance of their cities. However, several questions arose:

- What exactly is citizens' or people's or public participation?
- How can motivated groups or individuals be identified for participation?
- What methods can enable such participation?
- Can a single public interest represents cities?

Over 50 years ago, in 1968, the renowned French writer on cities, Henri Lefebvre, introduced the concept of the 'Right to the City' in his book "Le Droit a la Ville". He defined it as "a right of no exclusion of urban society from qualities and benefits of urban life" (Lefebvre, 1968). Subsequently, social movements emerged in some western cities as "a call to action to reclaim the city as a co-created space: a place of life detached from the growing effects that commodification and capitalism are proposed to have had over social interaction and the rise of posited spatial inequalities in worldwide cities throughout the last two centuries" (Harvey, 2008). Drawing significant attention from developing countries in Asia and Latin America, the 'Right to the City' approach primarily addresses social exclusion. In broad terms, it advocates for the creation of just and equal cities.

Participatory Planning

The World Bank (2019) recognised Participatory Planning as "a process that convenes a broad base of key stakeholders, on an interactive basis, in order to generate a diagnosis of the existing situation and develop strategies to solve jointly identified problems". It serves as a viable management tool that emphasises: (a) establishing a mutual partnership and interaction between government officials, elected representatives, and the community for convergence of knowledge, skills, and resources for plan development, and (b) ensuring that decisions are relatable, instill a sense of ownership, and generate interest among the people who will ultimately benefit them.

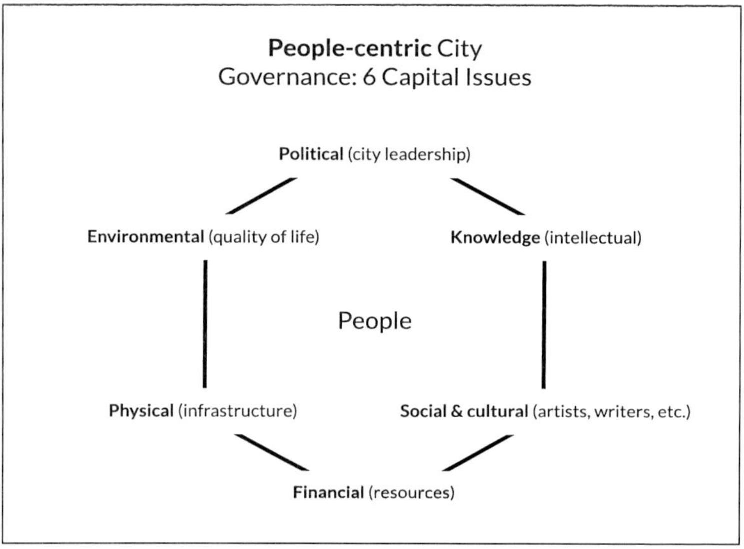

Fig. 13.1: Six capital issues in people-centric urban governance.
Source: Author.

While the concepts and theories regarding people's participation in a democratic society may sound appealing, it is crucial to examine their practical implementation? Indian cities witnessed several public movements during the freedom struggle in the first half of the twentieth century. However, people were kept in the dark about the views they had expressed.

The voice of citizens initially emerged through small associations formed mainly to represent the interests of taxpayers. Over time, civic awareness grew, and civil society emerged as a strong force in some metropolises like Delhi and Mumbai, rallying against foreign power to achieve independence. Now, people had to contend with their own governments and the representatives they had elected. In a democracy, it was expected that these elected representatives would safeguard the people's interests and address their grievances. However, the reality fell short of expectations. Once in power, the elected officials' interests did not always align with those of their constituents. While there were exceptions, private interests gradually overshadowed public interests, leading to a conflict between the ruling class and the people.

To illustrate, the preparation of the master plan was conducted by the city planning authority in an opaque manner. The process involved publishing a draft plan for public comments within a specified time frame, followed by finalising the plan with the approval of the state government. Thus, it was a consultative rather than a participatory process, with decision-making power solely resting with the authorities. Citizen movements gained prominence in the 1990s when some citizen groups established citywide organisations to promote people's participation in civic affairs. Initiatives like the Citizens' Voluntary Initiative for the City (CIVIC) in Bangalore, Parivartan (Change) in Delhi, and Bombay First in Mumbai emerged. Swabhimana, launched in Bangalore in 1995, was a unique initiative that captured people's imagination as the first public-private partnership in civic affairs in India.

The 74th Constitutional Amendment recognised the importance of people's participation in city planning and development by introducing ward committees and district/metropolitan planning committees that could include members from civil society. However, the actual composition of these committees was left to the states, which have shown reluctance to democratise the planning process. The functioning of these committees leaves much to be desired.

The passage of the Right to Information Act in 2005 finally acknowledged the rights of citizens to know how the government functions, including its decisions, expenditure, potential misuse of public funds, and the benefits that accruing to the people.

The Act allows any citizen to seek information from government departments or agencies, with the agencies obliged to provide the requested information, except in matters related to national security. Additionally, the government has a responsibility to proactively inform citizens about new policies.

Recognising the importance of participatory planning, the United Nations, included it in the Sustainable Development Goals, which India has adopted. Goal 11, pertaining to sustainable cities and communities, aims to make cities "inclusive, safe, resilient and sustainable" by "enhancing capacity for participatory, integrated and sustainable human settlement planning". The government's first attempt to involve citizens in city planning was seen in the Smart Cities Mission, where selected cities were asked to prepare City Development Plans in consultation with the people. However, how people responded to the opportunity, and to what extent their ideas and suggestions were taken into account and incorporated into the city development plans remains unclear.

Measuring the effectiveness of participation is a challenge. Arnstein (1969) developed a Ladder of Citizen Participation consisting of eight steps: Manipulation, Therapy, Informing, Consultation, Placation, Partnership, Delegated Power, and Citizen Control.

The first three represent non-Participation, the second three Tokenism and the last two Citizen Control. Different cities are at different stages on this ladder, but no city in India or elsewhere can be said to have reached the top. It is necessary to recognise the limitations of participation, including conflicts of interest among participants, dominance of vocal groups, information gaps, and citizen apathy, as evidenced by low voter turnout in municipal elections in most Indian cities.

Data shows that voter turnout is usually lower in municipal elections than in any other kind of election. Turnout is lower in bigger cities than in smaller cities, i.e., in corporation elections as compared. Even the highest turnout in corporation elections, for example in Kolkata, is lower than the turnout for elections in smaller urban local bodies. (Fig. 13.2)

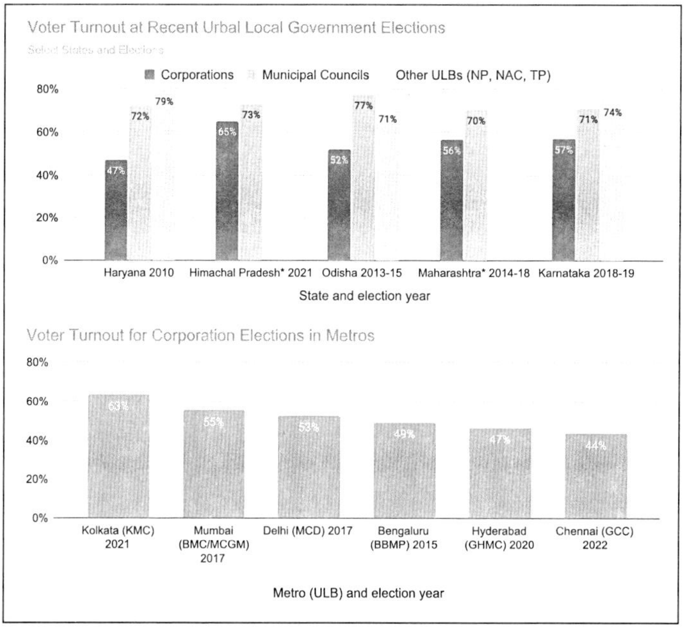

Fig. 13.2: Turnout in municipal elections, select states and ULBs.

Source: Swastik Harish, based on reports from State Election Commissions.

Citizen-centric governance demands that people's participation begins at the planning stage. Participatory planning can be defined as "a process that convenes a broad base of key stakeholders on an interactive basis, in order to generate a diagnosis of the existing situation and develop strategies to solve jointly identified problems" (World Bank, 2016). Ideally, a plan for the development of a ward must emerge from the interaction between elected representatives, government officials, and the community.

While speaking of citizen participation, it is also important to consider citizen responsibility in contributing to good governance. Respect for the law is generally low among Indian people, including the educated class. Compliance with laws in Indian cities is rather poor, be it the traffic rules or building regulations or payment of taxes. While law enforcement may be weak, it should not serve as a justification for violating the law. Voluntary cooperation is preferable to waiting for penal action.

It would be relevant to examine models of people's participation in developing countries in Africa and Asia, as they offer parallels with the conditions in India, rather than those in Europe and USA. Gautam Bhatia, the noted architect, has highlighted West African cities like Lagos in Nigeria and Kumasi in Ghana, which, like Delhi and Mumbai, are migrant towns whose development and future prospects are tied to the economy of day-to-day minor endeavours. These cities require temporary civic spaces for activities such as for vegetable markets, cattle fairs, and public festivals—features that make them strikingly similar to Indian cities. The combination of agricultural towns, rural outposts, and cosmopolitan centres provide the necessary value to a city's migrant economy. In Andhra Pradesh, during Chandrababu Naidu's tenure as chief minister, space was allocated in the city outskirts once a week for 'Raithu Bazar', or 'farmer's market'. This model gained popularity and was replicated in some other cities (Dey, 2012). The future 'urban' can also include 'rural' features where middle-class values like theatres, libraries, and stadiums coexist with temporary bazaars and open maidans for kabbadi and folk songs—a commingling of urban-rural cultures.

Ultimately, what we need is a cohesive and vibrant community that feels empowered to create an enabling environment for all sections of society to live in harmony, transcending differences of caste, community, language, and status. Can future Indian towns or cities reflect what the American urbanist Jane Jacobs called 'cultural cohesion', where the integration of economic and other disparities would lead to an unconscious mixing of interdependence, representing a finely woven carpet?

People's Ire Leads to People's Partnership

One of the most challenging tests I faced was during my tenure as Chairman of Bangalore Development Authority (BDA). Shortly after taking charge, I was surprised to see endless queues of people outside my office. As I listened to their grievances, which were many—years of waiting for site allotment, failure to receive a sale deed despite payment, long delays in land acquisition compensation, refund issues, and more—I realised the validity of their concerns. Meanwhile, the staff had their own explanations for the delays.

However, what appalled me was the utter indifference and lack of concern exhibited by the officials. I gradually discovered the awful state of affairs within the organisation, which was responsible for vast expanses of land in the burgeoning metropolis of Bangalore.

One afternoon, while contemplating how to address the situation, a few citizen groups approached me and invited me to a meeting to discuss their problems. Eager to gain a better understanding, I readily agreed.

When I entered the meeting hall at the Institute of Engineers in Bangalore, I was met with a huge gathering. I was unaware of what awaited me. After the initial welcome and presentation of a memorandum, the audience was invited to ask questions. What followed was an onslaught of inquiries, complaints, and an outright attack on the Bangalore Development Authority, branding it as 'a den of corruption'! I was at a loss for words to provide any meaningful response but mustered enough courage to acknowledge the maladies afflicting the organisation, including corruption. Emphasising that addressing the issue of corruption required not only the efforts of the BDA but also the cooperation of the people, I offered to carry forward the dialogue.

Soon after, I convened a meeting of concerned NGOs and citizen groups to explore effective ways of addressing the challenges people were facing. After extensive discussions, I proposed the idea of setting up a forum comprising government agencies and citizen groups to deliberate on specific issues and formulate workable solutions. The idea was welcomed, giving birth to 'Swabhimana', the first public-people initiative for city improvement and citizen welfare in Bangalore in 1995. It focused on issues like decentralised solid waste management and public grievances pertaining to BDA and the City Corporation. Some members called for increased transparency in the operations of BDA, a suggestion I readily embraced. They proposed that official files should be open for inspection. Despite strong resistance from the staff, I agreed, and we began making relevant files available for review by interested persons. We urged citizens to set up Resident Welfare Associations in their localities to improve their neighbourhoods and address local problems, leading to the formation of several new RWAs in Bangalore.

Overall, Swabhimana had a positive impact, but it encountered obstacles when elected representatives felt their importance was being undermined. This 'experiment' in a forging government-citizen partnership and promoting people's participation in city governance lasted for about a decade. Although the Forum no longer exists, the various RWAs formed during that time continue to operate. Civic activism in Bengaluru, as in many other major cities in India, has been on the rise.

Equity: Minimising disparities

Building upon the discussion in the section on poverty and inequality, it is evident that the core issue lies in ensuring equitable access to infrastructure and services for all segments of the population, without exclusion. Equity goes beyond providing the bare minimum and encompasses the necessary comforts for civilised living in urban environments. According to the latest World Inequality Report (2022), published by the World Inequality Lab based in Paris, the wealthiest 10 per cent of the global population earns 52 per cent of global income, while the poorest half of the population earns a mere 8.5 per cent of it. The report lists *India as one of the most unequal societies in the world*, with the bottom half of the population earning Rs. 53,610 while the top 10 per cent earns 20 times more at Rs. 11,66,520. The report further observes that the "Covid crisis has exacerbated inequalities between the very wealthy and the rest of the population. Yet, in rich countries, government intervention prevented massive rise in poverty. This was not the case in poor countries". Regarding India, it must be stated that the first long lockdown for two months and the sudden onset of the second wave of the pandemic did cause immense suffering to the general population, particularly the migrants. Subsequently, the government took strong measures to provide relief to the poor and upgrade the health infrastructure.

A disturbing phenomenon of the twenty-first century is the widening disparities in the education system, particularly in higher education. Many private schools, colleges, and universities, branding themselves as institutions of excellence, are becoming exclusive and elitist. With fee structures affordable only to the rich, they resemble luxury establishments, irrespective of the quality of education they provide (although it should be acknowledged that some of them are indeed centres of excellence). The proliferation of such institutions has significant implications for urban governance, including spatial inequality and infrastructure provision in urban agglomerations.

Some economists argue that rising inequalities need not be considered a big problem if economic growth raises incomes. Following the economic reforms of 1991, India's economic growth pulled millions of Indians out of poverty, although inequality widened (See Fig. 6.3).

Concentration of wealth in a few hands is certainly undesirable and can be dealt with through fiscal policy measures. The primary objective of public policy should be to ensure justice for the most disadvantaged population, especially in developing countries like India. This can be achieved by creating sufficient employment opportunities. The following measures have been proposed:

1. Introduce an Urban Employment Guarantee Scheme modelled after the Mahatma Gandhi National Rural Employment Guarantee Scheme (MGNREGS). This scheme would guarantee employment for a minimum period each year, providing economic security to vulnerable sections in cities. According to data from the Centre for Monitoring Indian Economy (CMIE), monthly unemployment has fluctuated between 6.56 per cent and 11.84 per cent over a year with urban employment surpassing rural unemployment in 10 of those months (*TOI*, May 30, 2022). A study by Azim Premji University estimated that providing100 days of guaranteed work at a daily wage of Rs. 300 for 20 million workers, with the overall wage bill capped at 50 per cent of the total outlay, would cost the Indian government Rs. 1 lakh crore (*TOI*, May 30, 2022).
2. Ensure a minimum wage for private employment that meets the requirements of a decent livelihood in urban areas. The minimum wage may vary based on different city classifications.

Instead of solely focusing on constructing new housing stock in far-flung areas that inconveniences those settled in one place, it is crucial to upgrade the housing conditions of the poor and marginalised sections to meet decent living standards, including access to water and sanitation facilities.

Rural-Urban Dichotomy

There is a noticeable disconnect between public policies for rural and urban areas, resulting in a rural-urban dichotomy. Planning efforts often fail to consider an integrated perspective that encompasses both rural and urban areas. The conflict is pronounced in the utilisation of resources such as land, water and energy. Agricultural land, an essential resource for rural communities, is extensively acquired for industrialisation and urbanisation, depriving the farmers of their livelihoods. This drives migration from rural to urban areas as people seek urban employment opportunities. River water that flows across the rural terrain is diverted to cities to satisfy the needs of urban dwellers and industries, while energy sources from forests and underground are exploited to drive economic growth, the fruits of which are enjoyed largely by the urban residents. This exploitation of rural resources to build an urban civilisation negatively impacts the farming community, the poor, and marginalised farmers and labourers, as well as food security and the environment. It results in the loss of farm and forest lands and contributes to pollution; ultimately affecting the entire rural-urban ecosystem, leading to unsustainable urbanisation, complex spatial distribution, and increasing social and economic inequalities.

The rural-urban conflict can also be viewed from the perspective of the rural-urban relationship. With increasing urbanisation, the boundaries between the two are becoming blurred, and there is a spatial transformation occurring through the daily flows of people, goods and financial investments in the regions surrounding cities. There is a noticeable shift from farming to non-farm sectors in village economies.. According to the NABARD All-India Financial Survey (NAFIS) of 2017-18, only 48 per cent of rural households are engaged in agriculture, while 52 per cent are engaged in non-agricultural activities. Managing the urban and rural ecosystems has become more challenging and ignoring these challenges can lead to disastrous consequences. It is essential to fully appreciate the interdependence between these two as well as adverse impacts that activities in one area can have on the other.

Agricultural Economy

Agriculture, which largely serves as the backbone of the Indian economy, cannot be considered purely a rural activity. Foodgrains and other agricultural produce from rural areas are marketed in cities, and the entire supply chain, with numerous linkages, is a rural-urban process. The spillover effects of farming activities, such as pollution and climate change, are significant. In Delhi, for example, air pollution is caused not only by local sources but also by the burning of crop residues from neighbouring states. Approximately 100 million tonnes of agricultural waste is burnt annually, in addition to 10-15 million tonnes of garbage burnt in the open. Moreover, a considerable amount of solid waste from urban areas is dumped in rurál regions, polluting the environment. The generation of farm and food waste in India is enormous and has adverse effects on both farmers and urban consumers. Annually, India produces an estimated 500 million tonnes of farm waste, 277 million tonnes of urban solid waste, and households waste about 50 kg of food per capita. The monetary value of harvest and post-harvest losses is estimated to be around Rs. 92,000 crores a year. Apart from the economic losses, the pollution of air, water and soil, caused by inefficient waste management is a major concern, especially its effects on public health.

Urban agriculture may also be considered for ensuring higher levels of food security. According to a 2017 report published in the *International Journal on Emerging Technology*, rapid urbanisation, population explosion and and climate change increases the risk of food shortage. Another report of 2010 by the M.S. Swaminathan Research Foundation reveals that 50 per cent of women and children in urban areas are anemic due to lack of nutrition. Globally, the UN Food and Agricultural Organisation acknowledged that urban and peri-urban farming can contribute to local food and nutritional needs.

It is interesting to note that about 60 per cent of Delhi's demand for meat, and 15 per cent of its vegetable needs are met by city-grown produce. Also, 25 per cent of its milk requirements is met locally. The Draft Citizen's Policy for Urban Agriculture in Delhi prepared by People's Resource Centre which aims to provide a holistic framework for urban farming has been submitted to the Delhi government. It has recommended building on existing practices, promoting residential and community farming through rooftop and kitchen gardens, allocating vacant land for agricultural use, creating a market, developing policies for animal rearing, and spreading awareness. In view of the increasing threat to food security, similar policies must be adopted in other states. State governments must also consider incentivizing urban farming practices. More research is certainly needed on food security and its relationship with urbanisation.

Land Degradation

According to the Global Land Outlook Report [United Nations Convention to Combat Desertification (UNCCD), 2022], up to 40 per cent of the planet's land is degraded, affecting half of the world's population, and costing 50 per cent of the global GDP. In India, 29.3 per cent of the total geographical area is affected by land degradation due to factors such as deforestation, urban expansion, population growth, pollution and improper waste disposal. This leads to the loss of top soil, which is essential for life. The consequences are alarming and include food and nutrition insecurity, water insecurity, rapid climate change, poverty, migration, and a reduction in ecosystem services. Restoring degraded land requires adopting regenerative practices for nature-positive food production in rural areas and greening urban areas. Under the UN Convention, countries have committed to restore one billion hectares of degraded land by 2030, and India has set a target of 28 million hectares. A tall order indeed!

Human-Animal Conflict

The invasion of animals into cities is an unexpected predicament, but that's precisely what is happening. Sightings of leopards in the outskirts of Bengaluru and instances of humans being killed by leopards highlight this issue. For a long time, it was assumed that cities and animals were mutually exclusive, except for pets and horses used for entertainment. Cows, buffaloes, and pigs, which used to be part of households about fifty years ago, have mostly been driven out of urban areas. As cities grew in population, animals were considered a nuisance that obstructed traffic and caused discomfort, leading to their banishment. In 1997, Tamil Nadu passed a law, The TN Animals and

Birds in Urban Areas (Control and Regulation) Act, prohibiting cows and other animals from the city. Similar laws were enacted in some other states. Gujarat has recently introduced legislation to regulate movement of stray cattle in its major cities due to the threat they pose to two-wheeler riders.

While striving for our own comfort, we forgot to safeguard the conditions necessary for animals, including wild animals, to live in their own habitat. Large-scale deforestation has deprived animals their sources of food and shelter, prompting them to venture into the 'civilised' world of human beings and prey on them. Elephants walking into agricultural fields and destroying crops is not an unusual occurrence, but wild animals rarely strayed into urban zones. Now, it is seen as a danger to human life. Finding ways to convert man-animal conflict into a positive human-animal relationship is a crucial aspect of addressing the rural-urban nexus.

There are many other areas of interface between the urban and the rural, such as climate change, education, and public health, that involve different types of exchanges and impact the overall economic and social development of the country. As India's urban population continues to grow and is expected to surpass 50 per cent of the coming decades, the future of urbanisation depends on the relationship between cities and their surrounding rural areas. Why not, therefore, develop an integrated approach that builds synergy between rural and urban areas by stitching together the sectoral policies? This would involve breaking down the 'silos' mentality and adopting a holistic approach to planning. This calls for a paradigm shift from the planning and development models of the past and a fresh perspective. In the pre-1990s socialist era, the State determined the development model and played a dominant role in driving the economy through the Five Year Plans. In the post-liberalisation period, deregulation opened the avenues for a more prominent role for the private sector and the market economy. However, both phases of development adopted a compartmentalised approach, treating "rural" and "urban" as separate sectors, with a strong focus on rural development and limited attention to urban development, as discussed in the introductory part of the book. The governance model evolved for rural areas through Panchayati Raj aimed at decentralisation of powers to local authorities, while urban areas remained largely untouched. Consequently, the colonial system of governance for cities and towns continued in the post-independence period, with states having the freedom to shape their own laws and plans. This resulted in a bi-focal approach to development process, creating sharp disparities between the rural and the urban.

Chapter
14

Reforming Urban Governance

Overhauling Municipal and Urban Laws

The first step in reforming urban governance in India is to thoroughly revise the laws governing municipalities, corporations, and the planning of towns and cities. State governments, that have originally legislated these laws, need to take up the responsibility of revising them. While some amendments have been made over time, the basic structure remains the same. The transformation from the predominantly bureaucratic system that prevailed during the British regime to a democratic system, which is the hallmark of post-independent India, has not occurred. The changes, if any, have been more cosmetic than substantive. True local democracy is virtually absent.

Revamping Governance Systems

The two systems of municipal governance—one where the Mayor and elected representatives are the key decision-makers, and the other where the Commissioner has a larger role in decision-making—have been the subject of much discussion. For instance, the former system is prevalent in Kolkata with a Mayor-in-Council system, while the latter is seen in Mumbai with a strong Commissioner system. This dichotomy between democratic and bureaucratic systems of local governance is not unique to India and has been observed in other countries as well.

In Britain, two traditions can be recognised: one of parliamentary sovereignty in a unitary state and the other of local independence, where local authorities claim the right to represent local opinion and resist state control. The former implies that local authorities act as agents of the central government, providing efficient administration in line with its policies. The latter advocates for greater autonomy for local authorities to manage their affairs while respecting national policies. In the USA, local government patterns have been influenced by three different thought processes: Thomas Jefferson's idea of direct democracy reflecting the will of the people, Hamilton's idea of a strong government promoting efficiency and effective public service delivery, and Madison's idea of balancing interests through discussion, negotiation, and compromise to achieve political consensus and social stability. As a result, the USA has four types of local administration: Strong Mayor-Council, Weak Mayor-Council, Commissioner System, and Council-Manager System (Pinto, 2000).

India inherited the system created by the British. According to the Report of the Indian Statutory Commission (Government of India, 1930), known as the Simon Commission, local self-government "in the sense of a representative organisation, responsible to a body of electors, enjoying wide powers of administration and taxation and functioning both as a school for training in responsibility and as a vital link in the chain of organisms that make up the governance of the country, is a British creation" (p. 298). However, in reality, the British administration in India was highly centralised, as noted in Part 1. The colonial legacy has continued to influence state governments, which are reluctant to decentralise power to city governments.

Local government in India is a state subject, and it is the responsibility of the states to implement the necessary reforms to empower urban local bodies. The 74th Amendment to the constitution has made provisions enabling state governments to decentralise power. However, what states have done so far is to make amendments to existing municipal laws to comply with constitutional provisions without substantially transferring power. In other words, the reforms are more in letter than in spirit. Hence, the following suggestions.

Revisit and Review 74th Constitutional Amendment

This exercise must be undertaken to establish urban local democracy on a firm foundation. Several provisions require amendments.

1. Delete the provision regarding the representation of Members of Parliament and State Legislature in a Municipality (Art 234R). Although it is stated that they shall not have the right to vote, some states like Karnataka have allowed them to exercise this right as before. This can distort voting results on specific matters or motions, as it happened after the municipal corporation elections in Bengaluru in 2015. Despite the Bhartiya Janata Party (BJP) securing a majority (100 out of 198 seats), the Congress Party managed to win the mayor's post with the support of MPs, MLAs and MLCs. Moreover, the presence of state and national representatives can be intimidating to local councillors and hinder their freedom to express their views.
2. Ensure the democratic character of the local government in unambiguous terms instead of leaving discretion to the states (Art 243W). This would imply that there should be a political executive at the city level with powers similar to that of the state government. This can take the form of a directly elected Mayor or an indirectly elected Mayor assisted by a Mayoral Committee or a Mayor-in-Council system. Each member could be assigned specific subjects/portfolios, similar to a cabinet at the state level. Along with political power, the mayor and their team shall be accountable to the people for providing efficient administration and effective delivery of services. They should be answerable for any omissions and commissions of the municipality.
3. Revise 12th schedule to the Constitution, which contains 18 items. Some of these items overlap with the functions of the state government or other organisations. For example, regulation of land use comes under the jurisdiction of city planning authorities, fire services are provided by separate agencies in some states, and urban poverty alleviation is the responsibility of the state government. This has led to confusion.
4. Thoroughly review the composition and functions of the Metropolitan Planning Committee (MPC) and District Planning Committee. The 74th Constitutional Amendment fails to recognise that metropolitan cities and even some smaller cities have a statutory planning authority constituted

under the Town and Country Planning Act of the state, which is responsible for preparing a master plan including zoning regulations. The only function entrusted to the MPC is the preparation of a draft development plan for the metropolitan area [Art 243ZE(1)]. However, sub-clause (d) of sub-section (2) of the same Article states that the state legislature may assign functions relating to planning and coordination for the metropolitan area to the MPC. Lack of clarity and overlapping jurisdictions have resulted in litigation, with courts issuing orders based on their interpretation. Regarding the District Planning Committee, its main function is to consolidate plans prepared by the Panchayats and the Municipalities in the district and prepare a draft development plan. Both the draft plans prepared by the MPC and the DPC are to be forwarded to the state government, but there is no clarity on what happens to the plans thereafter. It should be noted that state governments have been extremely reluctant to constitute the MPCs. Only repeated prodding by the central government and court directions have led to their establishment. However, they are given little importance due to the influential metropolitan planning and development authorities, which are parastatal organisations under the control of state governments.

In the urban sphere in India, decentralisation cannot be considered a willing and conscious decision on the part of state governments aimed at improving local administration. As Prud'homme put it, "decentralisation is a political strategy by ruling elites to retain most of their power by relinquishing some if it."

BBMP Ward Delimitation

The BBMP, which has been without an elected body for approximately two years, is likely to hold elections. In June 2022, the Government of Karnataka announced an increase in the number of wards from 198 to 243. This delimitation was carried out by an official committee of BBMP based on the 2011 Census data. However, this approach had an inherent limitation as it relied on population data that was over 10 years old. The Registrar General of India published the projected population of India in July 2020 which could have been utilised as a basis for the BBMP Act of 2020. Unfortunately, this opportunity was missed.

Another drawback of this Act is the provision for an official committee of BBMP to conduct the delimitation, rather than a Technical Committee headed by the Registrar General at the central level. It is difficult to expect objectivity from an official committee of a local body, resulting in an increase in the number of wards from 198 to 243. The delimitation exercise clearly exemplifies of how the state government exerts control over the governance of a large metropolitan city, as well as smaller urban areas, defeating the very purpose of decentralisation.

Restructuring Institutions and Delivery of Services

The 74th Constitutional Amendment is often hailed as the holy book of urban governance and its implementation as the panacea for the ills of local democracy. However, it is important to recognise that this reform measure primarily focuses on municipalities, which are elected bodies, while neglecting the parastatals responsible for urban planning, infrastructure development, water supply and sewerage, power supply, public transport, housing, and regulation of peripheral development of cities. Indian cities, especially metros and larger ones, are governed by multiple institutions and laws. In addition to parastatals, there are government departments at the state and central levels that provide various services such as security and traffic regulation (Police), inter-city transport (Railways, Airways), and telecom services, including private entities. Consequently, city governance has become complex, requiring innovative approaches to address emerging challenges.

As the UK City Growth Commission and Royal Society of Arts (2014) aptly stated, "A new global picture of growth is taking shape… It is about the rise of cities, the concentration of productivity, innovation, and creativity that will drive our economic future" (p. 2). Therefore, it is crucial to visualise the city as a unified entity and adopt a holistic view of its functions by reorganising its governance structures.

What type of an urban governance model would be suitable for Indian cities? It must be acknowledged that in a vast country like India, with states larger than many countries, decentralisation should be at the core of public policy, empowering local bodies—both urban and rural—with the necessary autonomy. The subsidiarity principle holds significant importance here. Kelkar & Shah (2019) articulated this aptly: "The subsidiarity principle is the essential foundation for cities that have local political arrangements for local public goods. When we see the city governance of New York or London or Sydney, we see a large array of functions being placed at the city level, which are found in India with the State or Union governments. The slogan of political thinkers in this field is the need to place 'funds, functions and functionaries at the local level'."

Committees on Urban Governance Reform for Bengaluru

Over the years, the Government of Karnataka has constituted several committees to examine the governance of Bengaluru and make recommendations for improvement. The first was the Committee on Urban Management of Bangalore City (1997), comprising four members, with myself as the Chairman, one member with a political background, and two officials. At that time, I also served as Commissioner of the Bangalore Municipal Corporation. In 2008, the Government of Karnataka formed an Expert Committee on 'Governance in the Bangalore Metropolitan Region and Bruhat Bengaluru Mahanagara Palike (BBMP)' chaired by K. Kasturirangan, the former Chairman of Indian Space Research Organisation, along with four other members, including myself. The most recent committee, formed in 2015, was called the BBMP Restructuring Committee, and consisted of three members, with a retired chief secretary to the state serving as the chairman, an official, and an expert.

The committees were tasked with addressing fundamental questions regarding Bengaluru's unprecedented growth, devising strategies for better governance and coordination of services, and proposing ideas for city management and restructuring of the local government framework. They extensively engaged with various civic agencies, professional bodies, NGOs, and individuals to gather insights from diverse perspectives. These committees also studied alternative models of city governance, both domestic and international.

While some of the recommendations put forth by these committees may be considered radical, others aimed to tackle fundamental issues in governance and service delivery. Yet, certain recommendations were common across the 1997, 2008 and 2015 committees:

1. Strengthening the local government through greater decentralisation of powers and ensuring financial resilience.
2. Having a directly elected mayor for the city corporation, serving a five-year term with executive authority (two committees).
3. Enhancing the effectiveness of ward committees to improve governance at the ward level and promote public participation.
4. Rationalising planning administration by expanding the scope of the Metropolitan Planning Committee (MPC) to encompass the entire metropolitan region and granting it the necessary authority.
5. Restructuring BBMP into five smaller independent municipal corporations.

It is disheartening to note that despite the Karnataka government's commitment to improve the governance of the capital city, there is a lack of willingness to implement their recommendations. Action has been taken on some matters, such as the establishment of the MPC or ward committees, only in response to public pressure or court directives. Unfortunately, political economy often takes precedence over public interest when it comes to relinquishing power.

Committees for Restructuring Delhi Municipal Corporation

The governance of Delhi, as a national capital with complex jurisdictional overlaps between a state, union territory, and metropolis, presents greater complexity than any other city in India. The Municipal Corporation of Delhi was established under the Delhi Municipal Corporation Act, 1957 and, in the first decade of the twenty-first century, it ranked as the second largest corporation in the world after

Tokyo, accounting for 94 per cent of the area and 96 per cent of Delhi's population.

Due to its immense size and seemingly unmanageable problems, the Government of India and the Government of National Capital Territory of Delhi were determined to restructure the monolithic municipal corporation into more viable units. Several committees were formed to examine this issue, starting with the Balakrishnan Committee, which recommended dividing the Corporation into eight parts. Subsequently, the Virendra Prakash Committee proposed dividing it into four parts, the Deep Chandu Committee suggested five independent corporations, and the Second Administrative Commission, viewing potential complications, discouraged divisions. Eventually, the Delhi government decided to divide it into three independent municipal corporations. In 2011, a committee chaired by K. Dharmarajan, IAS (Retd), was constituted to draft a new legislation for this purpose.

Interestingly, after a decade, the government decided to merge the corporations into one in May 2022.

City Leadership

Deliberations and literature on urban governance in India often emphasise decentralisation, fiscal devolution, infrastructure, environment, and services. While these aspects are undoubtedly crucial, one key element that is often overlooked is the role of leadership in transforming a city. Our cities are headless wonders with no one to lead, inspire, or unite people for a common cause. Though there may be motivated and dynamic commissioners who have brought about some change during their short tenures, they are not elected representatives who are accountable to the people. The prime minister leads the nation and the chief minister leads the state. The ultimate responsibility for governance lies with them. The question remains: Who is the leader of a city in India? Theoretically, it is the mayor, as she is an elected representative, but in reality, the mayor lacks both power and responsibility. While they may perform ceremonial functions and, depending on their personality, guide certain activities, they are not officially recognised as the leader of the city.

Looking across the world, whether it be well-developed cities in the USA and Europe or developing cities in Asian, African, and Latin American countries like China, Japan, Brazil, Argentina, and South Africa, transformative changes have taken place in all of them. They have strong mayors at the helm of affairs, who enjoy executive powers and provide leadership in city governance. The pioneering model of such leadership was demonstrated by Jaime Lerner, Mayor of Curitiba city in Brazil. As early as 1974, he caught the imagination of the world by introducing the first Bus Rapid Transit System (BRTS)—*Rede Integrada de Transporte*—one of the most successful examples of transit-oriented development that has been replicated in many other cities, including India, where such efforts are struggling.

Rudy Giuliani, Mayor of New York City from 1994 to 2001, is credited with significantly reducing the city's crime rate and reforming its finances. His leadership qualities came to the fore during the deadly terrorist attack on the World Trade Center towers on September 11, 2011. He was praised for his handling of the crisis and was fondly called 'America's Mayor'.

It is worth noting that in the pre-independence era, prominent national leaders and freedom fighters began their political careers in city local governments. For instance, C. Rajagopalachari (Rajaji), who became the Governor-General of India in 1948, served as the president of Salem Municipality in the then Madras Presidency in 1917. Chittaranjan Das became the first mayor of Calcutta Municipal Corporation in 1923, with Netaji Subash Chandra Bose as the corporation's Chief Executive Officer. Netaji also became the mayor in 1930. Jawaharlal Nehru, the first Prime Minister of India, was once the president of Allahabad Municipality. Unfortunately, in present-day India, politicians aspire to directly become legislators, parliamentarians, and ministers, skipping local municipal governance. The municipal governance system in India does not encourage local leadership either. Even in states where the mayor is directly elected and has a five-year term (Andhra Pradesh, Madhya Pradesh, and Uttar Pradesh) executive authority is vested in the commissioner, thereby weakening the mayor's authority.

It is high time that Indian cities, which significantly contribute to economic growth, generate employment, and serve as centres of higher education, knowledge, and innovation, also become vibrant centres of leadership. There is a strong case for introducing a system with directly elected mayors with executive powers for larger cities (corporations) and municipal presidents for smaller municipalities, providing leadership to both the municipal body and the city. The Second Administrative Reforms Commission (2007) has also expressed the view that "it is desirable to choose the Mayor/Chairperson through popular mandate in a direct election. Such a Mayor should have a fixed tenure of five years. The Council should have powers of budget approval, oversight and major policies... direct election of Mayor, which promotes strong visible leadership is an important source of recruitment of talent in public life and leadership development" (p. 217).

Importance of Politics in City Governance

One of the reasons why city leadership has not received adequate attention in India is because politics at the local level is often considered 'dirty' and 'corrupt'. Educated and qualified individuals tend to avoid participating in municipal elections, and they are often advised against doing so. It is crucial that the negative perception associated with local and higher-level politics gives way to a more positive attitude. With increasing representation of cities in state assemblies and the Lok Sabha, urban governance must be seen through a political lens, not just a municipal one. Out of the 543 Lok Sabha seats, 131 constituencies have an urban population of more than 40 per cent.

While the urban is still under-represented, this number will increase with future delimitation of constituencies, as will representation in state assemblies. Considering the economic importance of cities and their substantial contributions to GDP, politics within cities and city councils should receive the attention it deserves, which in turn, will promote better city governance. As K.C. Sivaramakrishnan aptly put it, "the new MPs and MLAs from metros need to realise that just as national issues cannot disregard a city's needs, local issues cannot be brushed aside under a national carpet". City councillors, who also serve as people's representatives living in close proximity to them, must be accorded the status and dignity they deserve. This recognition will go a long way in motivating them to better serve the people's needs and city's interests. Enhancing the capacity of municipal or urban institutions should not be confined to the bureaucracy or professionals, it must also include political capacity. This means that councillors and other political actors involved in transforming a city must be equipped with the necessary skills, especially leadership skills, to effectively govern a city.

From Metropolis to Rurbanopolis: Towards Urban-Rural Integrated Development

The approach advocated here is to create "sustainable human settlements and communities", and move towards "sustainable development" of a region, a state, and the country. Sustainable communities should encompass not only urban communities, but also those beyond municipal or urban boundaries, including rural and semi-urban areas within a defined region. While regional planning is being advocated in India, it is limited to large metropolitan regions such as Mumbai, Chennai and Bengaluru, and the NCR of Delhi. There is a need to develop a new strategy for the planning and development of the entire region, rather than compartmentalising it into rural and urban sectors. The 74th Amendment to the constitution, specifically in Articles 243ZD and 243ZE, reflects this concept by emphasising the preparation of District Development Plans (DDP) and Metropolitan Development Plans (MDP) respectively by the District Planning Committee (DPC) and the Metropolitan Planning Committee (MPC), respectively. These committees have a democratic character, with a majority of elected members from panchayats and municipalities. At least four-firth of the DPC should constitute elected members of the panchayats and municipalities, and in the case of MPC, two-thirds of the members should be from municipalities and chairpersons of panchayats.

The DDP includes both rural and urban areas within the district, while the MDP encompasses urban and rural areas, including municipal and village panchayat areas within the metropolitan jurisdiction. The DPC and MPC are responsible for "matters of common interest between the Panchayats and the Municipalities including spatial planning, sharing of water and other physical and natural resources, the integrated development of infrastructure and environmental conservation" (Art 243ZD). The concept of integrated development has been incorporated into the constitution, and its implementation details should be deliberated and decided by the respective committees.

Public policy in India has historically focused on countering rural-urban migration by creating more rural employment schemes, such as the MNREGA launched in 2006. However, there has been a lack of urban employment schemes, forcing migrants to take up jobs in the informal sector, mainly in construction. With urban development receiving little attention from the government, towns, and cities have experienced unplanned growth.

Rural-urban linkages have been recognised in the past, with various models developed based on these linkages. For example, Von Thunen's (Thünen, 1826) Regional Land Use model argued that market forces determine rural land use and urban demand was a key driver of spatial allocation of economic linkages of marginal returns to assets and labour. The Desakota model developed by McGee (1991), based on 'desakotasi' (desa-village, kota-town) of Indonesia, showed that the formation of territorial patterns was a mixture of agricultural and non-agricultural activities of the region, the five main regions being main cities that are big, peri-urban areas within commuting range and exhibits high interaction, desakota region, i.e., the areas along the corridors, densely populated rural regions, and sparsely populated rural regions. The Networked Model of Douglas (2006) proposed clustering settlements, each with its own specialisation, rather than relying on a single large city as the centre.

The PURA (Providing Urban Amenities in Rural Areas) model, advocated by former President Abdul Kalam was initiated in 2012, with a focus on developing potential growth centres like census towns, stimulating local economic development, and enhancing basic services and creating well-planned "rurban" clusters.

In 2016, the central government launched the Shyamaprasad Mukherjee Rurban Mission to develop "a cluster of villages that preserve and nurture the essence of rural community life without compromising with the facilities perceived to be essentially urban in nature, thus creating a cluster of "Rurban Villages". Approximately 300 clusters for "rurban" development were approved by 2022, with nearly 39,000 projects/works completed, out of a total of 76,000 works entered in the scheme management system. However, these efforts they have focused primarily on rural areas without adopting a holistic approach.

The time has come to consciously shape urbanisation in India through appropriate policies and planning. Bogue and Zachariah (1962), in their essay on "Urbanisation and Migration in India", recognised rural-urban migration as the major component of urbanisation and the chief mechanism by which all of the world's great urbanisation trends have been accomplished. Understanding this process can deepen our understanding of urbanisation trends. Given the demographic dynamics and the political considerations associated with voting power, it is essential to examine and debate the potential of rural-urban migration. As observed by the authors, "a discussion of urbanisation in India is fundamentally a discussion of net rural-urban migration and an analysis of the migration-stimulating effects of the various demographic, economic and social factors that are at work". There is a need to explore the economic potential and other indirect benefits of rural-urban migration in India. Amitabh Kundu has emphasised the need to build an alternate macro-economic framework for understanding economic geography by recognising the process of rurbanisation and some small towns showing impressive growth rates. (Kundu, 2018)

Additionally, rural-urban linkages are manifested through continuous interactions, market flows and supply chains. The flow of people, commodities and information and the spatial distribution of economic activities establish a socio-economic interdependence between the rural and the urban. As urbanisation accelerates and urban land demand increases, urban market forces largely determine the rural land use patterns. The territorial patterns that emerge represent a mixture of agricultural and non-agricultural activities, urban uses gradually overtaking the farmlands and rural settlements. However, unplanned semi-urban settlements lacking civic amenities and infrastructure have emerged on the periphery of large cities. Simultaneously, the urban and industrial development authorities acquire large tracts of agricultural land for housing colonies and industrial estates. Thus, extended city regions in India often present a picture of planned and unplanned settlements, with the latter predominantly inhabited by lower middle-class migrant populations, including poor daily wage workers residing in slums or informal settlements.

China's cluster development system is worth considering in this context. Comparing the export trades of India and China reveals that while India exports a slightly wider range of products, China's aggregate export value is significantly higher at $3.36 trillion compared to India's $670 billion.

Efforts have been made to develop models based on the ideas of M.K. Gandhi and J.C. Kumarappa, who advocated local self-reliance for rural development. Elango Rangasamy, the former chairman of a village panchayat in Tamil Nadu, experimented with this concept and founded the Trust for Village Self-Governance in 2001. The trust aimed to develop a viable local economy by localising production and consumption, forming clusters of villages that could merge with nearby 15-20 villages with a population of 50-60,000. This approach provided employment opportunities, retained profits within the villages, reduced dependency on national and global markets and curbed migration to cities. Successful experiments in villages like Kuthambakkam village, comprising 1,050 households, increased family incomes from Rs. 3,000-4,000 to Rs. 20,000-25,000 per month. According to Rangasamy, "the Network Growth Economy concentrates on prosperity creation rather than poverty eradication...A new world order will become possible with strong and self-sustaining village-based local economies" (Chamaraj, 2022).

The obvious question is whether such a model is sustainable. While claims of a new world order may be far-fetched, these new models can inspire the development of a new urban-rural model based on concepts such as Local Economic Development, Local Self-government, and the integration of the local and the global. This model aims to reconstruct the concept of agglomeration, identify rural areas/villages with local resources and potential for growth to develop them as productive regions, and build urban-rural linkages that address issues relating to employment, migration and provision of basic amenities like water supply, sanitation and housing for vulnerable sections of society in urban settings. Planning for such growth presents a significant challenge for policymakers, technologists, and stakeholders.

Capacity to Govern

As urbanisation gathers pace and villages grow into towns, towns into cities and cities into metropolises, new structures of governance will emerge, requiring new skills to govern these evolving cities. Therefore, it becomes crucial to enhance capacities, both at the institutional and individual levels. This demands a thorough examination of the existing systems, skill levels, and future requirements of urban and rural organisations. Strategies and programmes must be devised at macro and micro levels.

A committee on Reforms in Urban Planning Capacity in India (2021), constituted by Niti Ayog, has highlighted the disparity between the growth of urbanisation and the urban planning machinery, which has failed to keep up with the demands of urbanisation and global technological advancements. The town and country planning organisations in the country face a significant shortage of town planners, with only 4,000 sanctioned positions against a requirement of 12,000. Even worse, half of these positions remain vacant (varying by state). Another limiting factor is the poor quality of planning. The committee correctly identifies that lack of human resources and expertise as key challenges in planning for cities. Rural areas face even greater challenges due to the absence of dedicated courses for rural planning.

To overcome these issues, the committee has made several recommendations. The primary recommendation is the implementation of programmatic interventions for the '500 Healthy Cities Programme' over a five-year period, along with a sub-scheme to enhance Development Control Regulations. Other recommendations include increasing human resources in the public sector, ensuring qualified urban planners in services, mainstreaming capacity building and rejuvenation of capacity building institutions, revision of town and country planning Acts, involving the private sector to improve overall planning capacity, fostering local urban leadership, and strengthening the urban planning education system.

While the recommendations of the committee are not groundbreaking, is the key problem lies in the lack of action. The committee highlights the disconnect between the demand for urban planners and the availability of positions, despite numerous degree and postgraduate courses in urban planning across the country. The question arises: where are these young graduates finding employment? Why are they not being absorbed by the public sector, city planning authorities, municipal organisations, or other infrastructure development organisations? Some seek opportunities abroad or take up jobs in the private sector. The issue is not solely related to salaries, as the pay packages in the public sector in India are now relatively good, compared to two decades ago. Instead, it is linked to the recruitment process, fraught with dubious practices, the work culture and the working environment. The failure to attract well-qualified and bright young professionals to public service roles in urban planning reflects poorly on our capacity to place the right individuals in the right jobs. The government must earnestly address this issue and take corrective actions.

The Citizen versus/and The State—Where does Future Power Lie?

"Who will be more powerful in the future, the citizen or the state? Will technology make terrorism easier or harder to carry out? What is the relationship between privacy and security, and how much will we have to give up to be a part of the new digital age? How will war, diplomacy, and revolution change when everyone is connected, and how can we tip the balance in a beneficial way? When broken societies are rebuilt, what will they be able to do with technology?"

These thought-provoking questions posed by Schmidt & Cohen (2013) of Google prompts us to reimagine the future of Indian cities and the country's development trajectory While grappling with issues related to local governance, we must also remain acutely aware of global events that impact cities and smaller human settlements.

We must confront the challenge of accommodating the increasing number of people who will reside in our cities and towns. According to the United Nations, India's urban population will reach 607 million (40.1%) by 2030 and 2.2 billion by 2050 (Firstpost, June 2022). In planning for the future, we must reckon with three factors.

Firstly, contrary to popular belief, net rural-urban migration has only contributed to relatively low percentage (20%) of urban population growth in recent decades. Secondly, we are witnessing a significant rise in urban-urban migration. Lastly, there has been a substantial decline in the rural population (Mathur *et al.*, 2021).

Let us delve into India's demographics. Over the past two decades, population growth has been declining. Live births have consistently decreased since 2003, and by 2019, fertility rates had fallen below 3, below the global average (Saran, 2022). The Indian family is shrinking rapidly, with urbanisation being a key factor.

Despite the declining trend in population growth, majority of India's population is composed of youth, with 43 per cent under the age of 25 and nearly 60 per cent under the age of 35. This demographic dividend presents both opportunities and challenges. The employment rate has fallen from nearly 43 per cent in 2016 to 37 per cent in 2021. The pandemic has added 10 million unemployed individuals in just two years, bringing the unemployment figure to 30 million. So, where will the youth find jobs, as more and more of them migrate to cities?

As we address these issues, we must also consider the global scenario. Khanna (2021), in his thought-provoking book, "Move: How Mass Migration Will Reshape the World and What It Means For You", presents a future defined by mobility—mobile phones, the internet, medical consultations, and finance will all be mobile. Mass migration will become inevitable. Urbanisation within countries has already sparked the largest migration in history and will increasingly occur across borders. Migrants represent 10 per cent of global GDP (World Migration Report, 2018). Young individuals tend to move where there are better job opportunities, income and prospects. It is estimated that about five million students worldwide migrate annually for educational purposes. The long queues at American embassies in India indicate the aspirations of the youth to pursue higher education and better incomes in the United States. Technologically advanced nations compete to attract young talent. North America, Europe, and north-east Asia (Japan, South Korea, Taiwan, among others)—incidentally the three wealthiest regions in the world—are keen to attract migrants due to their declining populations. They have reached sub-replacement fertility levels. Factors such as increasing life expectancy (expected to reach 107 years for those born today) and high dependency ratios (the number of old people each working-age person supports financially, contribute to Japan losing five lakh individuals annually. South Korea's fertility rate has dropped below one child per woman, while Europe faces rising spending on pensions and elder care combined with a shrinking workforce.

In this scenario, youth in developing countries, unable to find jobs in their own countries, have the option to migrate to places where opportunities await. The immigration policies of host countries play a significant role. Canada, for instance, has made entry processes easier, as have Australia and Japan. Many European countries are in desperate need of more people, including unskilled migrants, to care for the elderly, handle waste management, and address infrastructure needs. These countries offer excellent social services—free education and healthcare, reduced pollution, affordable housing, and public transportation. Some countries in eastern Europe and Asia are also attracting migrants. Armenia, Azerbaijan, Georgia, and Kazakhstan offer good educational facilities. The UAE has emerged as the world's most 'post-national' economy, where everyone is a minority, with the local Emirates numbering only one million in a country of 10 million. Therefore, it seems that the future belongs to those willing to move to cities that offer the promise of a better life, regardless of their location. Globally connected cities, inclusive environments and increasingly mobile populations, may become the trend in future urban civilisation.

We must address the issue of rising inequalities, which appears to be worsening. While there are no quick solutions, can we convert it into an opportunity to generate resources for the renewal of our cities? Can we consider implementing progressive taxes on the wealthy? Oxfam has suggested that a tax of just 1 per cent on the increased wealth of India's top 11 billionaires during the pandemic would be sufficient to increase the allocation of Jan Aushadi scheme, which provides affordable medicines, by 140 times.

Anthropologist Ruddock (2021), explores the perpetuation of social hierarchies and health inequalities in medical education in her book, "Special Treatment: Student Doctors at the All India Institute of Medical Sciences". She argues that the narrow norms and conceptions of excellence at AIIMS hinder the potential of the MBBS programme and its students. She calls for a re-evaluation of the purpose of undergraduate education, which could make graduating from India's most prestigious medical college more meaningful. While her study is confined to AIIMS, the argument could potentially be extended to other institutions. The question is whether medical education, and education in general, can be used as a social equaliser?

In terms of urban health, the cost of medical treatment is a serious concern. The corporatisation of the medical profession, coupled with the emergence of luxury hospitals, has rendered healthcare unaffordable for a significant portion of the urban population, resulting in a substantial social divide. Moreover, private hospitals have attracted most of the well-qualified and competent doctors and healthcare professionals, depriving government hospitals of quality manpower. Most private hospitals have turned exploitative. It is essential to prioritise comprehensive health reforms, including medical insurance, standardised test rates and treatments in private hospitals, provision of adequate facilities in government hospitals, and improvements in medical education.

As we envision the future, we must grapple with the most complex question of how technology will shape and impact life and work in cities. While technology has played a key role in material transformation, we are now witnessing its negative influence, especially on urban youth. As the nature of work continues to change rapidly with technological advancements, we must realign our education and human resource development policies.

The most significant technological revolution is the recent leap in the capabilities of Machine Learning and Artificial Intelligence (together called AI/ML), and its applications, such as ChatGPT. These advancements have raised inconvenient though profound questions about the future of cities, life on the planet and humanity in general. Will AI/ML lead to large-scale unemployment by taking away manual and low-tech jobs such as code testing, image and content creation, and interpreting laboratory reports, etc.? Will AI/ML be able to answer larger questions on urban problems, and if so, with what efficacy and accuracy? Can AI/ML also create new jobs? These questions have given rise to serious debates about the future. The only thing that remains certain is that there will always be uncertainty, and we must grapple with this issue—urban planners, technology experts and policymakers—even as we work towards making cities better in terms of infrastructure and physical facilities. The social impact of AI/ML will also be a key determinant of the future, of tomorrow's cities and non-urban areas, and of human civilisation.

The State will play an important role in regulating access to technology. In India, the State continues to be the main vehicle of empowerment, as it has been for quite some time, and the citizens' power may be limited depending on security issues. The Digital Data Protection Bill, 2023, that has already been passed in the Lok Sabha, claims to safeguard and make available data under all circumstances, giving the government the power to control the use, transfer and disclosure of personal information. It has thus raised serious concerns about data privacy issues. What Edward Snowden, the American technology expert and whistleblower said is worth considering: "We trusted the government not to screw us... They did. We trusted the companies not to take advantage of us... They did. This is going to happen again, because that is the nature of power." (*ToI*, 8 August, 2023, p. 12). The citizen today and in the future is therefore squeezed between state power and corporate power. Can he really assert himself?

Continual engagement and deliberation are necessary to find the right answers, whether the questions are old or new.

SUMMING UP

Governance as a concept is fundamentally different from government. The idea of governance, especially in cities, includes many stakeholders such as central and state governments, municipal bodies and urban parastatals, along with what can be called parallel state systems, such as the judicial and quasi-judicial, as well as legislators. On the other hand, private interests, such as corporate and real-estate organisations, as well as NGOs, CSOs and associations of residents also contribute to the governance of a city. At its core, governance is an exercise of power by these stakeholders. Given the complex web of stakeholders in urban governance and the explicit and tacit ways in which they wield power, governance of Indian cities has been quite fragmented, and the results achieved have been less than satisfactory. Scholars argue that city planners seem to have an 'anti-big city bias', and the reality of Indian cities indicate that land and labour markets seem to drive urban growth, rather than planning.

The National Urban Policy Framework (NUPF) identifies ten focus (sectoral) areas in urban life and infrastructure and suggests an outcome matrix to capture the progress on each of them, and yet treats them as separate spheres of activity. In planning for the future, it may be useful to consider the work of scholars who emphasize the process of governance, one that may overcome simple territorial or jurisdictional categories such as urban and rural. As of now, we have failed to provide systems of urban governance, develop adequate infrastructure, protect the environment, decentralise effectively or include citizens in decision-making. Several of these imperatives may appear contradictory, but choosing the right processes and locations of governance can overcome some of these complex challenges. In many ways, there is a need for a paradigm shift in our governance systems, primarily in two areas. Firstly, in the planning process, instead of planning only for urban areas, there is a critical need for a holistic approach that looks at the urban along with the rural, and the linkages therein—working towards creating 'rurbanopolises' rather than metrolpolises. The other would be to centrally involve citizens and residents more effectively in decision-making, by truly empowering them for participatory planning, making cities more people-centric, and creating an enabling environment for their participation in governance.

Municipal and urban laws need to be overhauled to be made more effective in ensuring local democracy. Many reforms are more in letter than in spirit. States (which still largely govern cities by default) need to truly decentralise their power, and also make a choice between mayoral and commissioner-led systems with more confidence. The 74th CAA also needs to be revisited and a clear line of leadership needs to be instituted. To a large extent, this would also resolve the deeper question of who wields power in the city—the state or the people.

Bibliography

Abu-l-Fazl (1902). *Akbarnama* (Vol. 1). Asiatic Society of Calcutta. http://www.indianculture.gov.in/rarebooks/akbarnama-abu-l-fazl-history-reign-akbar-including-account-his-predecessors-vol-i-0

After Bombay High Court's rebuke, Maharashtra govt orders demolition of Nirav Modi's "illegal" Alibaug bungalow-Business News, Firstpost. (2018, August 21). Firstpost. https://www.firstpost.com/business/after-bombay-high-courts-rebuke-maharashtra-govt-orders-demolition-of-nirav-modis-illegal-alibaug-bungalow-5011341.html

Ahluwalia, I.J., Mohanty, P.K., Mathur, O., Roy, D., Khare, A., & Mangla, S. (2019). *State of municipal finances in India.* Indian Council for Research on International Economic Relations.

Ahmad, T. (2018). The role of cultural interactions and resident Indian communities in the GCC countries in shaping Gulf-India ties. *The Milli Gazette.* https://www.milligazette.com/news/7-analysis/16244-the-role-of-cultural-interactions-and-resident-indian-communities-in-the-gcc-countries-in-shaping-gulf-india-ties/

Ambedkar, Dr. B.R. (1949). *Constituent Assembly Speech.*

Amirtahmasebi, R., Orloff, M., Wahba, S., & Altman, A. (2016). *Regenerating urban land: A practitioner's guide to leveraging private investment* (Urban Development Series). World Bank. https://www.worldbank.org/en/topic/urbandevelopment/

publication/regenerating-urban-land-a-practitioners-guide-to-leveraging-private-investment

Arnstein, S.R. (1969). A ladder of citizen participation. *Journal of the American Institute of Planners*, *35*(4), 216-224. https://doi.org/10.1080/01944366908977225

Asian Development Bank (2013). *Municipal finance matters: India municipal finance study.* https://www.adb.org/projects/documents/municipal-finance-matters-india-municipal-finance-study-tacr

Baru, S. (2021). *India's power elite: Class, caste and cultural revolution.* Penguin Random House India Private Limited.

Bell, J.A., & Nuzzo, J.B. (2021). *Global health security index: Advancing collective action and accountability amid global crisis.* Global Health Security Index. https://www.ghsindex.org/report-model/

Bengaluru tops in water bodies with chemical pollution. (2018, March 22). *The Hindu.* https://www.thehindu.com/news/cities/bangalore/bengaluru-tops-in-water-bodies-with-chemical-pollution/article23324428.ece

Berry, B.J.L. (1973). *The human consequences of urbanisation: Divergent paths in the urban experience of the twentieth century.* Macmillan.

Bertaud, A. (2010). *Land markets, government interventions, and housing affordability* (No. 18). Brookings. https://www.brookings.edu/research/land-markets-government-interventions-and-housing-affordability/

Bertaud, A. (2014). *Cities as labor markets* (Working Paper No. 2). Marron Institute of Urban Management. https://marroninstitute.nyu.edu/blog/alain-bertaud-cities-as-labor-markets

Bertaud, A. (2018). *Order without design: How markets shape cities.* MIT Press.

Bhalla, S.S. (2017). *The new wealth of nations.* Simon and Schuster.

Bhushan, C. (2021). Just EVs won't clear air pollution: Coal, biomass and degraded land are main contributors. *The Times of*

India. https://timesofindia.indiatimes.com/blogs/toi-edit-page/its-not-fossil-fuel-stupid-coal-biomass-and-degraded-land-are-main-contributors-to-indias-air-pollution/

Blake, S.P. (1991). *Shahjahanabad: The sovereign city in Mughal India 1639-1739*. Cambridge University Press.

Bogue, D. J., & Zacharaiah, K.C. (1962). Urbanisation and migration in India. In Roy Turner (Ed.), *India's urban future*. University of California Press.

Boston Consulting Group & Michael & Susan Dell Foundation. (2021). *Unlocking the potential of the gig economy in India*. https://www.bcg.com/unlocking-gig-economy-in-india

Brenner, N. (2004). *New state spaces: Urban governance and the rescaling of statehood*. Oxford University Press.

Brenner, N., & Schmid, C. (2014). The 'Urban Age' in question. *International Journal of Urban and Regional Research, 38*(3), 731-755.

Burn, S.R. (Ed.). (1937). "The Cambridge History of India", Vol. IV, *The Mughul Period* (Vol. 4). Cambridge University Press. http://www.indianculture.gov.in/ebooks/cambridge-history-india-voliv

Castells, M. (1996). *The Rise of Network Society*. Blackwell: Oxford.

Cauvery issue: The shocking story of Bengaluru's dried up '1,000 lakes'—India News, Firstpost. (2016, September 19). Firstpost. https://www.firstpost.com/india/how-city-of-1000-lakes-dried-up-the-shocking-story-of-bengalurus-ailing-water-bodies-2671706.html

Chamaraj, K. (2022, May 12). Building prosperous villages. *Deccan Herald*. https://www.deccanherald.com/opinion/comment/building-prosperous-villages-1108761.html

Chandra, K.K. (2021, September 12). Dholavira: The lost & found civilisation. *Deccan Herald*. https://www.deccanherald.com/sunday-herald/sh-top-stories/dholavira-the-lost-found-civilisation-1028649.html

City Growth Commission & Royal Society of Arts. (2014). *Unleashing metro growth: Final recommendations of the City*

Growth Commission. https://www.bl.uk/collection-items/unleashing-metro-growth-final-recommendations-of-the-city-growth-commission

Climate change 2021: The physical science basis (Working Group I; Sixth Assessment Report). (2021). Cambridge University Press. https://doi.org/10.1017/9781009157896

Climate Change 2022: Impacts, Adaptation and Vulnerability (Working Group II; Sixth Assessment Report). (2022). Cambridge University Press. https://doi.org/10.1017/9781009325844

Comptroller and Auditor General of India. (2022). *Performance audit on functioning of Karnataka state road safety authority* (No. 5). Government of Karnataka. https://cag.gov.in/en/audit-report/details/115561

Dalberg, Clean Air Fund, & Confederation of Indian Industry. (2021). *Air pollution in India and the impact on business*. https://www.cleanairfund.org/resource/air-pollution-in-india-and-the-impact-on-business/

Dandekar, V.M., & Rath, N. (1971). *Poverty in India*. Indian School of Political Economy.

Darin-Drabkin, H. (1977). *Land Policy and Urban Growth*. Elsevier Science & Technology.

Darlymple, W. (2019). *The anarchy: The East India Company, corporate violence and the pillage of an empire*. https://www.goodreads.com/book/show/42972023-the-anarchy

Datta, V.N. (1986). Punjabi refugees and the urban development of Greater Delhi. In R.E. Frykenberg (Ed.), *Delhi through the ages: Essays in urban history, culture, and society*. Oxford University Press.

Davis, M. (2005). *Planet of Slums*. Verso Books.

Deepak, J.S. (2021). *India, that is Bharat: Coloniality, civilisation, constitution*. Bloomsbury Publishing.

Department of Economic Affairs. (2019). *National infrastructure pipeline: Report of the task force*. Ministry of Finance, Government of India. https://indiainvestmentgrid.gov.in/

Devas, N., Amis, P., Beall, J., Grant, U., Mitlin, D., Nunan, F., & Rakodi, C. (2004). *Urban Governance Voice and Poverty in the Developing World.* Earthscan Publications.

Dey, S. (2012). Rythu bazaar: A study of the supply chain of the farmers' markets of Andhra Pradesh. *The IUP Journal of Operations Management, XI*(3), 43-66.

Douglass, M. (2006). A regional network strategy for reciprocal rural-urban linkages: An agenda for policy research with reference to Indonesia. In C. Tacoli (Ed.), *The earthscan reader in rural-urban linkages* (1st ed., pp. 124-154). Routledge. https://doi.org/10.4324/9781315800486-7

Dunford, Michael & Aoyama, Yuko & Diniz, Clélio & Kundu, Amitabh & Limonov, L. & Lin, George & Liu, Weidong & Park, Sam & Turok, Ivan. (2016). "Area development and policy: an agenda for the 21st century". *Area Development and Policy*. 1. 1-14. 10.1080/23792949.2016.1158621.

Dunn, R.E. (1986). *The adventures of Ibn Battuta: A muslim traveller of the 14th century*. London : Croom Helm. http://archive.org/details/dli.pahar.3594

Dutt, R.C. (1901). *Indian famines, their causes and prevention.* P.S. King.

Edwardes, M. (1967). *British India, 1772-1947: A survey of the nature and effects of alien rule*. Sidgwick & Jackson Ltd. http://archive.org/details/in.ernet.dli.2015.135833

Finance Commission India. (2000). *Report of the eleventh finance commission.* https://fincomindia.nic.in/ShowContent.aspx?uid1=3&uid2=0&uid3=0&uid4=0

Finance Commission India. (2009). *Report of the thirteenth finance commission.* https://fincomindia.nic.in/writereaddata/html_en_files/oldcommission_html/fincom13/tfc/index.html

Food and Agriculture Organisation. (1996). *World Food Summit Report.* https://www.fao.org/3/w3548e/w3548e00.htm

Francis, W. (1988). *Gazetteer of south India* (Vol. 1). Mittal Publications.

Friedmann, J. (1986). "The World City Hypothesis". *Development and Change*, 4, 154.

Frug, Gerald & Barron, David (2013). *City Bound: How States Stifle Urban Innovation*. 10.7591/9780801460081.

Geddes, P. (1947). *Patrick Geddes in India* (J. Tyrwhitt, Ed.). Lund Humphries.

Ghose, A. (1973). New Lamps for Old-3. In *Bande mataram: Early political writings.*

Ginsberg, Allen. (1970). *Indian Journals*: March 1962-May 1963. City Lights Books & Dave Haselwood Books: United States

Goldman, M. (2011). Speculating on the next world city. In A. Roy & A. Ong (Eds.), *Worlding cities: Asian experiments and the art of being global* (p. 376). Wiley-Blackwell. https://www.wiley.com/en-us/Worlding+Cities%3A+Asian+Experiments+and+ the+Art+of+Being+Global-p-9781405192767

Government of India (1930). *Report of the Indian Statutory Commission* (No. 1). http://www.indianculture.gov.in/rarebooks/report-indian-statutory-commission-vol-i

Government of India (1976). The Urban Land (Ceiling and Regulation) Act, 1976. https://mohua.gov.in/upload/uploadfiles/files/ulcra_1976.pdf

Government of Karnataka (1961). *The Karnataka Town and Country Planning Act 1961*. Department of Town and Country Planning, Government of Karnataka.

Goyal, R., Reiche, C., Fernando, C., Serrao, J., Kimmel, S., Cohen, A., & Shaheen, S. (2018). *Urban Air Mobility (UAM) Market Study* (HQ-E-DAA-TN65181). https://ntrs.nasa.gov/citations/20190001472

Gulyani, Sumila. (2016). *Success when we deemed it failure? Revisiting sites and services 20 years later*. World Bank Blogs.

Gupta, N. (1991). Urbanism in south India: Eighteenth/Nineteenth centuries. In I. Banga (Ed.), *The city in Indian history: Urban demography, society, and politics*. Manohar Publications.

Habib, I. (1963). *The agrarian system of Mughal India, 1556-1707* (1st ed.). Department of History, Aligarh Muslim University.

Hardin, G. (1968). The Tragedy of the Commons. *Science*, *162*(3859), 1243-1248.

Harish, S. (2009). "Dholavira: Ancient Water Harnessing System". *Context-Built, Living and Natural*, VI(1).

Harish, S. (2021). "Affordable Rental Housing Complexes and Private Rental Housing in Indian Cities". *Economic and Political Weekly*, LVI(16), 15-19.

Harvey, D. (2003). *The New Imperialism*. Oxford University Press.

Harvey, D. (2008). The right to the city. *New Left Review, 53*, 23-40.

Heitzman, J. (2004). *Network city: Planning the information society in Bangalore*. Oxford University Press.

Hettne, Bjorn. (1978). *The Political Economy of Indirect Rule: Mysore 1881-1947*, Curzon Press Ltd., London.

High Powered Expert Committee (HPEC) (2011). *Report on Indian urban infrastructure and services*. https://icrier.org/pdf/FinalReport-hpec.pdf

Honasoge, K.S., Jagadeesh, K., Kalloor, V.J., & Anand, S. (2020). *Inclusive growth and the informal food sector in Bangalore, India* (No. 20; Hungry Cities Reports). Indian Institute for Human Settlements. https://hungrycities.net/publication/hcp-report-no-20-inclusive-growth-informal-food-sector-bangalore-india/

Housing, Town Planning, etc., Bill (Hansard, 12 May 1908) (n.d.). Retrieved December 1, 2022, from https://api.parliament.uk/historic-hansard/commons/1908/may/12/housing-town-planning-etc-bill

Howard, E. (1902). *Garden cities of tomorrow*. Swan Sonnenschein & Co. Ltd. http://archive.org/details/gardencitiestom00howagoog

Hunter, W. (1898). *The Indian empire: Its people, history, and products* (3rd ed.). W. H. Allen & Co. Ltd. http://www.indianculture.gov.in/rarebooks/indian-empire-its-people-history-and-products

IPCC, 2022: *Climate Change 2022: Impacts, Adaptation, and Vulnerability. Contribution of Working Group II to the Sixth Assessment Report of the Intergovernmental Panel on Climate Change* [H.-O. Pörtner, D.C. Roberts, M. Tignor, E.S. Poloczanska, K. Mintenbeck, A. Alegría, M. Craig,

S. Langsdorf, S. Löschke, V. Möller, A. Okem, B. Rama (eds.)]. Cambridge University Press. Cambridge University Press, Cambridge, UK and New York, NY, USA, 3056 pp., doi:10.1017/9781009325844.

Jagadeesh, M. (2016). *Gustav Hermann Krumbiegel: Renowned Horticulturalist and Landscape Architect*. https://ia801003.us.archive.org/29/items/Krumbiegel/Krumbiegel.pdf

James, L. (2006). *The middle class: A history*. Little, Brown.

Janaagraha (2015). *Street quality score*. https://www.janaagraha.org/files/publications/Street-Quality-Survey-2015.pdf

Jones, E. (1966). *Towns & cities*. Oxford University Press. https://www.biblio.com/book/towns-cities-jonesemrys/d/274919933

Joshi, S. (2017). India's middle class. In *Oxford Research Encyclopedia of Asian History*. https://doi.org/10.1093/acrefore/9780190277727.013.179

Kaggere, N., & Prakash, H. (2020). Recurring urban floods elicit quick-fix solutions, no concrete action. *Deccan Herald*. https://www.deccanherald.com/specials/insight/recurring-urban-floods-elicit-quick-fix-solutions-no-concrete-action-915697.html

Kalecki, M. (1999). Observations on social and economic aspects of intermediate regimes. In J. Osiatynski (Ed.), *Collected Works of Michal Kalecki: Volume V: Developing Economies* (Vol. 5). Clarendon Press. https://www.abebooks.co.uk/9780198286677/Collected-Works-Michal-Kalecki-Volume-0198286678/plp

Kamath, Suryanath U. (2001). *A Concise History of Karnataka: from Pre-historic Times to the Present*. Bangalore: Jupiter Books.

Kaza, S., Yao, L.C., Bhada-Tata, P., & Van Woerden, F. (2018). *What a Waste 2.0: A Global Snapshot of Solid Waste Management to 2050*. World Bank. https://doi.org/10.1596/978-1-4648-1329-0

Kelkar, V., & Shah, A. (2019). *In service of the Republic: The art and science of economic policy*. Penguin Random House India Private Limited.

Kellock, J. (1990). Mahadev Govind Ranade: Patriot and social servant. In V. Grover (Ed.), *Mahadev Govind Ranade*. Deep and Deep Publications.

Khanna, P. (2021). *Move: How mass migration will reshape the world and what it means for you*. Orion Publishing Group Limited.

Kidwai, A.H. (1991). Urban atrophy in colonial India: Some demographic indicators. In I. Banga (Ed.), *The city in Indian history: Urban demography, society, and politics*. Manohar Publications.

Kulkarni, C. (2022). How land mafia grabbed Chikka Kallasandra lake. *Deccan Herald*. https://www.deccanherald.com/city/top-bengaluru-stories/how-land-mafia-grabbed-chikka-kallasandra-lake-1091387.html

Kundu, Amitabh. (2018). Rurbanisation. In Patel, S. & Goyal, O. (Eds.). (2018). *India's Contemporary Urban Conundrum* (1st ed.). Routledge India. https://doi.org/10.4324/9780429023996

Lefebvre, H. (1968). *Le droit à la ville*. Anthropos.

Leite, D.N. (2014). *The Two Revolutions : Land Elites and Education during the Industrial Revolution*.

Maddison, A. (2001). *The world economy: A millennial perspective*. Organisation for Economic Co-operation and Development. https://www.oecd-ilibrary.org/economics/the-world-economy_9789264189980-en

Malghan, D., Kemp-Benedict, E., Goswami, R., Muddu, S., & Mehta, V.K. (2013). *Social ecology of domestic water use in Bangalore*. *48*(15). https://www.epw.in/journal/2013/15/special-articles/social-ecology-domestic-water-use-bangalore.html

Marya, G. (2018, September 25). *Indian housing market to contribute 11 percent to GDP by 2020*. Latest Real Estate News, Articles, Property Insights. https://www.99acres.com/articles/factors-catalysing-real-estate-sector-enabling-huge-demand-in-residential-market.html

Mathur, A., & Cunha, D.D. (2006). *Deccan Traverses: The Making of Bangalore's Terrain*.

Mathur, O., Abbas Haider Naqvi, Akanksha Laroiya, V. Sai Samyukta, & Himani Verma (2021). *State of the Cities India* (p. 199). Institute of Social Science.

Mathur, O.P. (Ed.) (1999). *India: The challenge of urban governance.* National Institute of Public Finance and Policy. https://www.environmentandurbanisation.org/india-challenge-urban-governance

Mazurek, M. (2018). Polish Economists in Nehru's India: Making Science for the Third World in an Era of De-Stalinisation and Decolonisation. *Slavic Review, 77*(3), 588-610. https://doi.org/10.1017/slr.2018.201

McAfee, A. (2019). *More from less: The surprising story of how we learned to prosper using fewer resources—and what happens next.* Simon and Schuster.

McAuliffe, M., & Ruhs, M. (Eds.) (2017). *World migration report 2018* (World Migration Reports). International Organisation for Migration. https://publications.iom.int/books/world-migration-report-2018

McGee, T.G. (1971). *The urbanisation process in the third world.* G. Bell & Sons. https://www.abebooks.co.uk/9780713516234/Urbanisation-Process-Third-World-Mcgee-0713516232/plp

McGee, T.G. (1991). The emergence of desakota regions in Asia: Expanding a hypothesis. In N. S. Ginsburg, B. Koppel, & T. G. McGee (Eds.), *The extended metropolis: Settlement transition in Asia* (p. 339). University of Hawaii Press.

McKinsey Global Institute (2010). *India's urban awakening: Building inclusive cities, sustaining economic growth.* https://www.mckinsey.com/~/media/McKinsey/Business%20Functions/Operations/Our%20Insights/Urban%20awakening%20in%20India/MGI_Indias_urban_awakening_executive_summary.pdf

Mehta, S. (2004). *Maximum city: Bombay lost and found.* Alfred A. Knopf.

Mills, C.W. (1956). *The power elite.*

Ministry of Finance (2018). *Economic survey 2018.* https://mofapp.nic.in/economicsurvey/economicsurvey/index.html

Ministry of Housing & Urban Affairs. (2019, August 11). *Inaugural conclave on "National Capital Region-2041" to be held in Delhi*. https://pib.gov.in/pib.gov.in/Pressreleaseshare.aspx?PRID=1591023

Ministry of Housing and Urban Affairs (2006). *National urban transport policy*. https://mohua.gov.in/upload/uploadfiles/files/TransportPolicy.pdf

Ministry of Jal Shakti (2022). *Number of Water Bodies*. https://pib.gov.in/pib.gov.in/Pressreleaseshare.aspx?PRID=1805815

Ministry of Road Transport & Highways. (2019). *Annual Report 2018-19*. https://morth.nic.in/annual-report-2018-19-0

Ministry of Urban Development. (1988). *Report of the National Commission on Urbanisation*. http://indianculture.gov.in/reports-proceedings/report-national-commission-urbanisation-vol-i

Misra, S. (2022, September 5). *Is Shimla story over? Bengaluru-like jams, no water, collapsing buildings, swelling crowds*. https://theprint.in/features/is-shimla-story-over-bengaluru-like-jams-no-water-collapsing-buildings-swelling-crowds/1116455/

Mohan, V. (2022, June 11). What India is doing to tackle its water crisis. *The Times of India*. https://timesofindia.indiatimes.com/india/what-india-is-doing-to-tackle-its-water-crisis/articleshow/92141578.cms

Moorhouse, G. (1971). *Calcutta: The city revealed*. Weidenfeld and Nicolson. http://catalogue.bnf.fr/ark:/12148/cb41402114r

Mumford, L. (1938). *The culture of cities*. Harcourt Brace.

Muthiah, S. (2008). *Madras, Chennai: A 400-year record of the first city of modern India*. Palaniappa Brothers.

Narain, S., Srinivasa, R.K., Pandey, P., Banerjee, S., & Chaudhuri, J. (2012). *Excreta Matters: How urban India is soaking up water, polluting rivers and drowning in its own waste*. Centre for Science and Environment.

Narayanamoorthy, A. (2022). Groundwater Irrigation in India: Development, Overexploitation and Sustainability. In A. Narayanamoorthy (Ed.), *The Irrigation Future of India:*

Development, Resource and Policy (pp. 73-95). Springer International Publishing. https://doi.org/10.1007/978-3-030-89613-3_4

National Buildings Organisation (1987). *All India standard schedule of rates, 1986* ([2nd ed.]). Govt. of India, Ministry of Urban Development, National Buildings Organisation and UN Regional Housing Centre, ESCAP.

National Commission on Population, Ministry of Health and Family Welfare (2020). *Population Projections for India and States, 2011-2036.* https://ruralindiaonline.org/en/library/resource/population-projections-for-india-and-states-2011-2036/

NITI Aayog and RMI (2021). *Turning Around the Power Distribution Sector.* https://www.niti.gov.in/sites/default/files/2021-08/Electricity-Distribution-Report_030821.pdf

NITI Aayog (2018). *Composite Water Management Index: A Tool for Water Management.* NITI Aayog, Government of India. https://smartnet.niua.org/content/49afbaf0-9c5c-4daf-82b0-52dd6fe60c97

NITI Aayog (2021). *Reforms in Urban Planning Capacity in India.* https://niti.gov.in/sites/default/files/2021-09/UrbanPlanningCapacity-in-India-16092021.pdf

Observer Research Foundation. (n.d.). *India's Smart Cities Mission —An Assessment.* https://www.orfonline.org/research/indias-smart-cities-mission-an-assessment

Ostrom, E. (1990). *Governing the commons: The evolution of institutions for collective action.* Cambridge University Press.

Pani, N. (2022). *The City as action: Retheorizing urban studies.* Routledge.

Pareto, V. (1916). *The mind and society.* http://archive.org/details/ParetoTheMindAndSocietyVol4TheGeneralFormOfSociety

Philips, C.H., Singh, H.L., & Pandey, B.N. (1962). *The evolution of India and Pakistan, 1858 to 1947: Select documents.* Oxford University Press. https://www.cambridge.org/core/journals/bulletin-of-the-school-of-oriental-and-african-studies/article/abs/c-h-philips-and-others-ed-the-evolution-of-india-and-pakistan-1858-to-1947-select-documents-edited-by-c-h-philips-with-the-cooperation-of-h-l-singh-and-b-n-pandey-select-documents-on-the-history-of-india-and-pakistan-vol-iv-xxi-786-pp-london-etc-oxford-university-press-1962-4-10s/DB43460BA04EAF3DF0406589931D46F2

Phillips, D., & Williams, K. (1999). *Literature Review on Peri-Urban Conceptualisation and Management Approaches.* (p. 233). Department for International Development. https://www.gov.uk/research-for-development-outputs/literature-review-on-peri-urban-conceptualisation-and-management-approaches

Pillai, M.S. (2021). *False allies: India's maharajahs in the age of Ravi Varma.* Juggernaut. https://www.goodreads.com/book/show/59073557-false-allies

Pinto, M. (2000). *Metropolitan city governance in India.* SAGE Publications.

Plato (360 C.E.). *The Republic.*

Prakash, G. (1965). *Report of the committee on urban land policy.* Ministry of Health, Government of India. http://indianculture.gov.in/reports-proceedings/report-committee-urban-land-policy

Prakash, G. (2010). *Mumbai fables.* https://press.princeton.edu/books/paperback/9780691153179/mumbai-fables

PricewaterhouseCoopers. (2020). *AI: An opportunity amidst a crisis.* https://www.pwc.in/consulting/technology/data-and-analytics/ai-an-opportunity-amidst-a-crisis.html

Raban, J. (1974). *Soft City.* Hamish Hamilton and E.P. Dutton & Company.

Ramachandra, T.V., Aithal, B.H., & Sreejith, K. (2015). GHG footprint of major cities in India. *Renewable and Sustainable Energy Reviews, 44*, 473-495. https://doi.org/10.1016/j.rser.2014.12.036

Ramanujan, A.K. (Ed.). (1985). *Poems of love and war: From the eight anthologies and the ten long poems of classical Tamil.* Columbia University Press.

Randstad (2021). *Annual salary trends report.* https://newsmeter.in/pdf_upload/randstad-salary-trends-report-2021-312722.pdf

Randstad. (2022). *Talent trends report 2022.* https://www.randstadsourceright.com/talent-trends/

Rao, V.L.S.P. (1979). *The structure of an Indian metropolis: A study of Bangalore.* Allied.

Rao, V.L.S.P. (1983). *Urbanisation in India: Spatial dimensions.* Concept.

Ravindra, A. (1996). *Urban land policy: A metropolitan perspective.* Concept Publishing Company.

Reddy, Y.M. (2022). Newly-built market lying unused for 2 yrs. *News Trail.* https://www.newstrailindia.com/inner.php?id=6574

Reserve Bank of India (2022). *Report on Municipal Finances.* https://rbidocs.rbi.org.in/rdocs/Publications/PDFs/01OVERVIEW88D43E7D95D444A187D2F0B18F724E84.PDF

Revi, A., Ray, M., Sami, N., Anand, S., Mitra, S., & Malladi, T. (2020). *The potential of urbanisation to accelerate post-COVID economic recovery: Report to the XV Finance Commission* (p. 192). Indian Institute for Human Settlements. https://iihs.co.in/knowledge-gateway/the-potential-of-urbanisation-to-accelerate-post-covid-economic-recovery-report-to-the-xv-finance-commission/

Rifkin, J. (2014). *The zero marginal cost society: The internet of things, the collaborative commons, and the eclipse of capitalism.* St. Martin's Publishing Group.

Rowe, J. (2007). The parallel economy of the commons. In Worldwatch Institute (Ed.), *State of the world 2008: Ideas and opportunities for sustainable economies :* (25th ed., pp. 166-178). Routledge. https://doi.org/10.4324/9781849772600-18

Roy, T. (2021). *An Economic history of India 1707-1857.* Routledge.

Ruddock, A. (2021). *Special treatment: Student doctors at the All India Institute of Medical Sciences.* Stanford University Press.

Saran, R. (2022). Problem ... solution ... problem: India's population will start to collapse in two decades. It's a matter of celebration – and concern. *The Times of India.* https://

timesofindia.indiatimes.com/blogs/toi-edit-page/problem-solution-problem-indias-population-will-start-to-collapse-in-two-decades-its-a-matter-of-celebration-and-concern/

Sassen, S. (2001). *The Global City: New York, London,* Tokyo, rev. edn. (originally published in 1991). Princeton, NJ: Princeton University Press.

Sassen, S. (2009). Cities in today's global age. *The SAIS Review of International Affairs, 29*(1), 3-34.

Sassen, S. (2014). *Expulsions: Brutality and complexity in the global economy*. Harvard University Press.

Satterthwaite, D. (2021). How can transport contribute to other urban agendas? In G. Tiwari & D. Mohan (Eds.), *Transport and safety: Systems, approaches, and implementation* (pp. 303-318). Springer. https://doi.org/10.1007/978-981-16-1115-5_15

Schmid, C. (2014). Networks, borders, differences: Towards a theory of the urban. In N. Brenner (Ed.), *Implosions/explosions: Towards a Study of Planetary Urbanisation* (pp. 67-85). Jovis.

Schmidt, E., & Cohen, J. (2013). *The new digital age: Reshaping the future of people, nations and business*. John Murray.

Scott, A. J., & Storper, M. (2015). The nature of cities: The scope and limits of urban theory. *International Journal of Urban and Regional Research, 39*(1), 1-15.

Second Administrative Reforms Commission. (2007). *Local governance: An inspiring journey into the future* (No. 6; Second Administrative Reforms Commission Reports). Government of India. https://darpg.gov.in/en/arc-reports

Sharma, R.S. (1991). Urbanism in early history of India. In I. Banga (Ed.), *The city in Indian history: Urban demography, society, and politics*. Manohar Publications.

Singh, N. (2022, January 3). Work from anywhere: Tier-2 cities to earn big. *The Times of India*. https://timesofindia.indiatimes.com/business/india-business/work-from-anywhere-tier-2-cities-to-earn-big/articleshow/88654293.cms

Sivapriyan, E.B.T. (2021, September 19). In Keeladi, archaeological finds that validate Sangam corpus. *Deccan Herald*. https://www.deccanherald.com/special-features/in-keeladi-archaeological-finds-that-validate-sangam-corpus-r-balakrishnan-1031815.html

Smailes, A.E. (1969). *The Indian city: A descriptive model.* Geographische Zeitschrift.

Smith, S.H. (2018). A slice of history: What a British city plan tells us about late 17th century Madras. *Scroll.In.* https://scroll.in/article/867288/a-slice-of-history-what-a-british-city-plan-tells-us-about-late-17th-century-madras

Smitha, K.C., & Pal, B.D. (2018). Spatial Reproduction of Urban Poverty in Global City: Gender, Informality and Mobility in Bengaluru. *Economic and Political Weekly, 53*(3). https://www.epw.in/journal/2018/3/special-articles/spatial-reproduction-urban-poverty-global-city.html

Sposito, Maria Encarnação Beltrão. Capitalismo e Urbanização. 1998. Geografia Contexto, 1998.

Srinivas, L. (1991). Land and Politics in India: Working of Urban Land Ceiling Act, 1976. *Economic and Political Weekly.* https://www.academia.edu/es/682440/Land_and_Politics_in_India_Working_of_Urban_Land_Ceiling_Act_1976

Swinburn, Gwen; Goga, Soraya; Murphy, Fergus (January 2006). *Local Economic Development: A Primer Developing and Implementing Local Economic Development Strategies and Action Plans.* Washington D.C.: World Bank.

Taylor, P.J. (1997). Hierarchical tendencies amongst world cities: A global research proposal. *Cities, 14*(6), 323-332. https://doi.org/10.1016/S0264-2751(97)00023-1

The World Bank (1983). *World development report 1983.* World Bank. https://doi.org/10.1596/0-1952-0432-8

The World Bank (2009). *World development report 2009: Reshaping economic geography.* World Bank. https://doi.org/10.1596/978-0-8213-7607-2

The World Bank (2016). *Social Development—Social Accountability E-guide.* https://saeguide.worldbank.org/sites/worldbank.org.saeguide/files/documents/1_Participatory%20Planning.pdf

The World Bank (2019). *Social accountability E-guide.* https://ppp.worldbank.org/public-private-partnership/library/social-accountability-e-guide

The World Bank (2014). *Urban Transport. World Bank.* https://www.worldbank.org/en/country/india/brief/urban-transport

The World Bank (2022). *Financing India's Urban Infrastructure Needs: Constraints to Commercial Financing and Prospects for Policy Action*. https://documents1.worldbank.org/curated/en/099615110042225105/pdf/P17130200d91fc0da0ac610a1e3e1a664d4.pdf

Thomas, F.C. (2016). *Calcutta Poor: Inquiry into the Intractability of Poverty*. Routledge. https://doi.org/10.4324/9781315479255

Thünen, J.H. von. (1826). *Isolated stat* ([1st ed.]). Pergamon Press. http://books.google.com/books?id=yNuFAAAAIAAJ

Times Evoke (2021, October 9). 'India's economy is the informal economy—The rest simply can't work without it.' *The Times of India*. https://timesofindia.indiatimes.com/indias-economy-is-the-informal-economy-the-rest-simply-cant-work-without-it/articleshow/86874878.cms

Tinker, H. (1954). *The foundations of local self-government in India, Pakistan, and Burma*. University of London, Athlone Press.

Trevelyan, Sir G. (1863). *Quoted in Calcutta: Old and New by H.E.A. Cotton*, edited by N.R. Ray, General Printers and Publishers Pvt. Ltd. Originally published 1909, Revised edition 1980, p. 194.

UNCCD (2022). *Global Land Outlook Report* (No. 2; Global Land Outlook). https://www.unccd.int/resources/global-land-outlook/glo2

UN-Habitat & UNESCAP (2010). *The State of Asian Cities 2010/11*. https://unhabitat.org/the-state-of-asian-cities-201011

UN-Habitat & UNESCAP (2015). *The state of Asian and Pacific cities 2015: Urban transformations shifting from quantity to quality*. https://unhabitat.org/the-state-of-asian-and-pacific-cities-2015

UN-Habitat (2003). *The challenge of slums—Global report on human settlements 2003* (p. 345). https://unhabitat.org/the-challenge-of-slums-global-report-on-human-settlements-2003

UN-Habitat (2006). *State of the World's Cities 2006/2007* (p. 202). https://unhabitat.org/state-of-the-worlds-cities-20062007

UN-Habitat (2008). *State of the world's cities 2008/2009—Harmonious cities* (p. 224). https://unhabitat.org/state-of-the-worlds-cities-20082009-harmonious-cities-2

UN-Habitat (2009). *Planning Sustainable Cities: Global Report on Human Settlements* (p. 338). https://unhabitat.org/planning-sustainable-cities-global-report-on-human-settlements-2009

UNICEF, Food and Agriculture Organisation, & SaciWATERs. (2013). *Water in India: Situation and prospects.*

United Nations Department of Economic and Social Affairs. (2004). *World urbanisation prospects: The 2003 revision.* https://unesdoc.unesco.org/ark:/48223/pf0000137892

United Nations (2019). *World urbanisation prospects: The 2018 revision*. United Nations.

Vaddiraju, A.K. (2021). *Urban Governance and Local Democracy in South India*. Routledge India. https://www.routledge.com/Urban-Governance-and-Local-Democracy-in-South-India/Vaddiraju/p/book/9780367219208

Varley, A. (2013). Postcolonialising Informality? *Environment and Planning D: Society and Space*, *31*(1), 4-22. https://doi.org/10.1068/d14410

Venkatarangaiya, M., & Pattabhiram, M. (Eds.) (1969). *Local government in India: Select readings*. Allied Publishers.

Wateraid (2018). *State of urban water supply in India*. https://www.wateraid.org/in/sites/g/files/jkxoof336/files/state-of-urban-water-supply.pdf

Watson, V. (2014). African urban fantasies: Dreams or nightmares? *Environment and Urbanisation*, *26*(1), 215-231. https://doi.org/10.1177/0956247813513705

Wilbur Smith Associates (2008). *Study on Traffic & Transportation Policies and Strategies in Urban Areas in India.* Technical report, Ministry of Urban Development, New Delhi, India.

World Economic Fourm (2022). *Why Are These Coastal Cities Sinking?* https://www.weforum.org/videos/why-are-these-coastal-cities-sinking/

World Health Organisation (2021). *WHO global air quality guidelines: Particulate matter (PM2.5 and PM10), ozone, nitrogen dioxide, sulfur dioxide and carbon monoxide*. https://apps.who.int/iris/handle/10665/345329

World Inequality Lab (2022). *World Inequality Report 2022.* //wir2022.wid.world/

Index